Authors Note

This is a memoir of the authors time spent in a southern jail and prison from December of 1975 to July 1985. Though written from memory I can with good conscience promise that all events written in these pages are true and free of embellishments. Quotes from the trial portion were copied directly from a certified copy of the court record currently in my possession. Where the phrases "heard, saw, or rumor" are used that is where my information came from. More information on the validity of my story is accessible online at www.053803.com on the documents page. Thank-You for sharing my story.

053803 a memoir / Robert J Gagnon-paperback
ISBN-10: 0-9778662-0-3
ISBN-13: 978-0-9778662-0-5

Book cover is a Photo of a Florida Correctional Institution taken by R J Gagnon.

053803

Life at Fifteen

By

Robert J Gagnon

The Crime

December 19, 1975

The bank was a small building, about the size of a convenience store. Double glass doors swung outward from the entrance. Ten paces past these doors; the patrons waited at a counter that spanned the width of the interior. At the far right, a small cluster of desks faced outward, awaiting the day that business warranted additional staff. This bland building served as the temporary branch, in the shadow of the main building still under construction. Zig had chosen this particular bank for its unimposing size and location. Standing out near the South West corner of Commercial and Federal Highway in northern Fort Lauderdale, this small building had caught Zig's eye, and I'd agreed this would be a good practice run. On an overcast Friday evening, Zig and I sat in the parking lot alongside of the bank debating whether we should cancel our mission.

The Camaro we had planned to use for our get-away had broken down the day before and our back up, a red, white, and blue AMX, had a starting problem. Zig had brought this last minor technical problem to my attention as we entered the bank parking lot. The vision of us trying to push start the car while the cops stood around laughing, played itself out in my head, along with the realization that one of us would have to stay with the car. Since Zig was the better driver, it was now up to me to either go in alone or cancel the robbery. My gut feeling was

to just walk away and forget the whole thing, until my partner evoked the magical word "chicken". I told him to keep the engine running and began walking towards the front entrance.

A strong wind had sprung up during our debate, impeding my every step and making it unusually hard to pull the glass door open. How amusing I thought with a smile, it's as if the elements themselves were trying to stop me. I sensed that familiar tension in my stomach, that stuffy tightness that reached up my spine into the back of my head. It's always like this at the start, sometimes referred to as the butterflies. This feeling would pass once the actual robbery started. Then I would get the RUSH. The rush that makes you feel god-like with infinite authority, all too soon followed by the overwhelming need to run like hell, to get away, to haul ass out of there.

Inside the entrance, I took a moment to scan the layout and the position of everyone inside. An average looking teller stood before me to my left, a frail Asian girl in the middle, and a tall dorky character was leaning over one of the desks off to my right. The lone guy in line ahead of me was kind of on the big side, but he'd be out the door and gone before my thing started.

The Asian girl's nametag identified her as "LISA". She would have been cute if not for her love of potato chips and rebellious complexion. She was my best bet. Get her squealing in fear; and the other employees would do whatever they're told to protect her. I thought this would be an easy in and out, as I approached the counter.

"Can I help you?" Lisa asked. With a smile I responded, "Yes Ma'am, I'd like to make a withdraw." Then I handed her the note:
I have a gun, give me all the money
you have in ten seconds or I will kill!!!

She read the note, then studied it for a few moments before asking, "Are you serious?" Still smiling I replied, "As a heart attack, now if you could hurry it up please, I have someone waiting for me outside." She looked at me for a very long moment with those expressionless Asian eyes then announced, "We have no money."

I had planned for any conceivable statement the teller might make after reading the note, but this response threw me for a loop. I imagined myself pulling the gun out and shooting her for being so blatantly stupid, I decided instead to be a little more assertive.

"Now look," I said, "this is a bank, and a bank has money, so give it up!" Lisa said, "I must ask boss for money."

She then walked over and handed the note to the tall skinny guy whose nametag identified him as "Kim" the Branch Manager.

This guy was no bomb threat. Tall and skinny with glasses, a better name for him would have been 'Poindexter.' I pondered how a guy could have a name like Kim. (Maybe he was a Savings and Loan cross-dresser.) I watched him read the note, look at me for a second or two, then tell Lisa, "Give him the money." "But we have no money," Lisa still insisted. Kim repeated himself, "Give him the money. . . . NOW!"

Very slowly, Lisa unlocked the cash drawer and put a stack of bills on the counter in front of me, then slammed the drawer shut. "What's this," I asked, "I said all the money!"

Lisa retorted, "I tell you we have no more money. You go now!"

I realized at this point that I'd lost control of the situation.

This wouldn't have happened if I'd have followed my plan. My partner Zig was the one that insisted on the note idea. The good thing about the note was that I didn't have to pull a gun. If by some chance things did go wrong, the charge would be simple robbery, not armed robbery. Now a big gun and a cold voice give you the power of command where people do as they are told without a hassle. All I had was a little .22 stuffed in the front of my pants that wouldn't scare anyone if I did wave it around. Either way, I'd already been inside too long. Getting away with something was better than not getting away at all.

"OK then, keep your damn money!" I said, while grabbing the stack of bills from the counter and hurriedly flipping through them. There was a Hundred, a Fifty, and what looked like fives and fifties mixed. There was about a grand or so from the looks of it. Turning away to leave I noticed the camera in the upper right corner near the door. I couldn't tell if it was on or not, but I had to smile in its direction while stuffing the money into my pocket. Ten more feet and I would be out the door. It was hard to casually stroll outside with every muscle screaming to run. Were the cops outside waiting? Would they jump out as I'm getting into the car? There was only one way to find out...

Pushing the door hard against the wind, I made my way outside. Dusk had turned into night during my mission, and walking from light into darkness left me temporarily blinded. I stumbled towards the parking lot straining for any sign of Zig, but I couldn't see him or the car anywhere. Then I stopped, realizing that something else was wrong. The door hadn't slammed shut behind me. As I started to turn for a look back, something heavy slammed into the middle of my back knocking me forward. I barely got my hands in front of me to break my fall as the ground rose up to meet my face.

I was face down with a knee in my back and an arm around my throat. I turned my head expecting to see a cop, but instead I caught a glimpse of a white shirt. IT WAS POINDEXTER! He'd decided that I wasn't going to get away with this. Not only did he have me pinned from behind and in a yoke hold, but the heavy jacket I wore severely limited any defensive movements.

Wrestling was not an option, I'd already been here way too long, and it was a sure thing the cops were on their way by now. No way would I let this geek hold me until they got here. I reached for the gun, but it was gone! The gun had fallen into my crotch, loaded and cocked with the business end warming itself between my testicles.

Thoughts of unpleasant possibilities passed through my mind as I shook my leg and tried to work this destructive little problem out of my pants. We were about ten yards from Federal Highway in North Lauderdale and a crowd was starting to form. Some were the people from the bank, and a few curious passer-bys. A couple of people were sitting through the green traffic light in their cars, to watch this odd spectacle. I could see a security guard from across the street unholstering his gun and running towards us from across the Highway.

One of the girls standing over us tried to kick me and got Kim instead. I would have thanked her for the help, but I was too concerned about the whereabouts of my partner. It was starting to look like I was on my own. The gun was almost to my ankle and I began to shake my leg like a dog to get it out. Kim changed his grip and started grunting and growling like some kind of an animal. I began to laugh at the thought of how much he sounded like a poodle fighting over a sock you're trying to take away. Then the gun was out and on the ground somewhere behind us. Kim reached back and

grabbed it first, putting the barrel up to the side of my head.

Now I was screwed, there is nothing scarier then a Dork with a gun, and the advantage. I reached up with both hands and wrestled the gun away from my attacker. A woman's yell, "Oh my God, he's got a gun," came from somewhere in the crowd. I heard the sounds of feet moving as everyone ran away in different directions. I could see the traffic dodging guard from across the street, run all the way back across the highway and duck behind a car, his gun drawn, peering from around the bumper. I pointed the gun at Kim's head and said, "Get off me man, or I'll shoot your ass!" He answered with some more persistent growling.

This was his big chance to get his revenge for all the times he'd been slapped around in gym, or didn't have lunch money because someone else wanted it more than him. Either way I was not about to be caught by some Mamma's boy, wanna-be hero. I didn't want to kill him. Hell, I didn't even want to shoot him. I couldn't shoot his arm that was around my neck, since .22's tend to follow the bone and might get me instead. Someone in the crowd got brave and kicked Kim again trying to get me. Soon, they would be trying to get the gun away.

I switched the gun to my left hand, reached behind my back and aimed as best as I could at his ass. No way was he getting a dignified wound out of this! I fired the gun, which sounded more like a cap pistol in my moment of need, but the bullet had missed its target. There was the sound of more feet scurrying around and a scream or two from the women nearby, as Kim tightened his grip around my throat.

Something popped in my neck, as a flash appeared somewhere to my left. I squeezed off another shot. Had someone in the parking lot just fired a gun at me? The grip around my neck relaxed, and Kim slid

off my back and onto the ground. Lying next to me on his belly, some funny gurgling sounds emanated from him. 'Can't see any holes or blood, he must be faking it,' I thought as I rose to my feet. The temptation to shoot him for making this whole thing such a mess was overwhelming. Instead, I kicked him once, as everyone else had. Now it was time for the get away.

It appeared as if my partner had left the scene after shooting Kim, leaving me surrounded by a semicircle of people. There were twenty extra bullets in my pocket. I noticed a few had fallen out during the fight when I bent down to scoop up the spent shells. Standing upright, I pointed the gun into the crowd and yelled, "I'll kill every damned one of you!" They all looked more stupid then scared, as if they were not sure if they should run or hit the ground. Then one guy put his hands up. The others looked at him and did the same. This was how it was supposed to have started out. As I pondered my next move, I heard a voice from the parking lot, "Over here man, come on!" It was Zig!

I ran over to the car and jumped in. Zig asked what had happened. "I shot the hero man; now get us to hell out of here!" I yelled, closing the car door behind me. Zig calmly stated, "I'm pulling out nice and slow so we don't draw attention." I replied, "It's a little late to worry about that right now, just go!" I started counting the money from the bank and realized there were only a couple of hundred bucks in the stack. Now I was really pissed off, this idiot (Kim) had about got himself killed over a couple hundred dollars. What a moron, and thinking of what I went through for the same, didn't make me much brighter.

We had planned to play Bad Co.'s theme song for our get away. But the AMX didn't have a tape player. So there I was being driven down a side street

heading west with a tone-deaf driver singing out of time and key, 'Man, it can't get any worse than this'.

Turning north, we had to wait for the parade of cop cars racing eastward to the bank to cross Commercial Blvd. We jumped the median in front of two cruisers, which ignored us. They were on their way to a shooting.

I heard later that when the first cars arrived at the scene, the officers approached the crowd and saw Kim on the ground. Someone in the group stuttered that there was a robbery, and a gun went off, and then pointed at Kim. Assuming the man on the ground was the now subdued robber, they told Kim to get up. When he didn't move, they kicked him a couple of times. Kim wasn't having a very good night.

Zig dropped me off at Randy's house; this would be part of my alibi if one became necessary. Randy was a twenty-four year old epileptic that lived in his garage, black lights and various paraphernalia lined his walls. I'd hung out here most of the day making sure his very religious mother was aware of my presence.

She was a pillar of the community and a very convincing witness. I made a point of asking her the time both when leaving and returning. Randy and I retreated to party dungeon where I filled him in on my where a bouts for the past hour. Looking at the money under the black light, he brought to my attention some florescent paint where they had been marked.

Randy didn't believe the story behind the money, nor did he care, as long it would buy something to drink. With one of the marked bills, he bought a case of beer, and we celebrated for a couple hours. Getting home about midnight I flopped onto my bed and dropped into a restless sleep filled with dreams of the robbery.

Saturday morning I sat straight up in my bed with a sore neck and a bruise on my lower back. Well that would explain the weird dream, too many good drugs especially the PCP. I'd been using the stuff so long now that dreams and imagination were easily mistaken for memories of actual events. On the flip side, what I sometimes mistook as daydreams or hallucinations turned out to be actual memories at times. The repetition of doing things you don't remember and remembering other events that never occurred had taken away my responsibility of having a conscience.

I'd adapted to my present condition of reality deprivation, but that last dream was painfully real. I would have been more concerned if not for how ridiculous it was. There was no way in hell things could go that wrong. Unless it was a sign to let me know I was about to screw up. Nah, I wrote it off as just another dream and continued lying in bed thinking about the actual robbery to come.

We'd been planning this robbery for a couple of months now. Neither one of us were in it for the money. I wanted to be the youngest bank robber in history, or so I had convinced myself. Actually, this had become my only way out. By age fifteen I had both a drug, and an alcohol habit, and I couldn't quit either. The only way to get into a clinic was if your folks had a lot of money or the courts sent you. In my house, asking for help is a sign of weakness. Less than a week before, after asking my dad about seeing a shrink, I was accused of being a flake.

Robbing a bank was my only option. If caught, they would force me to dry out, get my act together. If I were killed in the act, I'd become a piece of local history. Robbing a bank was a sign of strength, the perfect solution. No matter what the outcome, the mere act itself would leave a profound message.

Zig on the other hand didn't drink or use anything. He was just nuts. My partner actually thought he was John Dillinger reincarnated. That same character flaw was what made him such a good partner. A fanatic dedicated to an idea is the most loyal person you could have at your side.

Last night's dream had instilled some doubt; maybe this really wasn't such a hot idea after all. No one ever gets away with a bank robbery, that's why I picked this solution. Zig planned to rob a slew of banks, the temporary savings and loan was just a rehearsal to him. To me it was a one shot deal, a means to an end. But my partner did have an infectious enthusiasm that sometimes tainted my intentions. This avalanche of random thoughts was still running through my head as I stumbled into the living room and asked the Old Man what we were doing for work that day.

He sat in his chair holding a newspaper looking somewhat perturbed, he asked, "Where's the money?" What money?" I stammered. You robbed a bank last night, I want my cut." He then held up the front page with the headlines- "Manager in critical condition after shot by fleeing bank robber". "You're right there in the picture. That's your walk, your clothes, and your shit-eating grin. How could you be so stupid?" After looking at the picture and reading the article, I attempted to explain how it couldn't be me. "Look Pop, they describe the robber to be approximately two hundred pounds and between twenty-eight to thirty-five years old. Besides, he got away in a rusted blue car, or a sedan and you know my driving couldn't get me out of the parking lot. On top of that I'm only fifteen years old, how could I pass for someone ten years older?"

"If you did it you had better tell me now and we'll send you up North to live with your mother's family

10

for a year or so until this cools off. If this guy dies, even that might not be far enough."

"No, Dad, it's not me, now are we going to work or do I actually have a day off?" "Just stay around the house for right now," he growled at me as I walked out front to gather my wits. Once outside I leaned against the garage wall, staring down my street without seeing any of the well-manicured lawns or neighbors taking their morning walk. I recalled the previous night's events that had until a few moments before been dismissed as a bad dream.

So far, I'd managed to get away with it for a night, which meant we hadn't been followed leaving the bank. The description of the robber was way off, taking the age and weight profile into account. But that picture on the front page was damning to say the least. If the Old Man could pick up on it that fast, so could anyone else in this upper class neighborhood. I wasn't exactly all that popular around here. The best thing for now was to lay low and try not to draw any attention to myself. If it looked like the cops are getting too close then I'd bolt.

My thoughts were disturbed by what looked like a skinny old man way up the street swerving from one side of the road to the other with a pile of something on the handlebars of a bicycle. This odd spectacle served as an amusing distraction for a few moments. As he came closer, the face became familiar. It was Zig with a stack of newspapers. He peddled up in my driveway, jumped off the bike, and started tearing off the front pages.

Panting for breath Zig stammered, "Here, this is your half, Oh shit man, you did shoot the Hero. Hey, I want to see some of the money." I told him that the money was marked and that we should burn it. "Screw that, I'll get the car fixed and we'll go on a rampage robbing banks cross country, this is my dream man, we can't stop now, this is our destiny!"

"No, this is my ass and that's not enough money to get us out of the state." Zig, "Hey, I drove the car, and I want some of the money, just for a trophy." I told him that I'd bring some of the marked bills to a mutual friend's house that afternoon, where we could talk. But not here or now, "My Dad's already asking me about the front page, so I'll have to see you later. And get away from me with those damned papers!" " No problem, I'll hold onto your half for you", Zig replied.

Later that afternoon, at a friend's house, Zig got some of the money and we took a few of pictures with the get-away car and the two of us holding up one of the bills for the camera. Zig's new idea was to buy a Thompson and walk in leaving no witnesses. That way we could just pick up the money without all of the hassle. But my mind was on how long it would be before the cops caught up to us.

My plan had failed miserably, not only was the robbery slip shod, but someone had been seriously hurt. And now my partner was busy organizing a crime spree. I convinced him to wait a week until things cooled off, we'd act as if nothing happened. This turned out to be harder than I thought.

I had no idea what it is like to be wanted. During the next few days, I couldn't walk into a store or down the street without feeling on the verge of panic. Whenever anyone glanced in my general direction, it felt as if they knew who I was, and what I did. Any second I expected them to raise their finger and point me out like in that body snatchers movie. With each stare, I anticipated the mob of people that would rise up and run after me, shouting to the people ahead, "That's him, grab him, and call the cops!" I couldn't sleep or hold food down, my stomach stayed knotted with sharp pains akin to an ulcer.

After a week, these symptoms eased and the paranoia faded. I began to believe that we'd gotten away with it. A feeling akin to invincibility rose to the surface of my conscious thoughts. I felt almost compelled to test this newfound power by seeing just how far I could go before getting caught. In fact, Zig's new plan was starting to sound pretty damn good to me, now that a week had passed.

The Bust

It had been exactly one week and one hour since the robbery. Sitting in the Old Man's chair, my mind was working at warp speed trying to analyze the events of the past week. Somehow, in spite of all the screw-ups, we'd managed to escape the legendary "long arm of the law." It seemed reasonable that if they hadn't caught us by now, then they weren't going to catch us. I had to find Zig to let him know that next time we'd have to be more professional. Where to hell was Zig anyway? No one had seen him since early in the morning; it was as if he'd dropped of the edge of the earth never to be seen again.

Watching my eleven-year-old sister had tied me to the house on this particular Friday night. The dog kept barking at something in the back yard for the past fifteen minutes or so, but when I looked outside, I couldn't see what he was barking at. Then there was a knock on the door.

Opening the door, I saw a group of guys in suits, at first they looked at each other and then me as if sharing a common thought only they were aware of.

"Are you Robert?" Yes. "Can we come in?" No, I stated flatly, and shut the door. They came in on their own flashing various badges identifying themselves as FBI, and Broward County detectives. "Where were you December 19th"?

"Probably home watching TV, where were you?" "Don't get smart, we know you robbed the Savings and Loan so you might as well tell us now, it will go easier on you." With that, they tossed a blown up picture of me from the bank in my lap. "That's you; we also have Zig and the AMX!"

"What's that supposed to be, some kind of code, or something? Now look here guys, I'm not the one you're looking for, I'm only fifteen years old, and I did not allow you in my parents' house. I suggest you leave and wait until my folks get home otherwise you're here illegally, so I suggest that you go."

"You're not fifteen and we can go wherever we want during an investigation because we have the FBI with us. Besides you were ratted out by your partner, we know everything."

"BULLSHIT," I yelled, "get out of my house!" Then one of the detectives leaned over the chair, and put his handgun in my face. "WE KNOW you did it," he whispered. I smiled back.

When this had no effect, he pointed it at my balls and asked, "Now you did do it, didn't you?"

"Yeah, and I shot Abraham Lincoln too, get the gun off my nuts. What ever happened to good cop, bad cop anyway?"

My younger sister began chanting, "Robert's getting busted, Robert's getting busted," repeatedly, so I sent her to her room.

Then they asked, "So where is it?" "Where's what?" "The gun." "What gun?" "The gun from the robbery." "Oh yeah." "Well, where is it?" "Where's what?" "The gun?" "What gun?"

I saw the Detective pointing his gun at my nuts again and said, "Here I'll show you where the gun is." I got my ass off the chair and started walking towards my bedroom. They followed like a row of ducks in suits. Reaching for a .38 I had on the top shelf of my closet, I muttered, "I'll show you a gun!" I was grabbed by one of the feds, and slammed to the ground before my last word was out.

"Now look guys, there might be a gun similar to the one you're looking for in one of those boxes, but I am

15

not giving you permission to look without a warrant. So if you do happen to find one in there you can't use it in court." Ignoring my ranting, they started searching my closet and came up with a gun. "We've got you now!" One of the detectives said rather proud of himself. I was taken downtown after they read me my rights.

Handcuffed and dragged into the Lauderdale Police Station, I saw Zig halfway across the room, with his Dad on one side, and a lawyer on the other. I could hear him saying, "I don't know what you're talking about old man, I don't know nothing about no bank, and no one named Zig. My name is Dillinger, John Dillinger. You can put the thumb screws on me and you can't make me talk!" I yelled over and held up my cuffs. He responded with, "Oooooh, what are you doing here?" "I was gonna ask you that." I replied.

"Hey, they picked me up twelve hours ago, and I haven't said shit." I was then ushered away from Zig and into an office. Various detectives came in playing the game. How Zig told them where to find me, and how they knew everything. My only response was that I wanted a lawyer, if they wouldn't give me a lawyer then send me to juvenile or let me go! This went on for over an hour until, my Dad walked in.

He casually explained that they already had enough to put me away until I turned eighteen. The cops had offered him a deal, get me to give them a statement and they guaranteed I'd only get one year in State School. They told him that since I was a juvenile, there wasn't much they could do to me. Just give them a statement, "besides it's Zig they want not you, he's an adult.

Then it occurred to me how I could fix everything in one shot. I could take all of the heat for the shooting, since there was nothing they could do to me anyway. This would save my partner, and get everyone off my back until I had a chance to sort things out. So, I gave them a statement.

Rambling into a small hand held recorder, I described the wrong ammo, knowing that I'd dropped some unspent shells that night. I went as far as saying I couldn't remember my age. The conversation with the teller I described in detail, then I altered the part about the shooting. Instead of the actual events, I told them the story from the newspaper. Sounding cold and callous I described how after being tackled by the manager, I had flipped my assailant, pulled the gun from my belt and coldly shot him in the back while he lay face down on the ground.

Zig was portrayed as an unknowing accomplice. Once the recorder was turned off, I signed some kind of form saying everything on tape was true and not coerced. When asked why the top of the form was left blank, the detective said that they print the transcribed tape in that section, it saves time to fill in the blanks later. After signing the last form one of the detectives said, "You're fucked now asshole!" I had no idea what they meant.

Pompano Detention Center was located on Hamondville Road, it served as a midway point between the crime and the sentence. The building was rectangular with the entrance on the long side about midway. Once inside I was led through a hallway with a couple of offices, and into the chow hall via a steel door. The control room covered the far wall of this room.

This was where the "counselors" could watch the whole place from one location. The boys were on the one side, girls on the other. Leading into each side outward from center was the TV room with a couple of chairs in each. The girls had a few more chairs than us since they tended to beat each other with them less then the boys. Then out into an open courtyard encased in Plexiglas. Behind the clear shielding, were the cells. Originally built for two people each, they sometimes had as many as five guys in each of them.

Cigarettes were very scarce. If you were lucky, you could find enough butts to roll up some tobacco in Bible paper. John Edgar always seemed to have something to smoke. He was a malformed character who was also fifteen. Very bony with long hair you could always look for him curled up in a corner; his limbs always at unnatural angles as if a train had hit him and deposited him there. Rumor was his mom had been feeding him LSD since he was a year old. It made him easier to handle. But she took good care of him now, smuggling him cigarettes and Quaaludes. Apparently, his raping an elderly woman at gunpoint hadn't changed this caring mother's opinion of her son.

I spent my first day hanging out and getting the feel of my new home. Asking how things worked, inquiring about the drug, and counseling programs, I was answered with puzzled looks or laughter. Things here weren't quite as I had imagined them.

Bank robbing made me somewhat of a celebrity, and coming from a nice neighborhood made me a little different than the rest of the guys. One other kid stood out from the rest. The boy's name was Kenny.

He was very passive and mellow compared to everyone else. There were scars on top of scars covering his arms from trying to kill himself. The quiet persona may have been from the massive amounts of thorazene; they fed him a couple times a day. His Mom never really wanted him and I guess some her boyfriends did. Between beatings and other forms of abuse, he spent most of his time pondering the end of his existence.

I'd spend hours talking to him, trying to meet the person behind the monotone voice and blank eyes. I could almost see a real person buried deep inside, but somehow that part of him always eluded contact. On rare occasions, a small part would start to rip its way to the outside in the form of a smile or some emotion in his voice. But the scars of his life created a wall that quickly absorbed these few instances as if they never happened. His life sucked more than anything I could ever comprehend. The futility of his existence fascinated me.

Early Monday my court-appointed lawyer paid me a visit. He started the conversation by informing me how bad things looked, between the pictures from the bank, witness ID, and the taped confession; the state had a very good case against me. I explained that the confession was not a great concern of mine, and that the gun was confiscated in an illegal search. I figured if the witnesses couldn't describe me immediately after the robbery, then what good would they be in court?

My main concern was how long it would take them to realize that they had violated about every civil right I had. And would it take more then a month before my release. The Attorney said we'd have a better idea of where we stood after court that afternoon.

That same morning some of us were bussed over to juvenile court. This was more like a PTA meeting than the traditional courtroom. The judge sat behind a long table facing rows of chairs where we sat with our families seated behind us. They stated my name and read off the charges. Armed robbery, attempted murder, illegal possession of a firearm, discharging a firearm in public, conspiracy, leaving the scene of a crime, and some other charges I couldn't fathom. They didn't ask for a plea of guilty or not guilty, since they were considering a Grand Jury indictment.

I asked my lawyer about this Grand Jury thing, and he said they might try to make me stand trial in adult court.

"How's that when I'm a juvenile?" I thought you could only be tried as an adult for a capital crime like murder. He explained, the law now read that any crime involving a gun carried a life sentence, so I could be indicted as an adult. "How about I plead guilty now and we push it through Juvenile?" The judge didn't even want to hear the motion. He made a note that I had asked for the chance to plead guilty, but the court wouldn't accept it at this time. As far as being released to my parents' custody, that was denied also.

Back at the detention center, I asked some of the guys what the deal was with being indicted. A few of them said they take you to court to enter your plea of guilty or not, then you spend the night in a steel two man cell. Next morning you're back at the center waiting for trial. Still the most anyone got was a year in the county jail. Then they make you a trusty and that's the end of it. The only exception was if you had a murder charge.

The idea of being here at the center for thirty days sucked, a year in state school was worse, but a year in the county was a little bit hard to go for. I'd heard the food was inedible, and that they served the coffee and tea from big trashcans as you hold your cup through the bars. But knowing that a year in the County Jail was the worse that could happen left me with the hope that I'd get off easy, hopefully with just a year in State school.

Two weeks had passed in the juvenile center. I was amazed at how easy it was to adjust. My first weekend I hadn't been able to hold any food down and my hands shook uncontrollably. The other guys had said this was common if you had a daily habit of drugs or alcohol. The hallucinations were still there, but it was becoming easier to identify them and treat them as such.

I should have done this robbery thing a long time ago. Another month or so and I'd be over these cravings and on my way to getting my act together. It looked as if my plan was going to work, if a year in the county jail is what it took then so be it. They'd done me a favor by locking me up after all. All I had to do was keep myself amused and enjoy the ride.

We'd always find some thing to do or someone to pick on for our entertainment. I averaged about one fight a day. Most of them victorious, some never finished. The counselors were quick to stop any fight that got too serious and at other times let them go just to see who would win. There was one short but big built black kid called Kojak. He'd put his baldhead down and charge his adversary like a bull. I'd seen him knock the wind out of a couple of big guys. One day for some odd reason he came my way, head down and at full steam. As his shoulder hit my side, I looped my arm under his and fell backwards onto the concrete, his head sticking out behind me. I couldn't believe it when he got back up. He asked, "Why'd you do that?" Then his eyes glazed over and he toppled backward unconscious. That would have killed the average person but it only gave him a headache.

That little move cost me a day confined to my room. Later that evening one of the counselors (guards) came by the door and told me I'd been indicted. A week earlier, this would have worried me, but by this time I really wanted to see if all I'd heard about the County Jail was true, it was worth a one-night stay just to find out. The next morning an old burly deputy came and put me in handcuffs and shackles and off we went, in a crowded van to the Broward County jail.

County Jail

At the courthouse, we took a steel elevator upstairs to a narrow waiting room with bench seats on each side and just enough room to walk in the middle. We were cuffed in groups of five and taken to a hallway like area with a single long bench just off from the courtroom itself. As your turn at court came up, they'd cuff you separately and lead you before the bench.

My judge was Tyson. I'd already heard the stories about him while waiting in the back. Rumor had it; he'd been shot in a robbery, and burned anyone that was involved in one. In actual appearance, he didn't look all that bad. The bailiff started with the case number and my name. Then the Judge looked at the papers on his desk and said, "I can't believe this, there must be a mistake, how old are you boy?"

"Fifteen, Sir."

"Do you have any idea what the charges are against you?"

"No Sir, not exactly."

Tyson, "You are hereby charged with robbery in the first degree, with a firearm." He then sat there staring down at me waiting, as I wondered what had happened to all of the other charges.

He asked, "Well now, what do you have to say for yourself?"

"Is that all?" I asked.

"What do you mean is that all, isn't that enough?"

"Man, you should have heard what they had me charged with in juvenile court!"

The judge's demeanor changed, His voice shook as he yelled to the bailiff, "Get him out of my courtroom."

My lawyer, Wade, interjected, "But your honor we haven't entered a plea yet?" "What do you plead?"

"Not guilty." Bail was denied, as I was led from the courtroom.

We went up some stairs and made some turns past rows of cells. Then into a short side corridor that had two big steel doors with Small Square hatches about six inches across mounted at face level. At the bottom was a fold up lid about four inches high where the food was slid in on the floor. The guard opened a square gray box on the wall pulled some levers and turned a wheel. Loud clanks and grinding sounds came from inside the steel wall and then the door popped open to the rear cell.

Inside, to the right, were two bunks and straight back was the combination commode and sink. I walked in and felt the door shut behind me, the walls shook with the sound.

My new roommate was an older heavy guy that was more concerned with sleep than anything else. He told me everyone in this section was Federal prisoners. After a pitiful dinner, some of which was still sticking to the bottom of the door, a trusty came by and asked where the young bank robber was. After identifying myself, packs of cigarettes and Apple pies came sliding under the door. Wait a minute; I think I'd heard of this one before.

Then I saw the note from Zig. "Looks like we're going to the big house. No more jive in seventy-five! Let me know if you need anything." I sent a note back saying, I was just there for the night, but thanks anyway, we don't get to smoke in juvy.

My cellmate had some wine he'd made and it was damn strong stuff. He was convinced there were microphones hidden in the cell, and that there was something "they" were hoping to find out from him. Yeah, well I could believe any thing at this point. But one thing he said did make sense, that since this was Friday and they didn't move prisoners on the weekend then I might be here for a few days. Looked like my one night visit had been extended to Monday.

An insufferable amount of noise went on constantly in the jail. The continuous slamming and clanking of metal doors and the yelling, hollering, and loud conversations of almost a thousand people, echoed off the miles of steel walls. Adding to this were the sounds of a hundred TVs and radios all blasting at once, the average person might find it hard to sleep.

Looking out of the small upper portal, I had noticed a hand poking out of the cell next to us with a ragged tattoo on it, this guy had been constantly yelling over to the Fed cell around the corner. From what I could gather, they figured him for a snitch, and it was the guys in the Fed cell that had forcibly held the man down and tattooed the word SNITCH across his hand. He ranted on and on about killing everyone in the Fed cell. The Feds retorted by chanting 'SNITCH!' in unison.

This banter continued until around midnight when the noise reached an even higher level. It was election time, and Reagan was in town running against Carter. Apparently, the fool they were bringing in had pulled a toy gun out near Reagan at the Miami Airport. I caught a glimpse of the guy as he was brought by my cell door.

Wearing a party shirt, he stood well over six feet tall with a medium build. The cops where throwing him around a lot. He fought them for every inch of ground as they pushed him up to, and then into the next cell. He went in and the snitch came out. Once in the max cell, the new guy started screaming bloody murder about how he was a claustrophobic and that the walls were closing in on him. Maybe he should have thought of that before this career move.

He emphasized his condition by kicking the walls for hours until everyone on the floor started yelling for him to cut it out or he'd get his ass kicked. The cops came back and told him if he could stay quiet for a few hours they'd put him in regular population, this seemed to calm him down a bit. The cell around the corner asked who was in the cell with this new guy, and was answered by a frail wimpy voice. "Just me, Little Jim". "Hey guys, they put the nut in with the Bitch!"

The wimpy voice answered, "I am not a bitch!" "You'd be my bitch if I was in that cell!" the voice from the Fed cell replied.

Now it sounded interesting. So I started yelling down the hall at the Feds, "What's up?" "Who are you?"

"I'm the fifteen year old bank robber, who are you?"

"I'm the guy that tattooed SNITCH on that snitches hand. See if you can shut that other asshole up next to you!"

I spent the next couple of hours talking with The Nut. He asked for something to smoke and some aspirin. I sent it over and soon smelled something funny. I asked what it was and the Bitch replied that the Nut was smoking aspirin rolled up in a cigarette.

In the morning the cops came to put the Nut in population somewhere downstairs. They had him at the top of the steps when he decided to fight them; they gave him one warning before letting gravity assist his descent.

In the morning we could hear his whining from downstairs, he kept calling out that he was dying and needed the nurse. The nurse finally came and slapped the hell out of him while yelling, "What the hell are you doing drinking bleach, how much of this did you drink?" When there was no answer, the sound of another slap rang out. They took him away for most of the day, but when they brought him back, he was cuffed spread eagle, his butt facing the bars. He howled and whined for a while, and then he whimpered and eventually started sobbing. Sometime during the day, he just stopped making noise all together. Maybe he was moved or made bail; I didn't really care what happened to him. He was weak, and there was no sympathy here for the weak.

Monday morning came and went with no hint of when I was to go back to the Juvenile Center. Come noontime, I was resigned to consume some of the food. They did come for me, but instead of going down stairs, I was moved next door to where the flaky voice had been emanating from. The voice came from a skinny little guy who was very happy to take the top bunk if I wanted the bottom one.

He informed me his name was Jim, and that he was gay. Personally, I thought gay was a very polite word for a dick-sucker but as long as he kept it to himself, I really didn't have a problem with it. It was a fair assumption that Jim was lonely, from the way he talked endlessly. I found myself telling him to shut up more than a few times. He mentioned that he was ten years older than I and that he should get more respect then just being told to shut up. I stood up and explained that unless he could kick my ass he should just keep his mouth shut.

Evening came, and with it shower time. We showered with the Fed cell from around the corner that I'd been talking with. I finally had the chance to meet the people behind the voices. The first guy introduced himself as the houseman. Every bullpen has a houseman. A bullpen is a square cell that serves as a living area, where if you're lucky there's a table for eating and playing cards or whatever. Sometimes called a day room, this is where most of your time is spent in population.

The pen is ringed with small two or four man cells where you sleep and keep personal property. The houseman is elected by his cellmates. His job is to make sure the cell gets enough trays for everyone at chowtime, also coffee, tea, laundry, or whatever the cell needs. He chooses his own assistant houseman and between the two of them they manage the internal problems like what channels the TV is on

27

etc. For this they are paid ten and five bucks a week prospectively, to buy what they need out of the commissary. Of course, in the case of the snitch, they had asked him to leave peaceably. When the guy refused, the cell remedied the problem with a tattoo party.

Being in a Max cell as I was, I'd been missing out on the population routine, but my new associates were more than happy to fill me in. They told me that Jim was scared to take showers because of them. "You mean I'm in a cell with someone that doesn't bathe, I don't think so!" I went back and convinced him to come down with us. The Feds explained some good hustles for making fast money. They said I had balls but banks were outdated, the money now was in white-collar computer crime. It's high return with low risk. And if you're caught, the sentences are a joke, making the risk well worth the money.

Then he asked me if I was getting any. "Any of what", I asked. "Any ass off that bitch you're in a cell with? Man that's a prime opportunity." "I'm not getting any closer to that faggot then I have to!" "You just haven't been in long enough. Any real man has to get off. After you're in a while you'll see what I mean."

"No, I don't see what you mean, but you're welcome to him if that's what you want."

After a small huddle in the corner of the shower cell, they surrounded Jimmy and tried some unfriendly persuasion. I'd already washed and was drying off when the houseman came up to me and asked, "Hey, she says that she doesn't want to do anything for us. You got her to come down here, see if you can talk to her about hooking us up with some ass."

"Man, I'm not getting involved in this kind of stuff. What makes you think I can change its mind?"

He responded, "Hell, I don't know but it's worth two packs of cigarettes from each of us if you can talk her into it." It looked like I was going to have a little talk with my cellmate.

"What's the problem with you and my friends there?" I asked.

"They want to hurt me!" "No they don't, they just want to give you some of what you want, and you're not getting near me with that stuff. Why don't y'all just work together on this, you have my word they won't hurt you."

The next thing I knew, there were two of the guys poking the fag at once. I tried not to stare at this odd performance as I counted my cigarettes. Only two of the packs were Menthols, some Cowboy smokes, and some non-filtered. But what to hell, the non-menthols would still get a weeks worth of extra trays from the trustees.

Four of the Feds screwed the boy; a couple of them weren't interested, and one guy got a piece of ass on credit, with the promise of payment in menthol. Later that night back in the max cell, I had to repeatedly tell Jimmy to shut up; he kept saying how nice I was to make sure they didn't hurt him. I had already started reading a self help book, and was about a third of the way into it, when a note was handed down to me. I open it up and read the contents. Jimmy had hand written a formal request to suck my dick.

"Now look, I told you before I'm not into that. If you bug me about it again, I'm going to kick your ass all over this cell. Do you understand that? We have a good thing going here and everybody is happy with the arrangement. So be happy with what you get, OK?" She asked, "What if I won't do that any more?"

"Then I guess I'll have to let them hurt you, and there will be no extra food for you. In fact, I might not let you eat at all!" If this is what a pimp goes through, it's no wonder they beat their bitches. He was quiet for an hour or so, then he handed down another note. "This better not be what I think it is," I said, while unfolding the second note. It started with a formal apology and then a request to see my Dick, "Hard" of course.

That's it, I'm kicking his ass! I put my boots on and jumped up to see this ugly, boney little guy quivering under a blanket. He asked all teary eyed, "What are you so mad about, I didn't do anything wrong!" I grabbed him by the hair and threw him against the steel door. There were thick horseshoe cleats on the heels of my boots. I raised one foot, with the intent to kick him in the face. But as he raised his hands to cover his face the blanket fell, he was buck-naked! Then a two-foot long Dick came rolling out.

No wonder he was queer that thing had been propping his ass up like a kickstand all his life. I hesitated a moment not sure to stomp his face or throw something at the snake. Screaming like a girl he begged, "Please don't hurt me, I have Demerol!" "What's Demerol?" "Just ask the Trusty, he knows what it is!" "OK, you just bought yourself a couple of minutes, now get over in the corner and don't move until I check on this."

When the trusty came to the door, I asked him what Demerol was worth. He said, "Anything you want." I told the trusty to check back with me later, I then told my cellmate, "OK, now, put your clothes on bitch! From now on, you do what you're told, you speak when spoken to, and you do not touch the trays when they come in. Do you understand this?" With a girlish grin she replied, "Oooh I like it when you're mad!" "And no more of that shit either!" Damn, this sicko gets off on this.

I had a good life for a week or so. I'd never had a servant before, lot less one that hung onto my every word and was thrilled if I just talked halfway nice to him /her. I was beginning to see that the rules were different in here than on the street.

Outside these walls, weaker people have an even say with the stronger and the laws enforced that. But here the stronger ruled the weak, and the weak had to be ruled otherwise they'd just do what ever they wanted, all of which involved disrespecting their superiors. Besides, the weak enjoy being controlled; it takes away their sense of responsibility. It's as if you're the Daddy and they're the kid, when problems arise, your say is final. Sometimes you might have to beat them a little just to remind them of their place, but for the most part, it's understood who runs things. The Feds got a big kick out of this, and said that I didn't have a thing to worry about if I did go upstate. I took this as a compliment.

Word came that I was being transferred, and that afternoon I was moved to a holding cell. This is the cell everyone comes to first until their regular cell is assigned. I was standing around talking when an unusually big black guy walked up and asked, "You in here for robbing a bank?" "Yeah." "Well someone wants to talk to you." "Who's that?" "The houseman in the first cell." I looked into the first cell and saw a foam mattress laid on the commode like a recliner, then I noticed Zig doing the reclining. Smiling he said, "What's up partner?"

"Hey Zig, you the houseman of the holding cell?" "Yeah, this is the worst cell in the jail; it's the cops' way of screwing me over." The big guy came in and - Zig said, "This is Moe my assistant, and the cell enforcer. Moe, this is my partner that went in and did the robbing." Moe smiled, exposing his gold teeth, and shook my hand, exclaiming how he'd heard all about me. Zig told me to sit on the throne, and with that, I checked out the recliner. Moe handed me a cigar from a large box under the bunk that was full of stuff, and lit it for me. Zig went on to explain how his Dad had spent a lot of money on an attorney. The court wanted to burn at least one of us. If I didn't get any time then Zig would get it.

What we were hoping to get was about five years each and sent to ACI, a jitterbug camp. A jitterbug is a young guy out to prove himself. Quick to start a fight but lacking in common sense, normally more of an annoyance than a threat. A whole camp full of them could be a real pain in the ass.

I asked Zig how he managed to get himself caught that day. It seems he was driving the AMX to get parts for his Camero, when a cop pulled him over for a taillight. Zig was trying to stuff some of the marked bills into the shifting boot as the cop walked up to the window. When the cop asked what he was trying to hide, Zig slapped him with his wallet and tried to pull out. Two other cop cars pulled in front of him, leaving no way out. We both looked enough alike that they thought he did the robbery. So they put him in a lineup. He was identified as looking a lot like the guy, but not being him. The detectives asked around the neighborhood to see if anyone recognized Zig in the picture. When they got to Larry's, he told them, "That's not Zig, it's Robert; here I'll show you where he lives." And if that wasn't enough, Larry was now testifying for the state.

Our conversation was interrupted when I noticed the guards taking some guy with one leg down the hall. Zig told me how the one legged guy and some buddies had run a tollbooth, and then shot two troopers that pulled them over. After a bunch of cops caught up to them, they threw their guns out the window and gave up. The cop on the driver's side pointed the gun in the window, then down at the driver's knee and blew his leg off. Or at least bad enough where they had to remove it. The papers said it happened when they tried to run. But I had already learned the papers print what they are told, or whatever sells better.

I still found it hard to believe that I would get much of a sentence. Even five years sounded ridiculous to me. Everyone's trying the old scare tactics. I assured Zig of this, but I could see in his eyes that he didn't share my confidence. An hour or so later they came and took a vanload of us to the Annex.

The Annex

The Annex was located on the third floor of the Ft. Lauderdale City jail. It had one hallway with five big open cells to one side. Inside each cell, a ten-foot deep area in the front near the bars served as a day room. Behind that were double bunks on both walls leading to the back, and four bunks in the middle, twenty-two in all. Looking in from the hallway into the back left were a single shower stall and two commodes. A steel table was our entertainment center where we could watch the TV.

There was four feet of space between any of the bunks; so most everyone stayed on their bed. The exception being chow time, then there was only enough room for half the cell to be up at one time. I was in cell two, known as the school cell. We had a teacher come in once a day to help prep us for taking the GED test. Being fresh out of school I figured what to hell, I'll get my diploma and no more school for me when I get out in a month or two. The houseman was called "MG" for his initials. He did a good job and was the first to fill me in on the cell rules. "Everyone gets along, no jitterbugs, no stealing. Any one breaking the rules gets court held on them in the cell. And whatever everyone decides on for sentence is quickly carried out. If you got a problem with any of this, let me know now!" "Sounds good to me, I don't think we'll have a problem with any of that." He stared hard at me for a moment, and then walked away.

34

I took a bunk in the far back right corner. It was hard to see the TV from there but it was a low traffic area. The bunks near the front got crowded when everybody went for chow. I preferred to have a little more personal space when I ate.

Most of the guys in there were good people at least by our standards. We had no stealing and very few fights. It was easy to tell the druggies apart. The potheads were mellow, the acidheads were kind of bug eyed, and so on. I met Shorty, the guy in the next bunk. About twenty years old from Boston, Shorty looked much younger than his age. He was just a little bit crazy and would fight anyone, real or imagined.

Shorty was telling me how the new guy they just brought in wasn't right in the head. "You can tell by the way his eyes are sunk back in his head." Shorty explained. Sure enough, he was right. The new guy had told someone how he'd been walking through a mall parking lot and decided he needed the cigarettes sitting on the dashboard of a truck. When the owner of the truck, a rather big cowboy from Davie came out of the store, he found Crazyman sitting in the truck, broken glass and all, smoking away. From the looks of things, the cowboy won. And Crazy wasn't no little kid either, About 6'3 with a big build he could be threatening. Back and forth, this guy paced, talking to himself.

Most of us were getting annoyed at this point. MG asked the guard to get him out of the cell and was told, "No, the boy had as much right to be there as everyone else". Shorty asked him if he kept moving because he was scared the cowboy was still after him, "He's coming, and you know he wants another piece of your ass." Shorty taunted. Crazy man jumped! With one hand, he hoisted Shorty off the ground by his throat.

The little guy swung at his attacker but his fists fell short a couple inches from Crazies face. A couple of us tried prying them apart, but crazy people have unlimited strength. Finally MG grabbed the mop wringer and drew back with it telling Crazyman he was about to get wasted if he didn't let Shorty down. A sudden look of realization passed over Crazies' face, as he dropped Shorty to the ground. Then Crazy went back to his pacing, as if the incident never happened.

Late that night, we put a blanket over Crazies head and everyone took turns beating the shit out of him. As long as everyone got a shot in, no one could snitch. At least we used that excuse for our "blanket party". The now bloody and whining Crazy stooped at the bars crying for the guards to let him out, while everyone in the cell pretended they were asleep. He was promptly removed, and the cell once more reached its previous level of harmony for the rest of the night.

Early in the morning, four guards came in yelling shakedown and transferred everyone to the other end of the building. There was one large cell and two little ones on the opposite side. In one of the little ones sat the one legged guy I'd seen at the county before I'd left. Everyone was spitting on him and throwing cups of water in his direction with amazing accuracy. Someone said how yesterdays' paper told how this guy was testifying against his partners. Then the chant of snitch started up.

It was like some kind of a ritual as the chanting grew louder, everyone got more wound up. You could actually feel the venom billow out of the crowd in a wave of pure malice flowing in the direction of this broken, one-legged man cowering in the farthest corner of his cell across from us. It was easy to get caught up in the moment.

The cops came and told us to quiet down or we'd be left in there all day. Once things cooled down a bit, we were led back to cell two. In our absence, the cops had torn everything apart. The idea is to find anything not allowed. This meant anything not on the canteen list, or listed as a personal item we came in with. Mostly it's a drug search but in this case, it was retaliation for Crazy falling out of his bunk and hurting himself.

Shorty was sent to the main county jail later that day and Bounty Hunter got his bunk. Now here was a character. He was kind of big with red hair and although very quiet, seemed always ready to jump into whatever situation that came up. He was the one that picked out who the cell snitch was. The boy in the top rear center bunk near the shower that never spoke much. While talking with Bounty about the different types of people in the cell, he pointed out how this one guy was just too clean. "Look at his clothes; they are always perfect, not a hair poking out of place, and way too quiet. That's your snitch right there."

It took a couple of days for Bounty to prove it, but he was right. When this kid went up to the bars for his medication (which only he got on request), he was leaving a small note on the bars. I told the houseman about it, and he agreed to check it out. That night he went to the bars and intercepted the note. It had the name of a trustee and "sells pot" written next to that. This scumbag was doing this in exchange for twenty bucks canteen money a week!

The cops had walked up at that time and instantly pulled him from the cell. They made him a trusty, but he never came near or waited on our cell. One of the other trustys' did get the pleasure of messing his hair up (by punching in his face), and came by to let us know the snitch hadn't totally gotten away with it.

During this time, I'd been going to different hearings for the technicalities in my case. Tyson had ruled for the state in everything that came up. In other words the gun, arrest, so called confession, and just about everything else would be used against me in court. Wade, my lawyer said my best bet was to try to convince a jury that since I never used the gun in the actual robbery that it was not an armed robbery. If the jury agreed then the county would have to send the case back to juvenile, since I could only be indicted for a capitol crime, (a crime that carried a life sentence).

He did tell me the state was offering a deal. If I pled guilty, they promised to give me no more than three years to life for this plea. Now I knew they were full of shit, and just trying a scare tactic. I told Wade, "Tell them in these words exactly as I say them, Kiss my Ass!" "I thought you might say that." Wade went on, "The judge and your prosecutor Chris Roberts are drinking buddies. A high profile case like yours gets Tyson reelected and Roberts possibly gets to be a judge. There is someone with a lot of money backing this thing that doesn't like you or what you did. You are being set up as an example, I don't have that much courtroom experience, and I'm not one of their boys. So if you want another lawyer I'll understand." " No man, you're too honest to let go, what's our next move?" Psychological Evaluation he said.

I was supposed to see three shrinks. The first one's office looked a little familiar. I was FBI cuffed, in other words hand cuffed and shackled with very short chains connected to a third chain that ran through my belt loops. This made it hard to walk in anything more than a shuffle, and impossible to even scratch your nose. The shrink opened with the usual questions like name, address etc. Then asked why people who live in glass houses shouldn't throw stones. My response, "Because if someone throws

38

them back, your house gets broken." "That's right." He said.

"But wait a minute there is a lot more to it than that. Although you don't have a house to live in anymore, you still have to pay taxes on the assessed value as if it was still there. The government is out to get you!" " Well, not necessarily." He stammered. "You mean nothing happens to anyone who refuses to pay their taxes?"

"No, you have to pay your taxes." "Then I'm right!"

Q. Do you ever hear voices or see things? A. Sometimes.

At this point, I realized where I'd seen this office front. We were across the street from the bank. I was staring out the window at the front of the building I had robbed!

Q. Do you hear any voices or see anything now?

A. Oh yeah, I see something.

Q. Would you care to tell me what you see?

A. Nope you wouldn't believe me anyway. END OF SESSION.

The next shrink was a trip. He asked the same questions as the last guy but acted the role of an analyst. He was a gaunt and wiry old man with a Star of David hanging off his neck. He constantly tugged on his thin white goatee, as if the secrets of the mind resided there. The office was nothing short of lavish, with a huge square desk at which we sat on opposite sides from each other. After the preliminary questions, the discussion turned to drugs...

Q. Have you ever used narcotics? A. No. Q. Have you ever smoked pot? A. Yes.

How much? A. How much you got?

The shrink reached over the desk shaking his finger in my face and yelled, "You're just a little punk, it's punks like you that have made the world what it is today!" I quietly replied, "Calm down Pops, and eat a pill before you have a heart attack, this isn't a good example of how adults should act around kids, I might get scared. Ha Ha".

He acted as if he was gonna try to slap me, that's when I lost it. I started crawling across the desk as quickly as my restraints would allow. "I'll get your old, half dead ass, you Jew bastard!" "Those cuffs will hold you." He said slinking backward into his chair. "Yeah, but I can still bite your face off!" And started snapping at him while I crawled. The shrink yelled, "Help, this inmate's crazy, help!" When the guard opened the door, I was on all fours in the middle of the desk. I calmly looked over and in my smoothest voice said, "Hey, it ain't like it looks." The guard dragged me off the desk and returned me to the annex. That session went rather well, I thought!

Time passed by uneventfully as my trial grew nearer. Wade had been by a few times with the new deals the state was offering. They went from life to fifty years, and then to thirty-five. My guess had proved right, calling their bluff was working but the numbers were still way too high. I had taken the federal GED test and passed it with a college sophomore level, or so they told me. But we argued over the diploma. They said I had to be Sixteen to get it and I was still fifteen. Hey, if I can be tried as an adult I want an adults' rights. They waited until my sixteenth birthday before giving me the diploma. The day before my trial was to start, Wade brought a deal that had him absolutely thrilled.

Plead guilty and you only get fifteen years! My response, "Do you know how old I am?" Answering my own question, "I just turned sixteen, "And do you know how long I've been alive?" " Sixteen years? Wade Stammered." " No, Three. I've only really been aware of the world around me for three years. And now you tell me that they want me to spend five times my life in prison! I don't think so. Tell them Five years stockade or probation, I'll do less than that if the case goes back to juvenile." Wade insisted I was making a very big mistake. Yeah, but it was my mistake to make, and they weren't about to scare me. They had no intentions of doing anything in the first place. Sure, I had a few doubtful moments now and then, but when it came right down to it, they were backing off. It looked like it was time for a trial.

Kangaroo Court

The first day of the trial started with my lawyer Wade, and the prosecutor, Roberts, arguing last minute motions in front of the judge. Up to this point, Judge Tyson had turned down everything Wade tried. What I had failed to remember was that upon entering the police station the cops had asked me to try on the heavy jacket from my closet. They took a picture, which they showed to the witnesses from the bank. Since this was how I was first shown to the witnesses, and I never had the chance to be picked out of a line up, Wade asked the court to eliminate the main witnesses on the grounds that the identification and recollection of the crime had been staged by the detectives. This motion was promptly denied.

Tyson then asked the shrink if I was competent to stand trial. The response was Mr. Gagnon is a paranoid schizophrenic, with self destructive and sociopathic tendencies. Tyson, "But is he competent to stand trial?" "Oh yes, he just has a few emotional problems."

Jury selection started with the first six people. Each one was asked if they knew or had met me at anytime. One guy said that he knew me from somewhere. My lawyer whispered, "If this guy is a friend of yours we could use him!" For the life of me, I couldn't remember who he was. So we bantered back and forth, do you hang out here or there, and do you know this friend or that one. Finally the

42

potential juror blurted out; "I used to be your bowling instructor when you were twelve!" "Oh yeah, you're Bob, how's it going man?" The juror continued "Not too bad, looks like you're in some trouble, hope you get out of it OK." Roberts immediately interrupted this dialogue and had him removed from courtroom.

The jury I did end up with was a casual mix of white and blue-collar common folks. One skinny black man seemed to be the brightest of the bunch. One white guy stuttered badly, two white women, one of them the victim of a purse snatching, and the other whose brother was hospitalized after being mugged. And one prominent businessman that seemed to have a negative opinion of me from the start.

The detectives testified that I gladly let them in the house and easily admitted to the crime. They went on to say how I led them to the gun and gave them the exact location of the weapon with permission to remove it. As for my father's claims that I had given them a statement because of their promises of leniency, one detective replied, "I would never make such a promise to anyone; for one thing I'm not authorized to make any deals. I'm just a detective."

Nothing in their story was true, but it sounded believable to the jury. They brought up some bullet casings that were recovered from the scene of the crime. These consisted of some live ammo and one spent shell. The spent shell was linked to the recovered gun by the FBI lab. According to the lab, the firing pin indentation from a .22 was like a fingerprint under an electron microscope. Because of impact, these indentations some times will not match even, from two shells fired one after the other. But miraculously in my case, they had a perfect match.

At this point, I mentioned to my lawyer that there was no way any spent shells were left at the scene. Wade asked the detective when this spent shell was recovered. He responded one week after the gun was confiscated. The worse part of this was that I couldn't jump up and say how I'd picked up my spent shell, or that the ammo in my pocket was a different brand than what was used in the gun!

This hoax of a trial was fixed. Roberts the prosecutor was running the show. He could do or say anything he liked with free reign while my lawyer was brow beaten and criticized at every turn. At one point during a break, he threatened my Dad in the hallway. This started an argument that continued into the courtroom.

The jury had just been reseated, when my father ran in being chased by two bailiffs and Roberts. Roberts, "I have a court order to keep the defendants father out of the courtroom!"

Dad, "I want the court to know how Chris Roberts threatened to make sure my son gets a life sentence and suffers for any delays in the case. He told me that he'd better just plead guilty now or it will just go harder on him!" Tyson told everyone to remain silent until the jury was removed from the room.

Dad continued, "Roberts approached me in the hall and stated that you the judge would sentence the boy to many more years for delaying the trial!"

Roberts, "That's a lie!" My Mom added, "It's true, I heard it too!"

Roberts, "That is not true, and that's the defendants mother your honor." And made a smirk with a half laugh as if to dismiss her credibility. At this response, my Dad darted towards Roberts who tried hiding on the other side of the prosecutors table. This turned into a small chase with Roberts breaking into a run to stay out of my Dad's reach.

Dad, "I didn't know that the prosecution could prejudge a case and speak for the court, meaning you. He was speaking for you judge!"

Roberts, "All I said was that the more this case was delayed, and the more I got upset, would influence what I would recommend in the presentence investigation."

Dad interrupted, "He spoke for the judge!" Roberts had by now surrounded himself with bailiffs producing a sudden surge of bravery, "Your honor, I have tolerated the defendant's family being allowed in the courtroom up until now. But after being called a liar in the hallway, and having already secured a subpoena I think the court should have the father removed from the room immediately." The Judge thought for a moment and decided to let my parents stay in the courtroom, turned down the motion for a mistrial, and made Roberts apologize off the record.

Next, they prepared to play the tape for the jury. At this point, I told Wade that we were home free. I was surprised they would offer this as a piece of evidence. As the tape played, everything began to make sense. The questions to my answers had been altered. I had given simple yes or no answers a couple of times, and those were to basic questions. All of my contradictory explanations had been removed, the sloppy editing was obvious. Half way into it I told Wade the tape had been altered. He advised the court as to my complaint. Robert's response was that any parts that had been removed didn't pertain to the trial and that we should stop wasting the court's time. Tyson let the tape play on. This was Florida justice, at its finest.

Somehow, I'd been fool enough to believe that court worked as it did on TV. Cops do their job, and no more than that. But what really matters is what people in the position of power want. If you're a judge, or a prosecutor wishing to be a judge and some kid comes along thinking he's smart, it doesn't take long for the money machine to start popping out ideas. The older people in the community that represent the majority of voters are appalled by a case like mine. Elections were coming up and what better way to get free advertising than to have your name in the paper as having saved the public from such a menace as myself. But the real reason behind why I was being persecuted instead of prosecuted was because of my partner Zig's father.

My partner was the older of the two of us, had typed the note, and in reality fired the destructive shot, it was he the courts originally focused on. But Zig's father had a lot of money, and hired the best lawyer money could buy. This lawyer took a rather large amount of money and deposited it in the campaign fund of an influential person in the prosecutors' office. Although no promises were made, the plan was simple; make a profound example out of me and Zig's involvement would be forgotten. Of course, if I weren't convicted then the attention would once again be placed on Zig.

My partners' Father was the moneyman my Lawyer had referred to before the trial. Zig had told me that he despised what his Father had done, and that it was all right for me to tell the court what was going on, but I was confident that the jury would know the difference between an armed robbery and what I had done. I saw no reason to expose Zig's payoff scam. Even without taking the stand, it was safe to assume that the jury would be able to figure out what was going on.

The story told in court was not the true one. Roberts depicted me as standing over Kim, pulling the gun out as he lay helpless face down on the ground and shooting him in the back. Lisa the Teller and Kim the manager had both changed their testimony to coincide with my now doctored statement. Being under pressure these two were not very good liars. They sounded like a couple of ten-year-olds making up a story.

(These are quotes from the certified court transcripts)

Kim"After we tussled a little bit, I was still lying on the ground on my back and the fellow who was tussling with me stood up and pulled a gun out and shot me."

Q. "Tell the members of the jury where you were shot Mr. Defreytas".

A. "I was shot in my back, just below my shoulder blade, and the bullet punctured my lung and it is now lodged in my chest, between my ribs". The jury asked him three times to repeat this testimony, but the Judge said to strike the other responses from the record since the witness was just being repetitive.

Only one of the witnesses from the bank told the truth. The other teller, Terry, had tried to say that her co-workers had changed their stories; Roberts quickly silenced her.

A friend of my fathers' had listened to the detectives coaching the witnesses on what to say out in the hallway. When he tried to inform the courtroom of what he heard, Roberts brought up old traffic tickets to prove that he was an unreliable witness. The Jury was instructed to ignore any mention of a second party being involved in the Robbery, and that any inconsistencies that may be viewed in my favor should be ignored.

My perception of reality and the world around me had suddenly been altered far beyond what any drugs could accomplish. I was in total shock. Even the return of the guilty verdict by the jury was just a muffled sound from far away that only distantly related to me, if at all.

I understood that a pre-sentence investigation took some time. That the PSI involved talking to my teachers and neighbors, and of course, there were a few other things on record. I had been in a little trouble before this. Although juvenile records are supposed to be sealed, someone was giving false records to the newspapers to print. To counter this move we had to explain in court what had really happened. Once we read into evidence the actual events my juvenile record was part of my adult trial. This was how Roberts used my juvenile records against me.

Post Trial Depression

I was back in the annex before my senses returned, padded with denial. They moved me two cells down to the college cell, where I had the chance to continue my education. We had a couple of college level books in the cell and an instructor that was there more to baby-sit than to teach.

The guys were pretty cool and a lot more organized in a political sense. Everything was voted on and majority ruled. The only violence came when a thief was discovered amongst us.

Everyone laid their property out in plain view while the houseman went over the week's commissary lists, which we kept to prove what property was ours in case of a shakedown. Before things had gone this far, it was explained to the whole cell that if the missing cartons of cigarettes reappeared, no search would be made. If the thief wanted to come forward there would be no penalty, but if caught at the inconvenience of everyone in the cell, then someone was getting hurt in a big way. The guy was caught and beaten near death before being ejected from the cell.

We did find some forms of entertainment from time to time. Like when they put an older Cuban guy in our cell. He made the mistake of acting crazy, such as putting all of his clothes in the laundry and wearing just a plastic bag wrapped around his waist. He ran back and forth across the cell like this yelling, "I'm CIA, I'm CIA." The cell met in small groups to

49

discuss if he was a real threat or just a little nutty. I had thought that maybe he was just scared, being in jail in another country maybe this was his way of dealing with us. So we decided on a test. If he could handle a practical joke and laugh about it, he'd be one of us. If he flipped out then he'd be squeezed through the bars like a thief.

The test involved a peanut butter sandwich laced with fourteen pink laxatives ground up into it. I was elected to give it to him since if he jumped me the cell was justified in protecting the juvenile against the wrath of a mad Cuban exile. The college cell had the same layout as the school cell, with the two open commodes in the back along side of each other, this was ground zero. Twenty minutes had passed since he'd consumed the sandwich with no response. We began making bets on how long it would take before the deluge began.

Thirty minutes after ingestion, he went into the back and took a normal dump. The debate now centered on the question, if that counted as the end of the bet, since it wasn't the torrential down pour we had anticipated. Then it came. This poor guy was jumping from one shitter to the other while flushing the one next to him. This went on for twenty minutes or so until he gradually rose upright and headed for the front of the cell.

Another ten minutes passed before he raced back to the commodes only to be beaten too his seat by two guys who really took their time getting off. The Cuban finally got his chance again after a lot of intense hopping and swearing only to find upon completion of his task that there was no toilet paper left. He ran to the front of the cell and used newspaper. His constant pleading at the bars finally brought the guards who promptly removed him. The sound of him saying 'I'm sick, I'm sick' faded into the distance as the bets were paid off. Later that night he was placed next door all the time swearing at our cell..."Mother fuckers Ex-Lax", repeatedly.

Outside of these few diversions time passed away uneventfully and I found myself feeling rather depressed. I now weighed 140 pounds compared to my normal 170. The lack of sunlight for almost half a year had left me a pale yellowish color. My only thoughts now, concerned my sentencing, which I had come to realize, would more likely be in the region of five years at ACI than of a year in county jail.

The day of my sentencing came, and I was transported back to the courthouse. I was standing with two other people, both who had stolen cars. The first one was given probation and the second one weekends in the county until the cars value was paid back. I was thinking that maybe today was the day everyone gets a break. And maybe I'll just get the minimum of three years possibly in the stockade near home.

I stood before the bench while the judge pronounced sentence.

"Robert Gagnon, you have been found guilty of armed robbery in the first degree by a jury of your peers and it is now for me to decide your sentence. Does anyone have anything to say for the defendant?" Wade asked that the court take my age into consideration, Roberts asked that I get a life sentence, and my mother crying, showed the judge my GED. Tyson replied, "I never said he was stupid, that's just all the more reason that I now sentence you to spend the rest of your natural life in a Florida state prison with a minimum of three years before parole. Has the defendant anything to say?"

I was in shock! One eye watered up as the other eye glared dryly at this pompous prick. All I could think was "I'll kill you," he looked startled as if he'd heard me, and maybe I did say it. He seemed to be growing closer maybe close enough to make my wish come true. Then I was grabbed from behind by a lot of hands and handcuffed. I was taken to a table at the edge of the courtroom, where I was again fingerprinted for the state. After being given a few moments to say good-bye to my family just outside the courtroom door, I was led back down the hall.

The hallway seemed to sway and have odd angles that I'd never before noticed. I no longer felt so light headed, I felt good, and actually, I felt great once the laughter started. I began laughing so hard, that I could barely walk. With all of my worrying about spending thirty days in juvenile, then a year in the county jail and finally the overwhelming possibility of maybe getting five years at worse in a state institution, the unimaginable had happened, I'd been sentenced to life in prison.

Looking back at the previous six months of constant worrying, without a single nights sleep, or appreciating one good meal, I had the mental image of a matador trying to avoid stepping in cow-shit while the bull spears him from behind with both horns. My self-imposed penance hadn't affected the outcome the slightest bit. The gross humor of it all was the feeling of relief. The unknown that had haunted me these many months was over. I now knew where I stood. The only sensible way to explain everything that had happened up to this point, and whatever was yet to come my way, could be explained in one simple phrase. I fucked up! My laughing had given way to somber contemplation by the time I had reached the all too familiar Max cell. Once inside I saw a familiar sight, it was Shorty.

Shorty was in Max for an escape attempt. They had managed to rip one of the commodes off the wall and get into the access hallway that ran between the bullpens. Out of this service tunnel, they found tools to bore through the concrete floor. During the day when the noise was at its peak, they would chip away at the concrete with a pick ax. The only thing stopping them from slipping away were steel reinforcing bars cast into the floor. Then some snitch had to run their mouth and the cell was hit with a shakedown. As the guard walked into Shorty's cell he stepped on the blanket placed over the hole in the floor. The cop's foot went through the floor and came out of a courtroom ceiling before breaking his leg. Shorty was picked out as the culprit and was now my new cellmate.

We exchanged ideas on how to make the best gas like flame from tightly rolled toilet paper set on fire on the edge of the commode. With this, we heated our coffee and tea in the milk jugs they gave us to store our drinks in. Twice a day they were refilled from the big plastic garbage cans that were rolled from cell to cell. We already knew the powdered creamer had sulfur in it, but it had to be tossed in the air before it really flamed up. On the bicentennial Fourth of July, this served as our homemade fireworks. We trashed the cell so badly, they ended up moving Shorty to the Max cell next door.

My next roommate was John Edgar from the Juvenile Center. Edgar might have been a strange character but he was no idiot. He showed me a handcuff key he'd made from a TV antenna. The key was made from the tube part with two tabs bent out for a finger grip and a single tab bent out to work the lock. I didn't think it would work but Edgar seemed confident in his locksmith like abilities. His plan was to eat a bunch of soap to make himself sick and get into the hospital where they'd leave him handcuffed to a bed. From there he'd use the key and be home free. The thing I couldn't understand was why he made so many keys. I then saw him hide a key in the seam of each piece of clothing that he owned. In this way, if the opportunity arose at an unexpected time he'd have at least one key already with him. He might have been crazy, but John wasn't stupid.

R.M.C.

At four in the morning, they loaded a bunch of us into a bus for the trip up state. This was a long hot ride as we headed towards Lake Butler in the Bluebird. The reception and medical center or RMC was the only processing camp in the state. Instead of walls, it was ringed with two high fences with about six feet in between them. These two fences were chain link topped with Constantine barbed wire. At each corner and gate of this semi octagon were the concrete gun towers. This is where the guards sat watching both the inside and outside of the camp.

Up until a few years before, the Florida penal system was known as the Dept. of Rehabilitation, this had been changed to the Dept. of Corrections. The reason for this being that the department was accused of not living up to its name with so few people leaving rehabilitated.

They cut our hair, took new mug shots, and fingerprints. This information was placed on cards along with our DC number. This card goes wherever we go along with a full file known as a jacket. They issued us state clothes or blues as everyone called them. Anyone assigned to the kitchen received white. After showering, we were led to the cellblock, which more resembled what I'd seen in the movies.

There were two tiers of two man cells. In the center was the control room, and on the other side were two other tiers that served as the box, or confinement. A steel door separated the last four cells on the confinement end. These cells were referred to as "Behind the Door." More than a few dark and sinister stories originated from this area. Even the guards used 'Behind the Door' as a threat, the same way a parent would refer to the Boogieman to keep bad kids in line. After putting our stuff away in the regular cellblock, they sent us outside to the chow hall where I had my first real food in six months.

They took our group through the administration offices as sort of a tour. At every turn, we were greeted by wolf whistles, and comments directed at our group. We stood out as new cocks with how pale we were.

Sherman was the old guy I hung out with. He was what they called "Old Chain-Gang" and had the scars on his ankles to prove it. He filled me in on how things worked, as far as keeping my mouth shut and not letting anyone disrespect me. I listened closely to everything he had to say. The man seemed to be aware of things I hadn't learned to see yet. He'd look out across the compound and point out who was selling the dope, which guys were going to fight, and which ones weren't going to make it.

The recreation field at RMC had an oval running track, with pavement in the middle. A low fence ran across this middle area where a couple of guys played tennis. This is the most open space I'd been in for months so I took off my shirt and ran around the track a couple of times. Sherman did get me to stop about the third time around, telling me I wasn't in shape for that yet, and to take it slow. I was inclined to disagree, but Sherman convinced me I'd probably enjoy watching a ball game first before doing anymore running.

There was a clay diamond with two teams already picked. Sherman advised I watch at least one whole game before wanting to play myself. The pitcher was a wiry old man smoking a pipe. Various other remarkable characters took their positions. One was a black sissy built like a linebacker, a couple weight lifters, and crazy George. George was a very short unhealthy looking guy with a constant nervous twitch. Supposedly, he was a heroine addict that kept getting more time for stabbing people. His reason for this being that he didn't like people messing with him. For all of that, he was the best ball player out there.

We watched chain-gang baseball for the better part of an hour. The basemen tripped the runners; the runners elbowed the baseman, and one time the pitcher nailed the runner in the head with the ball to stop him. Half of the batters took the bat with them to first base trying to hit the ball away. Before the game ended, a loud annoying buzzer sounded over the loudspeaker system signaling everyone to return to their bunks for count time.

Everyone was subjected to count every four hours or whenever the urge came to count us. In the event the numbers didn't match, they would roster count, meaning they would identify everyone by name and number. After dinner, they turned the showers on and let us roam around until lock down, that's when they locked our cell doors for the night.

I didn't see how this was so bad. Tomorrow we would move into the dorms where we'd stay until we were classified to what would be our permanent camps. So far, this had been a breeze. I might have to wait a year or two for my appeal to get me out, but in the meantime I could hang out for a while right here. At least my folks wouldn't have to worry about me, I was much better off in here than before in the county jail. An Old cock in our group said you couldn't judge the chaingang by RMC, and that our permanent camps would be a lot different. I found this info questionable, but then I hadn't been around long enough to comment otherwise.

I woke in the morning totally paralyzed. The short run the day before had sprung charley horses in every leg muscle I had. To add to this discomfort, was the sunburn that covered me from the waist up and the knees down. I managed to make it to breakfast where Sherman had his chance to say his told you so's. He said to go to the infirmary and get a pass from the doc to stay inside for a couple a days. That would also keep me off the work details. So pass in hand I returned to the cellblock in time to receive my new dorm assignment.

The dorms were rectangular, with the entrance in the middle of the broad side. Once in the door you stood in the day room that had the TV and some chairs. The back wall had the control room or the cop shop as we called it. Spreading out from center were the showers and latrine for each side. You could see directly into these from the dayroom through large plate glass windows. This design let the cops watch most of the dorm from one central location. In each side were rows of double freestanding bunks each having a steel drawer beneath them to keep your stuff in.

I had a bunk next to Church. He was a twenty year old American Indian and born again Christian. At first, I thought he was kind of weird but you just had to get used to him. His current goal was to convert this other guy Chuck to the Baptist style religion popular in the South. Both of them were on medical leave from the same camp called Sumpter. Once I told them how much time I had, they both insisted that Sumpter was going to be my permanent camp. They said that ACI was for youthful offenders with fifteen years or less. Anyone with more than that goes to either Sumpter or DeSoto. What the judge recommended meant nothing. Once remanded the DOC decides where you go.

Once the state has you, you become state property. If you're caught getting a tattoo, the charge is destruction of state property. They can do whatever they want to you. Once they get you, 'in the tank' they can beat you to death and no one can do anything about it. "We'll just have to explain this as best we can so you'll be for what's coming when you get there," Chuck continued.

Sumpter has fourteen hundred inmates, four hundred of them are white. And a quarter of the whites are fuckboys. This means that they are punks. Don't have anything to do with punks or the blacks or you'll end up being a punk. We call the blacks hamsters since they travel in packs and reproduce at random. If someone messes with you just hit them and keep on hitting them. Even if you get your ass kicked just keep on fighting.

Anytime you're losing a fight, never give up or try to run. Saying give is the same as saying "fuck me." Show them you got heart and eventually they will leave you alone. When other whites see you fighting like that, they'll jump in to help or break it up. And you better help them the same way or you'll end up alone. The Hamsters will try to act like friends and get you to hang out with them. If the whites see you hanging with the blacks then you're already considered a fuck boy. And you won't have any help when the hamsters make their move.

Then there's the Mind Games. There's the cigarette game, and the protection game. Most of the other games are derived from these two. In the cigarette game, it could be a pie or a cigarette, a soda or anything. They leave it on your bunk or under your pillow then you eat it or smoke it or whatever. Then later on, some big Guy comes up and says, "I want the same one back." Well of course, it's gone now so you have to fuck, fight or die. I couldn't see how anyone could be stupid enough to go for that. If I give someone something it's because I want them to have it, and if someone gives me something then it's mine. But Chuck insisted that it worked on a lot of people. Next I asked Chuck how the protection game worked.

That's when anywhere from four to ten guys surround you and start giving you a hard time. Or maybe they just jump you without warning. Then one guy comes out of nowhere and says that you're his partner, and backs the other Hamsters down. Then the others back off and say; "We didn't know man." This makes it look like he saved you. The idea is that he saves you a couple of times, and you end up not going anywhere or doing anything without your partner. The Whites see this and know what's going on, so they won't back you up. Then the "nice" Hamster turns on you and says 'Hey I did this for you, now you have to do a little something for me' meaning like a blowjob or something.

I asked, "And people really go for this crap, that's ridiculous." Chuck, "Yeah, it is, but you'd be surprised how many go for it. The idea for the protection game is to get at someone with some heart. The kind that will fight but isn't that complicated a thinker. It's being suggested that the good Hamster helping him out is feared by a whole group of Hamsters. This puts the idea in the Newcocks head that the "Good Hamster" is someone to be scared of. This way the hamsters break you down mentally by using fear." The more complicated games take three to six weeks from start to finish, the simple ones are almost immediate.

After listening to this I reached a rather profound conclusion, all of these games rely on one thing. That at the end of the game the so-called victim is expected to do what the game players predict. I could see an angle forming. The one thing I was always good at was using the rules against themselves. The rule for all games is that they only work if you do what is expected when expected. The players of the game have a lot of confidence in their ability to judge a victim and predict the games outcome. I always felt that confidence is a false assumption that should be taken advantage of.

I was almost thrilled when some Old Cock in the dorm tried running a game on me for the first time. I told Church about it and told him to watch how my theory on games worked out. It started simply enough, a rather tall Black guy offered me a cigarette, I gleefully accepted and then took it a step further and asked for one for the road. He made it a point to say hello and offer me smokes constantly and I in turn always said thank-you. He was very believable, if I didn't know better I'd probably like the guy to some degree, at least until the game ended. Then one day, wearing my boxers and heading toward the shower, he blocked my path and said we had to talk. I said," Go ahead and talk then."

"You owe me White Boy; I gave you smokes and kept the brothers from taking your ass!"

"I don't owe you shit. If you offer me something you're out of it, and as for your friends, I don't need you to look out for me. "

"Cracker you ain't listening, if you take something from me you owe me for it."

"Nope, if I borrow something then I owe you, if you give it to me it's mine, besides I said thank-you. So now, who ain't listening?" At this point, he grabbed me in some kind of an arm bar hold where both our arms were tied up and pushed me backwards into the wall of the latrine. "Man I'll fuck you up if you disrespect me like that again," he growled.

I responded, "Hey this pushing thing ain't gonna make it man, I don't feel like playing. But I'm gonna let it slide for now because you don't know any better." Trying to look mean he continued," Boy I'll fuck you up right here, you don't know who you're FUCKIN WITH!"

"Sure I do, you're a common thief that's trying to act bad. I checked into you. Now if you had any sense you'd cut me loose before I do something to you, I'm the one doing time for hurting people." "You threatening me Cracker? I've got you man, you can't hurt nobody."

Looking him in the eye I said, "For one thing you can't do shit because your arms are just as tied up as mine are. Now I'm going to count to three, and if you don't set me loose by three, you're gonna wake up in the morning with a pencil in you're eye." ONE......" Man you threatening me?" TWO......" You wouldn't really do that would you?" ......THREE, He cut me loose. "You better not be comin around my bunk Cracker, don't you ever come around me!" He hollered as he scurried away.

After taking my shower I walked over to his bunk and asked him for a cigarette, "Fuck You Cracker", was all he said. For the next few days he kept one eye open, whenever I walked near or stopped at the end of his bunk late at night.

Walking the track with Sherman one afternoon I asked about 'behind the door.' As previously mentioned the confinement part of the cellblock had a few cells separated at the end by a steel partition with steel doors. This is where you went if you really screwed up. The mere phrase held its own mystique as if to conjure up images of a medieval dungeon. Sherman said it was just some cells at the end of the block. As far as the beatings I'd heard about, those were known to happen in the understanding room, otherwise known as the control room.

A large group of cops called a goon squad would circle a guy and beat him silly with blackjacks and the large steel flashlights they all carried. In severe cases, they'd keep their victims in one of the downstairs isolation chambers and beat him at every shift change. This could go on until the inmate was broken, went mad, or died of some natural cause. If you attacked a cop, this treatment was guaranteed. The best way to avoid it was not to attract their attention.

Most camps had one place or another similar to RMCs Behind The Door. At the state prison there's a place called the flat top. Sherman said he'd seen the flat top himself. There's rows of small open cages some thing like what they put zoo animals in. The guys in the cages aren't very human anymore. They either cower in a corner or snap and grab at anyone that comes near. He told me how he'd seen someone he once knew in there. The guy did something to piss the cops off and they decided to break him. The mans spirit was too strong to break, but the mind can only take so much. Few people like to admit it but man is an animal before he's a human being. Animals have only two reactions to attacks, fight and flee. What makes people human is the ability to reason. An animal in a trap will chew off its own paw to escape, whereas a human knows to wait and see if it can fool the trapper.

When a human is abused beyond his ability to reason the instinct of the animal takes over to preserve the body. Only fight and flee are left as options, these people either cower or attack like a mad dog, anything that comes within reach. Sherman said he looked into his friends eyes and saw no recognition at all, just a snarl through teeth broken from trying to chew through the steel. He'd lost his humanity.

Once someone has reached this point, they will never be right again. They might seem themselves but when triggered by anything adverse the animal takes over. I was told to watch out for these guys and stay away from them. Not all of them had this happen in the system; maybe their folks beat them when they were kids, maybe Vietnam. It could even be the reason some of them are in here. But you can tell who they are by the eyes; the eyes are cold with no feelings behind them. When they look at you, it's as if you're being sized up as a threat, a meal, or something of no concern.

Gunshots from above our heads interrupted our conversation. The guard tower was shooting at two guys that hit the fence. The two escapees didn't know each other, and there wasn't much of a plan, except to get away. One had just read a letter from home the contents of which no one ever found out, and the second had just been told he was classified to the East Unit. Both had walked toward the fence simultaneously and started climbing. The cops in the towers were firing warning shots in the air. They couldn't shoot directly at them until they had reached the outer fence. They both went over the Constantine wire like it wasn't there.

One headed straight out in a zigzagging pattern and the second faded to the left, following the fence line. One of the other towers had opened up at this point and you could see the dirt kicking up around the heels of the furthest runner. The tree line was a few miles away in the distance and a couple hundred inmates lined the fence chanting run in unison, as if casting a spell. It was the most fantastic feeling, watching him run. I felt like that was me, and I was pumping my legs and getting closer to the trees, for some reason I pictured the tree line as a safety zone, and that reaching it represented a successful escape, apparently the runner harbored the same illusion.

An announcement came over the loud speakers warning everyone to move away from the fence and return to the dorms but it we ignored it. The second runner followed the fence line to some houses built right next to the institution. This didn't make sense to me. Why would anyone want to live this close to an Institution? Then Sherman pointed out that the officers and bachelor's quarters were in these buildings. The cops came piling out the front doors of the houses wearing shorts and flip-flops. Bats in hand with dogs leading them, it only took a few minutes to run down the second man and commence to beat the shit out of him.

The first man had reached the tree line by this time, and was beyond our vision for a couple of minutes before we heard a barrage of distant gunshots. A work squad escorted under shotgun was on its way back in when they spotted the farthest escapee. He never stood a chance. Sherman said, "Don't let your instincts to run get control over you. This is their trap and we're in it. Use your mind and play their game and one day they will have to let you out. That's the only real escape. Listen to your impulses and you'll end up like them." But, all I could think of was how much like a rabbit I felt, and how much like a dog I'd be shot down. For the first time the reality hit me that I was no more than a caged animal. What people do to dangerous animals that escape is no different from what I'd just witnessed. If I ever escape, it would be well thought out. And of course, I would be smart enough not to get caught.

It didn't take a genius to figure out that there was a lot more to be learned from the old convicts, than from the other new cocks like myself. Sherman was a very good teacher. When he wasn't schooling me in the ways of the chain gang, I had the opportunity to watch how he interacted with other old cocks. Afterwards he'd explain why business was conducted in a particular manner, or what message someone conveyed while speaking about a non-related subject.

Sherman had an untapped wealth of information, and he seemed to enjoy passing some of his knowledge my way. He seemed surprised that I had an interest in the way things used to be in the old prison system. Although reluctant at first, once the story started Sherman went on to explain the evolution of the Florida Prison system.

Originally, prisoners were called convicts; this was derived from being convicted of some crime or felony. The convicts called the guard's hacks, but never to their face, they were always addressed as Boss, Bossman, or Mister rarely by first name. The chaingang had been abolished for a few decades. But until the sixties the system's use of convict manual labor hadn't changed much. There are still road camps where crews work twelve-hour days, hand-tamping potholes in the road.

Different institutions had similar crews that were loaned out for various tasks from clearing woods to planting trees depending on whatever deal someone in authority has made with an outside interest. The present crews didn't work seven-day weeks; wear chains on their ankles, and normally didn't work under the gun. But the type work was still the same. Also under the old system, sentences were shorter. If you had a life sentence, the average time served was about seven years. The convicts were treated like dirt, and if you got out of line, the Bossman kicked you in the head. Escape was considered a natural reaction to inhuman conditions. And when you were caught, the punishment ranged from time in the box to maybe a few years added to your sentence. There was a unity between the convicts that the Hacks could never break into. On occasion, someone would turn snitch, but these snitches were shut out as soon as they were detected.

This turned the social interaction of convict to boss into an "us or them" situation. No one could play both sides. The Hack's only real job was to "secure the perimeter" or prevent escapes. For them, it was just a job they hated, that required no skills or education. Since most of the camps were in desolate rural areas, there was no shortage of this type of employee.

Once hired, the new Boss would get his first taste of power when he could tell a work crew what to do and it happens on command. What the new hack doesn't realize at first is that these work animals he's supervising on the average have a lot more intelligence then their masters. After a few bad experiences, the hack gets to resent the convicts and then gets jealous of how they stick together and follow a convict code even under severe punishment.

As dismal a group as this may be, the guards grow envious and then resentful, knowing that only the state and a gun make them superior in any way to their charges. Like being in a cage full of lions, they learn not to turn their back.

Then in the sixties, some group of intellectuals put together a fantastic theory. Criminals are emotionally handicapped people that given the proper help and opportunity could lead productive lives. So they renamed the prisoners, inmates like in the mental wards. Instead of being imprisoned the inmates were incarcerated in institutions where they could get the

67

help they required. Drug and alcohol programs were initiated, along with counseling groups and vocational training, which would lead to the rehabilitation of the inmates. This idea led to building camps with open dormitories that housed a lot more people then the old work camps of fifty or sixty bunks. They could house a thousand in a single camp with one guard for every hundred inmates.

Since the guards now served as counselors, the inmates could talk to them (in theory). This gave them the advantage of knowing what's going on from the inside, along with some degree of control over any possible events that may endanger their authority. Without a clear line drawn as to who is us and who is them the convict code almost disappeared causing the inmates to turn on each other. In some cases, one inmate selling pot will tell on a competitor to get control of his customers.

With the number of people in such a small area, there's not enough work to keep everyone busy. The idle time on dangerous minds created the mind games that I was now learning. In the early seventies, the intellectuals decided that rehabilitation was impossible to force on inmates and that it was up to the individual to seek his own help. The system was renamed the Department Of Corrections.

The programs were left in place and the DOC was left only with the responsibility of making sure the inmates were exposed to the available opportunities. Since the DOC was no longer a cruel place but a lower form of mental institution, longer sentences could be served out without being considered cruel and unusual punishment. Long terms of imprisonment were now interpreted as an extended opportunity to those that needed more help than others. The current punishment now for escape is up to fifteen years concurrent. Concurrent means that this new sentence doesn't start until the original sentence has been served.

Long-term punishment was now portrayed as a wealth of opportunity. The sentence given by the court sets the determined amount of time it takes for the individual to be properly exposed to these opportunities. Escape had now become a crime that someone commits to deprive the state of the allotted time it needs to perform its service to the individual and the public.

DOC has four levels of custody. The highest is maximum. The only two camps with this rating are the Rock, which is the original Florida state prison and the East Unit where the electric chair is kept. Next is close custody, these are the newer camps where the population stays in dorms but the outside perimeter has the same fences and guard towers as the maximum. Medium custody allows the inmates to go outside the fence but not without constant supervision. This applies to some road camps and the mobile work crews institutions send out on projects that need laborers. Minimum custody applies to work release, halfway houses, and various trustee positions. I was classified as close custody. Because of my age there were only two possible camps I could go to, Sumpter or Desoto.

The classification team decided Sumpter as the best place for me because of the violence involved in my case. Most of Sumpter's residents were violent offenders and the average sentence was fifty years. From the stories, I'd been hearing about the place, it was the king of gladiator schools. The common joke was that they give every New Cock a bat and a trash can lid when they first get there. If you make it through the first day then you get assigned a bunk. Life expectancy was about five years. I didn't give these stories much credence but I did believe about the food being the best in the system. This was the one common tale everyone agreed on. They were rumored to serve shrimp every two weeks. Church told me to look him up when I got there so at least I would know someone.

This unexpected change in my immediate future left me a bit nervous. It seemed that no matter what I prepared myself for, the situation kept getting worse. Why should I give a shit anyway? I have a life sentence and at least as much balls as anyone else I'll run into there. The rumors made Sumpter sound like the land of rampaging giants. I wouldn't believe any of this until I saw it for myself. My trip to my permanent camp would once again be postponed. With the growing problems of overpopulation, I would have to visit one more transient camp until room opened up at Sumpter. I soon found myself in a van heading towards BTU.

Attempted Escape

Butler Transit Unit was built next to the East Unit. Its main purpose was to house the overflow from RMC. Four long, dormitory like buildings made up the heart of the camp. Three were open dorms and one that served as the chow hall and laundry. Rows of tightly packed double bunks filled the dorms with a small area up front that served as a TV room. On weekdays only the orderlies stayed inside while the rest of us roamed the sandy field enclosed by wire topped fences.

Outside was a low wall with open commodes and a trough to piss in. A barn like structure served as a rec. hall but there was no recreation to be found there. Metal Quonset huts bought from the military were half assembled behind the main dorms. The plumbing hadn't been hooked up yet, and an opening into the roof of A-dorm let the wind blow down over the top of the back wall where we took our showers. While showering you could look up this wall behind the stalls and see stars. It was getting near winter and the cold wind that hit you made showers hasty, limiting sky gazing.

The kid in the bunk next to mine was named Billy. Behind the head of my bunk was Steve and across from him was Woody. Across the walkway from me on the top bunk was a sickly looking boy that was in for killing two cops. Woody was an old convict having been in the federal system, he'd somehow fallen into a loophole that let the state get their hands on him.

The first thing Woody told me was to stay away from the sickly kid because he was marked to end up as someone's boy. Anyone can kill someone else with a gun, that's the coward's way to kill. It takes heart to kill up close with your hands or a knife instead of just moving a finger.

Some of Woodys' other advice included you don't need friends, your friends need you. This meant that I was supposed to be able to handle anything on my own. I should never count on help from anyone, but my help to someone else makes me a desirable friend. Always do the right thing and I'll win in the long run.

Steve was state raised, this meant that he'd grown up in institutions and was quite at home finding hustles for making money or inventing ways to get hard to find contraband.

Billy was the easy mark. Eighteen years old, he came from a wealthy family and was a bit naive. I watched him give coffee and cigarettes to anyone that asked, so by the end of the week he was left without anything for himself. This aggravated me since I had begun to count on him for coffee. I preferred to spend my money on more extravagant things. One day he made the remark that he was going to quit smoking so people wouldn't ask him for cigarettes.

I had to explain to him that everyone was supplied with state smokes, so why should he give any tailor-mades away. He said he had a problem saying no. So I offered to keep his stuff in my locker and give him what he needed of his own stuff when he asked. I had no problem telling the leaches no. The old cocks got a real kick out of this and told me I was running the "free protection" game. Meaning that I guarded someone's property in return for the perks I wanted out of him.

At the time, I was honestly helping him out while protecting my own interests. I soon learned to take advantage of my newly acquired wealth. Billy's folks sent him more than enough money for himself, so as the locker filled I started selling some of the stuff at a high mark-up. This led to having more cash than we were allowed to have. So I could gamble a little, maybe even buy some reefer for a little buzz. This drew a more sophisticated crowd around me, which led to more opportunity. Every night a bunch of us would do the munchie and coffee thing. Smoking Menthols and playing cards, we'd discuss what was going on around the compound.

Billy started to get a little resentful that he was financing this constant party. He complained about me sending him to the store and making him hold the dope for my friends, which I got a share of for keeping for them. I had to explain that he was living better with me than on his own, and that he never went without anything he needed. But if he felt I was taking advantage of him, he was welcome to fend for himself and his problems could be his own. After insulting me with such an accusation, I told him I didn't want to see his face or hear his voice anywhere around me. He promptly apologized and I reluctantly accepted his apology with the condition that it didn't happen again.

Into our group came a short stocky guy from the next dorm. He was appropriately named Shorty. Shorty did tattoos on people and he was good at it. I had avoided tattoos although Shorty offered to do mine free. I gave him the story that in the event I ever escape I didn't want any identifying marks. He then said, "Let me show you something," and flashed what looked an awful lot like a gun. He went on to explain that his girlfriend would be waiting for him on a nearby highway in four days, all he needed was one person to help in the getaway. The plan was to grab the laundry truck that came in on a regular schedule. Shorty would drive it through the gate while I shot at the gun tower. Since they weren't used to being shot at, we'd have a head start in a vehicle without being fired on. Once past the perimeter road we'd meet up with the girlfriend and we were gone. I asked to get a better look at the gun and he said no way, I wouldn't see it again until we grabbed the truck. I wasn't supposed to tell anyone but I kind of hinted around a similar plan to bounce it off of Woody.

Woody asked if I had been talking to Shorty. Woody said there was no gun that's why I couldn't get a good look at it. "Shorty is crazy just stay away from him and his crazy schemes." Woody could be counted on for good advice, but I figured what to hell, I'll just be there when the truck comes in, and if there's no gun, I could walk away. Steve came up with a much better plan. He'd managed to get a set of bolt cutters. When the rain comes and knocks the power out (which it always did), we'd have a few minutes to scale the pipes leading to the opening in the roof from behind the showers. In the rain, we could crawl on our bellies under blankets until we could cut through the fence directly under the gun tower.

Then we go separate directions to confuse the dogs. The rain should also help cover our scent. So now there were two plans, both were feasible and one of them had to work. It looked like a busy weekend was coming up. Friday morning the truck was coming, so Thursday night I went into the next dorm to go over things with Shorty. I found him in the middle of a crowd, going over what we had talked about. He told me there were now several other people going with us. I told him he'd lost his mind. There is no way you can tell this many guys without letting the whole dorm know. We'd never get away with it. He said that these guys would be in the back to help stop any bullets from reaching us, once we get to the car

74

they'd be on their own. Let the dogs chase them while we drive away.

There was one other guy that would ride with us in the front and that was Butch, the canteen man. I instantly got that bad feeling in my gut about this guy. Butch wore pressed whites, was meticulously well kept, without one hair out of place on his head. "He's a snitch!" I said. No, he's not, look; he even gave me a couple hundred bucks to let him come along. And if he is a snitch, there is no time for them to do anything before morning. That's when we leave. I reminded him that he was crazy while walking away. This was going to be a trip.

In the morning, everyone went to breakfast as a group. I'd elected not to go, since rest seemed more important than food with our upcoming plans for the day. After chow, none of the guys came out of the chow hall. Finding this a little strange, I walked out behind the dorm and waited at the spot the truck always stopped at.

The laundry truck did come in, (with two cops in the back). They'd never before escorted the truck in or out. Something was very wrong. Steve came up and said they had Shorty up by the canteen, so I went around front to see just what was going on. Sure enough, they had Shorty and the whole crew from the night before handcuffed. I didn't see Butch, but I did notice his canteen window had remained shut this morning. When I shrugged at Shorty to signal the question, what's up? He just held his cuffs up and shrugged back. I slinked back into the watching crowd trying to make myself as small and inconspicuous as possible. Thank-God I had a back up plan.

A hard rain fell that night but the lights only flickered a few times, not long enough to make our move. Steve agreed Saturday night was better since everyone would be up late watching the tube in the

TV rooms. This would give us a chance to linger in the back without being noticed. Also being close to a shift change the tower wouldn't be as observant. The only thing we needed at this point was another good rainstorm and a little luck.

Saturday morning I skipped breakfast again and planned to lie in bed as long as possible. I needed whatever rest I could get before the long run I had planned for later in the evening.

A guard came by my bunk and asked how old I was. After I told him, he instructed me to get dressed and go to the Lieutenants office. I wasn't escorted there and this left me puzzled as to what it was about. I figured it must be my appeal. It had to be, why else would they want me?

Walking in the door, he asked me if I knew why I was there. I answered, "My appeal." "No, not quite, I heard you don't like it here."

"Well, I liked RMC better but I didn't think I have much to say about where you send me."

"No, I heard you want to escape."

"Sir I'm only sixteen, I'm not old enough to think about escape."

I also hear that you know where the gun is."

"A gun? You can't have a gun in prison that's ridiculous!"

"You can stop playing stupid, we know about the truck and we have everyone else that's involved in custody. It's just a matter of time before we know everything. And the inmate that helps us the most is the one that gets the least amount of time added to his sentence. You were the one we knew the least about. The only description we had of you was your age. You're the only sixteen year old that we've got".

It had to be the canteen guy that snitched, he was the only one that didn't know where my bunk was and that I hadn't talked to in person. Planning an escape is the same as attempted escape and they're all considered attempts since you eventually do get caught. The only way they can prove an attempt is to catch you in the act with the escape tools, or if you admit to it. I'm not saying anything; I'm not getting tricked into that one again.

In as calm and sensible a voice as I could muster I said, "Sir, you have the wrong guy, I'm waiting on an appeal. I have yet to see anyone successfully leave any of the places I've been in without getting caught or killed, and besides, there is no way in hell that truck could crash through that heavy a gate."

"I never said anything about the truck crashing the gate."

"I assumed that is what you meant, when you mentioned a truck full of people." "Boy, you just told on yourself. I wasn't sure about you for a minute there but I'll tell you what, you can kiss that appeal goodbye, you will be getting another fifteen years added on to your sentence, and... (He paused to look over my records) you will no longer be going to Sumpter. You are going to the East unit. Now if you want to help us out maybe I can help you get a shorter sentence but I can't promise anything. This is your last chance to save yourself."

"Sir I don't know a thing about it, you're turning an obvious assumption into a confession, Hell I didn't do anything!"

"Boy, I have a whole prison full of people that didn't do it, and I don't believe you anymore than I believe them. Take him away."

I hadn't eaten breakfast by choice. I didn't eat lunch or dinner because I wasn't given any. They had me in a very small steel cell that reminded me of the Max cell in county jail. The only light came from a single bulb hanging from the ceiling. The only furnishing was a narrow steel shelf on the wall not wide enough to sit on. So I elected to sit on the cold concrete floor.

Few people have any idea what it is like to be this alone unless they've been confined. There are no visual distractions, and what sounds reach through the door are very distant and not relevant to your world. I thought about the streets, and how I'd go off by myself to the hill by a church to be alone and think. Then, I always had the grass beneath me, trees to look at, the sound of birds or even traffic on the highway. And there was lots of open space, the knowledge of more things happening way beyond normal vision. All you had to do was go, and you were there. Being in a cell by yourself is a different kind of solitude. I had spent one night alone in the county Max cell once before. I had a real problem dealing with it then. It's like being a little kid trying to sleep with the light off for the first time. Without the distractions of other people or something to focus your attention on, the mind takes over. I've since come to refer to this as facing your demons.

With no external distractions, the mind turns inward and conjures up monsters from your past, both real and imagined. At first, you go nuts trying to ignore the images, some people panic. I still believe claustrophobics are a prime example of those who panic. But eventually you overcome the fear, and look the demons in the eye. The present is the foremost in the mind so that's what normally unfolds first before your eyes. In my case coming to BTU and how well I was doing until that conversation with Shorty, the talk in the office, and now here.

You concentrate on every mistake you made, everything you did wrong, and where saying something just a little bit different might have made the outcome a lot better. The demons won't let it go until you admit where the mistakes are and where the responsibility lies. Then it starts working its way backwards into the past which fortunately didn't get too far before the door opened and a Hack told me I was going for a little ride.

They wouldn't tell me where I was going, but I assumed the worst. It had to be the East Unit; everything else had gone sour, why should I think my next destination would be an exception. After what seemed like a long ride, they opened the doors and I found myself back at RMC.

If I had known this is where they sent you for screwing up, I'd have been a little less cautious in some of my activities at BTU. It was a fair assumption that they would keep me here until space opened up at Sumpter. This might just work out after all. They took me through the reception area to the cellblock just like the first time. Instead of going into the wing on the left, they took me upstairs and to the right, into K wing. We walked to what looked like the end of the wing up to a big steel door that opened with an old time jailer's key. I stepped into cell twelve, watched them close the cell door behind me, and then lock the big steel door separating us from the rest of the wing. I looked at my new cellmate and noticed he'd recently had the shit beat out of him.

Turning back to look out of my cell through the bars; the realization hit me that we were separated from the rest of the confinement wing. Something about this bugged me, and the edgy feeling wouldn't go away. There was something about that painted steel door that I was supposed to know. It was somehow symbolic. Trying not to sound too stupid I casually asked my cellmate, "Am I behind the door?" He simply responded, "Yup."

My new cellmate, (Dave) didn't care to talk much. Maybe he was antisocial or maybe it was just a little bit too uncomfortable with his lip being split. Dave was slow to leave the chow hall one day. When the guard told him to hurry it up, he responded with "Go

Fuck Yourself." He'd been counseled in the understanding room, and then deposited in twelve top cell. When I explained what they had me for he just wished me luck. Somehow I just didn't feel very lucky. If this was an example of what they do to people that cuss them, I'm in for a real ass whooping.

The Hacks liked to counsel people at shift change, the next one being around midnight, I figured it was better to just wait and see how bad I was going to get it. Hell, I couldn't sleep anyway. So I waited. At the midnight shift change, I heard the sound of many hard sole shoes walking toward the end of the cellblock.

Fortunately, for me, they were downstairs heading for one of the holding tanks. From the sounds of the footsteps there had to be four or five of the guards. Then the footsteps stopped, a door opened, "Time for your lesson, Boy!" Were the only words spoken before the sounds of the beating started echoing off the dark walls.

What made it worse was that you couldn't see what was going on. A few times I could hear some resistance from their victim and they almost seemed to enjoy these attempts of defiance. It seemed to make the guards a lot more enthusiastic to have a moving target to have some fun with, instead of just stomping a huddled mass. I couldn't tell if this ordeal lasted minutes or an hour, I caught myself secretly wishing it wouldn't end. As long as they were working on the guy downstairs, their attention was not on me.

When it ended the goon squad held a kind of hushed discussion downstairs. I couldn't tell what was being said but from the tones in their voices, I imagined they were looking for some new form of entertainment. The hacks began a slow shuffling walk back towards the control room. The steps leading to the upper tier were there. But they never came for me that night.

It wasn't until the morning that I had my first look inside the understanding room. It was a little after eight o'clock shift change and they had sent the population wings out on the compound leaving only the confinement side occupied. I was handcuffed and escorted by a single guard to the control room. I sat in a plain wooden chair while the five waiting guards encircled me holding various blunt objects that they persistently tapped against their own legs, the palms of their hands, or the chair I was sitting in.

The head Goon seated himself on the corner of the desk and started with the conventional questions such as name and DC number. He went on to explain how much trouble I was in, how I would be sent to the East Unit and have fifteen more years added on to my sentence. Maybe things would go a little easier if I cooperated. And I would cooperate either now or later through a mouth full of broken teeth. "Now tell me what you know about the escape." he started "I don't know anything about an escape, Sir." They all closed in a little tighter to form a semicircular wall that cast a shadow over me. One behind me said, "Let's not waste any more time on this lying piece of shit. Let's just kick his ass and send him to the judge for escape!" I interrupted, "Now wait just a minute officers, somehow there has been a mistake I really don't know anything about no escape!"

"So we ain't nothing but stupid hicks, is that what you're saying? We got the wrong guy because we're stupid. You're from the big city of Pompano and that makes you smarter than us like them Miami boys. Well if you were smart, you'd start talking before we make you tell us what we want to know. Understand me, BOY?"

"Yes Sir, I do understand. And I never for a moment thought that you were stupid. Hell, you're smarter than I am if you're free and I'm in here. But I really don't have anything to tell you."

"So, you never heard anyone say anything about an escape?"

"Everyone talks a little about escaping, but it never really happens."

"What you just said makes you guilty of attempted escape, you can get fifteen years just for admitting that you planned an escape."

"No Sir, discussing escape is not the same thing as planning one. Talking about it and planning it are two different things. I never planned anything with anyone. I'm waiting on my appeal, why should I risk losing that just to get shot down outside a fence?"

"Since you admit talking about it with a lot of people just who were these other inmates you discussed escaping with?" "Do you recognize any of these inmates?" They had pictures of Shorty, Turkey and some of the others I didn't know that well. They handed them to me and told me to look through them. I told them none of the pictures looked familiar. One of their steel flashlights contacted the back of my head pushing it forward. Just a little shove this time, not a hit. I wasn't too comfortable with the idea of all those D-cells hovering somewhere behind me.

"Now look," I said, "If you cut everybody's hair the same length and put them in the same clothes I have a hard time telling one person apart from another. I would really like to help you all out. But there's nothing I can think of to help. So, can I go back to my cell now?" "You ain't going anywhere until you tell us what we want to hear. Then we're gonna kick your ass around for a while for giving us such a hard time. It's time for your lesson city boy!" By this point, I was wound tight as a drum. The option of fight or flee didn't exist, and reason had no place in this room. I was on my way to a rather undignified beating with no way out.

It was hard to accept what was about to happen as reality, but between the condition of my cellmate and the guy downstairs the probability couldn't be ignored. The tapping on my chair had moved to my shoulders and seemed to be getting more persistent. I funneled all of my frustration through my voice and said, "I swear if I knew something I'd tell you! You can go ahead and beat me all you want but I've already told y'all everything I know. You'd be better off saving your energy for beating up on someone that knows something. You're just wasting your time on me. I'm just a dumb city boy!"

The room was silent for a long moment. . . Then they started laughing. I was tempted to laugh along with them but somehow I didn't think it would be appreciated. A little smack upside my head with a flashlight confirmed this, but they kept right on laughing, humored by the thought that I had come to realize their mental superiority. Then one of them asked, "What made you think we would beat you, did we say we were gonna beat you?" "No," I said, "but I could heard what you all did to the guy in the cell under me." They abruptly stopped laughing! "You're hearing things boy, we can't do that, it's against the law for us to beat prisoners. Now sometimes an inmate will fall down or give us a hard time where we'll have to use reasonable force. But we have never beat anyone, understand me boy?" "But I know what I heard," I insisted until another push on the back of my head along with the words, "Understand Boy?" interrupted my sentence. "Yes Sir, I understand".

"Now you see why this is called the understanding room. Let me explain a few things to you. Don't worry about anything you see or hear, just worry about yourself. You don't have any friends in here, just associates. And as far as the convict code, that's just a fairy tale the old timers invented to impress new cocks like yourself. When it comes down to it those old convicts will turn you in just to save their own ass."

"Now what do you know about the escape?" The head Goon asked. "I don't know anything about any escape, I swear to you I'd tell you if I knew anything!" They all looked at each other undecided as to what tact to take next. Then the headman said, "We're gonna talk to the others again, and if we find out you're lying to us you might find yourself falling down a lot. Understand Me, Boy!" "Yes Sir." "Take him back to his cell."

The next week or so was uneventful, every couple of days they would take me down to the understanding room, and we'd play through the whole thing again. I was actually getting bored with playing the scared sixteen-year-old kid role. As long as they had any doubts concerning my involvement, I seemed to be evading the whoopings like the ones I still heard taking place downstairs.

My cellmate was replaced by an oldcock with the same name. This Dave had a big crease in his head from a bat his stepfather had nailed him with. He went on to tell me how he was in a coma for six weeks, and how he saw the white light, and the whole bit about staying on here for some greater purpose. If doing time is serving a purpose then God has a perverse sense of humor. He was a clever old guy that filled me in on a lot of the chaingang rules, the games, and how the sex thing worked.

I will best explain it, as I understood it at the time. You are either a man or you're not. If you're not a man, then you're a bitch. A man fights for what he believes in, whatever that belief might be. Nobody tells him what to do or think. For anyone to attempt to tell you what to do is disrespectful and no man

84

will tolerate disrespect. If someone screws you out of money no matter how small the amount, you collect it in blood. If you don't then everyone will screw you out of it. Money is the same thing as your ass, if you let someone take your money and don't do something about it, then they know they can take your ass without the worry of retaliation. True rape is a very rare thing. The biggest meanest guy can get his ass taken either by a group or just one person knocking him out from behind. But, if this happens to a man he will get up afterward and kill the rapist. This is very rare, but it has been known to happen.

The old prison rape scenes you see on TV are mostly told from the punks' point of view. A punk or "pressure punk" as we call them, is someone that might put on the act of being a man, but when a knife is at his throat or a rape gang of four or five comes after him he will fuck or suck dick to avoid being hurt, or killed. A real man would rather be dead or beaten to death than to submit to another man.

Once submitting willfully, he becomes the sex toy of anyone that wants him. Unless he selects a daddy to protect him. This makes the punk the property of his protector. The Daddy has the obligation of protecting his property or loses the boy to someone more fit or willing to take care of him. I mentioned how this sounded like a bunch of queer stuff to me. Dave just stared at me a moment, and then went on to explain the basics.

A man has to have sex by nature. And being a man means having a female counterpart to carry out this need for sex. If there are no females, then he has to make one. This is where the punks or boys come in to play. They are latent bitches that can't come to terms with their desire to be a female for a man.

The threat of being hurt or killed or the presence of a couple of guys wanting a good time gives them the excuse to act out their desire to be a bitch. After all a man would rather be dead than someone's bitch. And death is a lot more dignified than being someone's woman. "How can they tell who to try this on?" I asked. They try you first. The first stage is a verbal threat to see how you react. If you get verbally disrespected and don't do anything about it then it becomes physical either by taking property from you or even trying to slap you.

Money and property are a part of you, if you give that up without retaliation then you won't do anything about them taking your ass. No man can let someone slap him without an immediate desire to kill or seriously injure the one that slaps him. If all of these requirements are met than it's time for a group to come and take the pussy. If you watch any of the old prison movies, you can see this process taking place long before the rape comes. But in here, it's not rape unless a man is forcibly taken in such a way that he can't do anything about it.

If they don't kill him when they're done, then he has to kill or maim as many of them as he can get at. In the case of the pressure punk, that has to be beaten a little bit or taken by storm, it is called a turning out. This means he has been given the opportunity let the bitch in him come out, by acquiring the proper amount of excuse he needs to appease his conscience. There are a few guys that don't get involved in any of this depending on what camp they are in, or if they're serving short time. The guys that have served a lot of time and don't screw sissies have a tense, crazy look about them like they're going to explode or something. This proves that it's not healthy mentally or physically, to deny the beast its basic needs.

The theory on younger guys is that they are not yet set in a mans ways. In addition, being more hormonal tend to be a bit on the freakish side. If a

86

young guy is not interested in getting laid it's because he's afraid that having a boy service him would bring out feminine desires he can't face.

If you're young like I was, it's a requirement to try to screw any boy you could corner or bribe out of some sexual favor. Although I wasn't interested, I had to put on the act that I was. Now there are different variations and titles of what kind of man you can be. One exception to all of the rules is the booty bandit. The original meaning of a bandit is someone that swings both ways. They'll intimidate or lure a guy in by giving him a blowjob, and when finished demand the same in return. A fight will ensue. Win it and you got some free sex, loose and you're fucked (in the literal sense of the word).

The new and improved definition of a Booty Bandit implies that you will chase down a boy or turn one out just because you've decided that you want him. This would make you one of the bad guys that play the games, set someone up, try them, and then take the ass when all of the requirements are met. The swap out artists also swing both ways they play the man role and may even be a dangerous guy to deal with but somewhere in secret they play both ends of the stick.

Boys are worse than women, once you own one, they can make life very comfortable. When you come back to the cell they'll have the place cleaned up and everything put away, rub your feet for you and wait on you just like a wife. But just like a wife they'll cheat, steal, and even try to cut off the sex to get their way. If not kept in line they may even try to get you to do a little sexual favor for them. The biggest thing a boy can accomplish is to lure a man down to his own level. That's their way of turning someone out, and it has been known to happen. The most important rule for a man to remember is never to fall in love with a boy!

I listened closely to everything my dent headed cellmate had to say, I had my doubts as to the validity of his portrayal of the prison world which had become my home. It had been a while since I'd gotten laid, but in no way did I have any interest in having sex with a guy. And I'll be damned if I'd be anyone's bitch. I'd rather be dead then have the judge and prosecutor sit back and say, "Yeah, you're not so bad now are you Bitch". If the chaingang worked the way Dave explained it, where the situation is screw or be screwed, then someone out there is gonna get fucked. There was a nineteen-year-old boy with a face like a young girl in the cell next to us. Dave recommended that I try to get in the same cell with him and turn him out. This would start building my reputation, before I got to my permanent camp.

He gave me some tips on how to give the boy a back rub, get him relaxed, talk him out of his drawers, rub his ass, spread his cheeks and I'm in. I tried talking the boy into asking for a cell change but he didn't seem interested. This was just fine by me but it gave me practice in pretending to have a desire to screw boys. Actually, I rather enjoyed the chase.

The idea of dominating someone mentally and physically was appealing to me. And I found myself getting off on the idea of entrapping the pretty boy in the next cell and making him my bitch. It must have showed, since my actions seemed to satisfy my cellmate that I was in the man category man and not a boy.

The cells in confinement were usually, meaning two men in each cell. The only time I had a chance to see other people was during shower time or when being escorted to the control room. There was one hell of an ugly black guy in one of the cells with a face that looked like a poorly assembled jigsaw puzzle. I'd heard him referred to by different names, but "Face" was one of the more prominent ones.

It was common when I'd first come to RMC to see some badly messed up people. Some of these deformities were birth defects that had affected these people's lives in a negative way. I hate to use the word freaks but under different circumstances, a few easily qualified for a circus sideshow. Not being able to lead a normal life, these poor souls tended to exhibit unacceptable behavior leading to their imprisonment. In some cases it was just their unpleasant appearance that caused them to be put away.

Since people as a whole, tend to fear monsters, they'll find some way of pinning a wrong on a malformed person to make sure they go away. Some of the other (freaks) were butchered jobs performed in surgery. I'd seen one guy that looked like a saucer had been implanted under the skin of his face that led from his brow to where the end of where his nose should be. Supposedly he'd caught a shotgun blast that took off that part of his face, and this was the states more economical form of reconstruction. The state values function more than appearance in most cases.

The story for Face varied in the fact that his deformity had been caused by his best enemy. A best enemy being a best friend that turns on you. This particular friend of his was nicknamed "Black." The story goes that Black and Face were running partners that had met at RMC. A partner is more then a friend in the system, more than a brother even. A partner shares everything under any and all circumstances. From making money, to jumping into an army of guys that are after you. Your partner is there to cover your back. True partners absolutely trust each other and take each other's side in any situation, with no regard for personal opinion or who's right or wrong.

Face it seems had betrayed his partner. The two of them were just a couple of skinny, little black Newcocks when they had reached Sumpter. Black being a good little hustler ran a canteen in the dorm and sometimes sold a little pot. Face backed him up on any conflicts or collection problems he had with customers.

Face felt that his best bet was to hit the weight pile and become a body builder. He wasn't very big or tall to start with. Since he couldn't make himself taller, he dedicated his time to getting bigger. And he did get one big solid build on him. Along, with the size came an attitude. Face felt he no longer needed his puny little partner, but he still wanted the things Black had to offer. So one night he took everything Black had in his store. Black tried to reason with him, and asked how he could do this to his partner? The response was, "Because I'm bigger than you, and from now on you'll do what I tell you. You're gonna be my boy from now on, you are working for me, and if you don't like it, then do something about it!"

Black wasn't about to be a punk and he couldn't physically overpower his ex-partner. With everybody watching him, he had to do something drastic before the booty hounds came after his ass. First thing in the morning he got some gasoline from the auto mechanics shop, mixed it with peanut oil from the kitchen, melted in a few Styrofoam cups, and took it to GED class in a coffee mug.

Face fell asleep in class like he always did, with his face down on his desk. Black waited a while to be sure he was asleep, then dumped the cups' contents on his partners' head. Face raised his head and stared at him half-awake, trying to figure out what was going on. Blacks' hands shook so nervously, that it took three matches before he successfully set fire to his partner.

The gasoline flared up, the peanut oil made it stick, and the Styrofoam kept it burning after being doused with water. Face was alight with something very similar to napalm. The fire destroyed his face and a good part of his scalp until it burned itself out. The skin he now had from the chest up, had come from the grafts taken off his ass. If you think white burn victims look bad, you should see black ones. After getting back from the burn unit he went back to the weight pile to keep his size up. Before long he was running around RMC trying to rough people off, this was how he'd ended up in the box. Now he was threatening to do a number on one of the white guys in the cell next to him.

Through out the weekend, these two had been verbally going at it and it was getting old. We looked forward to Monday when they could work out their differences.

To speed things up at Shower time, two or three cells were opened at the same time. Our end had already finished and the solid steel door had been left open. Everyone on the wing waited to see what was going to happen. I'd looked at both of the opponents when we walked by their cells, and I couldn't see how the white guy was going to cause much damage to someone as solidly built as Face.

When the doors opened the two of them went at it. The first punch from the white guy caught Face in the left cheek; the skin grafts hadn't taken very well and separated. The thin pink lines that zigzagged throughout his face widened into open fissures oozing some kind of clear fluid, the sheets of skin began sliding around as they were struck. The guys standing around them described this to us. The fight was over before it started. After the first punch, Face tried to cover his mug but the white guy stayed right on him, trying to knock as much hide off him as possible. The hacks broke it up and took face to the infirmary. They cussed out the white guy for how much it was going to cost the state to re-upholster the big hamsters face. Today I had learned a valuable lesson. No matter how invincible an opponent may seem there is always a weak spot. And once that spot is uncovered, everyone finds out just what to go for.

I was taken down to the control room once again and to my surprise they had changed their tactics. Instead of the somewhat tense persistent interrogation, they started off with a rather sad and somber revelation. It seems that I had been reclassified to the East Unit. This transfer was to take place in one week and nothing could alter this change in my destination.

It was kindly explained to me that I still had the opportunity to evade the extra fifteen-year sentence for attempted escape. All that I had to do was cooperate. When I stuck to my original story they all shook their heads and said that I was as good as dead already, but that I still had a week if I changed my mind.

Once I was back in my cell, I wrote a letter to my parents. I explained the present situation, as I understood it and asked if they could make a trip to see me one last time. Since people sometimes tended to disappear in the system, especially in the East Unit, I figured this to be the last time we might get to see each other. I also filled out a request form to my classification officer asking why I had been relocated to the East Unit. The idea behind this was that I wanted to know what kind of story was going on outside of the cellblock.

Until now, the only source of information I had was what my interrogators told me. I could deal with almost anything as long as I knew what was coming. Dave laughed and said, the cops read all of the letters before they go out, why should they let a request form reach its destination. And if the answer comes back negative what will that change? I told him that I wouldn't waste my time hoping for the better just to be let down again. Good or bad I just wanted to know where I was going.

The next day I received my answer. The form came back with the response, "You have been classified to Sumpter correctional, there has been no change at this time." My first response was one of relief, then I was pissed off. The realization that I'd been treated like a mushroom these last few weeks came crashing down like the bat that had dented my cellmates head. These hacks had been feeding me bullshit and I'd gone for it hook, line and sinker. This little piece of paper had changed everything. Instead of a hopeless wretch, waiting whatever fate was decided by the powers that be, I was now the 'Little Bank Robber that could.'

My confidence freshly restored, I prepared myself for whatever bullshit mind game the hacks were planning to run on me next. Everything they had taken away was an illusion. I made a promise to myself never to let anyone con me into being miserable again. These rather positive thoughts remained with me up until my last counseling session.

Once again, I found myself in the control room surrounded by my mental superiors. The room had a rather sad desolate ambiance, but I was now unaffected by the illusion of hopelessness. They began with telling me that I was going to the East Unit in less than an hour and how this was my very last chance to help them help me. I answered back with the same routine of not knowing anything, when a bright idea hit me.

I started, "You guys don't scare anybody. You all had me going for a while, but you're not gonna to bullshit me anymore. I'm not going to the East Unit, and I'm not getting no fifteen years. So go on and do whatever you're gonna do!" The room went dead silent. They all had this incredulous look of consternation that seemed to last an eternity. The headman said, "I don't know who you've been talking to, but you have been seriously misinformed. We have been cutting you slack because of your age. But it seems that you've mistaken our kindness for weakness!" They started closing in for the kill when I decided on another tact. "Hey now, wait just a minute guys! There's no reason for violence; I just figured that since we've spent so much time together that maybe we could do something a little different. You know, kind of like a joke!" The one answered back, "We'll see how funny you think it is when you get to the Unit, take him to the bus!"

I was ungracefully removed from the room and taken across the compound to the garage, then deposited in the back of a plain white van. Seven others were crammed in along with me. We sat on the narrow planks mounted along the inside walls in the back. The familiar steel frame and heavy diamond shaped grid separated us from the driver's compartment.

I strained my neck trying to see out the front. If I really concentrated and looked through the grid just right I could almost be out there, and not in here. The one hack put his head in the way and said, "Don't worry where you're going, we'll be there soon enough. Ain't no use in looking forward to it". So much for my special moment.

I noticed that everyone on the van had an expression of deep thought. We were all under the same dark cloud that sucked the colors from our world and drained the hope into the remaining grayness of our surroundings. This is what it must be like to be a ghost, to be able to think and see everything but not be a part of it. I could only look and long for the things I lost, and amuse myself with the thought that one-day I could rejoin the land of the living. This kind of thinking is called mind-fucking yourself. There were too many real threats in my present world that had to be dealt with. I had to deal with the here and now, and forget about the outside, or loose my mind. Of course, madness was always an option, but that was for the weak. I started this thing and I'd see it through to the end. Whatever that may be.

We rode mostly in silence with just a few bits of conversation exchanged. It seemed that this was the bus to the East Unit, and no one really felt much like talking. The ride didn't seem all that long before we stopped at the gate of the East Unit. A minute later, we were in the outer yard. The back doors were swung open and the guys got out as their names were read off. Only one other and myself were left sitting in the back. The driver kept shuffling through the files mumbling to himself about how he thought there was one more getting off. The other guy and myself took turns looking at the driver, each other and at the rear opening, until they closed the rear doors. We then stopped at BTU to pick up some more passengers for the long trip to Sumpter, my first permanent camp.

Sumpter

About ten of us were dropped off at the front gates of Sumpter CI. The bony boy from BTU that had killed the two cops was one of our group. They ushered us through the front gate and into one of two pavilions that graced the main crosswalk. Everyone looked worried and somewhat scared with the exception of myself. I asked what everyone was so bummed out about and was given some dirty looks. One guy said, "Man, don't you realize where we are? We're at Sumpter. This is the worst camp in Florida". Looking around, I said, "It don't look so bad to me, besides they were talking about sending me to the Unit and this has got to be better than there." A few of the guys nodded in agreement as a couple of rather roguish looking blacks came strolling into the pavilion.

These guys started asking what we were in for and what kind of time we had. When they asked me, I simply responded bank robbery. The bigger one said banks are Federal. I responded, "Yeah but they're on state property and they wanted me to suffer." He looked at me strangely for a long moment when the skinny kid chirped in that he'd killed two cops. The big guy snapped," Shut Up boy, we weren't talking to you!" About that time, a Sergeant walked up and chased our visitors off, before giving us a quick description of the camp.

Sumpter Correctional was a very large, modern, and well maintained camp. The main entrance housed the administrative offices, hospital and the confinement wings. A broad crosswalk leads through the middle of the compound towards the rear or sally port gate as they call it. The rear most building is for the print shop and vocational building. This was a long steel warehouse that spanned the back of the compound. In front of this lay the chow-hall to the right, and the school building to the left. The four main dormitories are in the middle of the compound evenly spaced from each other and positioned halfway between the crosswalk and the fence.

The dorms were square with an open courtyard in the middle. Three sides are living quarters with large windows covering the walls facing into the courtyard. The bunks were neatly lined up in even rows, single bunks towards the middle and double bunks towards the ends. In the middle are two sinks with commodes. At the end of each wing are the TV rooms that have a couple of wooden benches facing a TV mounted at head level. At the end of each TV room are the double doors leading into a small open corner separating the wings and open to the courtyard. The fourth side has the entrance gate, cop-shop, and latrine. The cop-shop being little more than a small cubicle with a heavy steel door and impact resistant Plexiglas.

Inside they have a phone to the main gate, a makeshift counter that serves as a desk, the mail slots, and the fuse box. Between the cop-shop and latrine is a six-foot wall space with the bulletin board and a pay phone for our use. Next is the latrine, which also has a wall of windows facing into the courtyard. As you enter the latrine, the shower room is to the right, laundry straight ahead, to the left are tiled walls reaching with sinks mounted on them. In the back left corner were the rows of commodes. We were each given a map of the compound and told to meet behind the laundry after chow.

The chow hall was impressive, with tiled floors and a high ceiling covered with florescent lights. The chow lines formed at the middle between two railings, we were standing when the fight broke out. I looked over to see one guy try to stab another with a fork. The attacker, a guy a little bigger than me went after another white guy about the size of a professional wrestler. They wrestled for a few seconds before the bigger guy picked up his attacker and slammed his head into the corner of the table with enough force to break the table and the smaller guys head. We grabbed their trays and moved away from the immediate area.

The cops broke it up before anyone was actually killed but it was obvious the smaller of the two had his lunch ruined. It was at this time I noticed that most everyone in here were victims of some massive growth spurt. Here I was sixteen years old at 5'11" and 175 pounds and I was puny compared to everyone in the chow hall. I was beginning to feel like I'd landed in the valley of the giants. And the giants didn't appear all too friendly. A few minutes after the fight, everyone went on about their business as if nothing had happened and I had my first Sumpter meal.

Everything I'd heard was true, the food was not only good but there was more than you could eat. One of the guys at our table explained that the inmates controlled the compound, and the only way to keep twelve hundred criminals with bad attitudes content was to keep them well fed.

A few times since getting here whites had come up to say one simple line. 'Don't talk with the Niggers and don't borrow any money.' And this guy at the table with us said the same thing. He went on to explain that we were all going to be tried in the next couple of days. Show some heart and fight like a mad dog and other whites will help you out. But associate

with the blacks at all, and that help will never come.
Exceptions to this being any kind of business transactions or once we were settled in. But for now no hanging with the Blacks. With whites being outnumbered five-to-one this should prove interesting

Church showed up next to me and repeated the same advice. He then advised me to try to get into B-dorm where he was at, when I saw my team officer. This being Friday I wouldn't have a chance to do that until the weekend was over. So I asked how bad D-dorm was, since that was my assigned dorm. He made a face and said that everyone in D-dorm was fucked up, even the whites. But we could hang out in B dorm over the weekend and he'd hip me to what all was going on.

After waiting forever at the laundry to get our clothes we had to report back to the pavilions by the main gate for count time, then we'd be escorted to our dorms. I knew a couple of the guys I'd come here with from RMC and BTU. There was crazy George, the little skinny cop killer, and Larry the black guy I bought sandwiches from when I hung out with Woody and the gang at BTU. I was assigned to D dorm C wing, and George went to B wing of D dorm.

D-dorm was nasty compared to the other dorms, it seemed to exude a filmy unpleasantness that permeated everything from floor to ceiling. I was assigned to a top bunk next to the TV room. On the bottom bunk below me sat a rather quiet guy that offered simple advice; "Don't talk to any Blacks, don't believe nothing you hear, and only half of what you see, and watch your ass". Then it was count time. Good, this would give me the chance to see everyone I had to deal with at one time.

I looked around and started to get a strange feeling. I hadn't yet developed my chain-gang sixth sense, but my instincts had sharpened significantly. If you've ever seen a mouse dropped into a snakes cage at feeding time you might understand the feeling I was presently experiencing. The mouse having never seen a snake only knows that it is little more than prey to a natural enemy that it does not understand, and has never seen before. I had the strong feeling that everyone in the wing was my natural enemy.

A small commotion was taking place a few bunks down from me. From my angle, I could make out someone laid over a bunk with his hands tied to the bunk rails. A sock had been shoved in his mouth and his pants were pulled down to his knees that were planted on the concrete floor. Various characters were taking turns corn-holing him from behind. When the Dorm officer came through for count time, everyone scrambled back to their bunks leaving the victim in this user friendly position. The guard stopped for a moment, took in the situation then continued counting. Once the guard was gone the butt party was continued.

After count time a couple of guards came in and untied the boy, removing him to the cop shop to ask what was going on. A few moments after that a little black guy came up to me with a lighter in his hand and asked "You know what this means?" While working the lighter. I responded, "You're either an arsonist or you're real good at lighting lighters". He retorted, "No, it means I might set you on fire while you're sleeping tonight!" I pulled out some matches, struck one and said, "I guess whoever falls asleep first is the one that gets burned. Got any lighter fluid I can borrow?" Then I smiled. This was not quite the reaction he'd expected. Or so I gathered from the look on his face. "I'll fuck you up cracker!" he mumbled over his shoulder as he retreated.

If this is their idea of trying me I wasn't very impressed, these guys will have to be a little more assertive than that. A Cracker from a few bunks down asked if I wanted to play some cards. I saw this as an opportunity to find out a lot of what might be going on from one of my own kind. We were playing hearts, a game I had no talent at. The stakes were for punches in the chest. There were three of us playing and the loser took punches from the other two. After about an hour of this I'd figured out that the cards weren't going my way intentionally.

I knew that I couldn't back out of the game without looking weak. I proposed that since I was new to the game I should get two swings for each of their one. Then as I got better at the game we could go back to one for one. They didn't want to go for this. I asked, "What, you're scared a little guy like me is gonna hurt some big guys like you?" This put them in the position of looking intimidated by me. But they couldn't give up their advantage. When the game ended, I could sense a little bit of animosity that a new cock had gotten over on them.

What little bits of information I did get out of these three guys was near useless. Tom, Ken and Steve did not impress me as being particularly bright. They did say that the incident with the little black guy after count time was just the first attempt by the Blacks at trying me. They added that the guy in the bunk under me was a strange character, but a hell of a fighter, and that the card game was a set up they used to see how tough I was.

They called themselves the D-dorm Klan. Each of them had a wheel and cog tattoo that identified them as members of a white power group called Thunderbolt. Their theme was to hate everybody except whites. After I proved myself in a couple of fights I might even be invited to join their merry group.

They showed me some of the propaganda they had slipped in from the streets. These pamphlets looked like Nazi newsletters touting small feats of racial resistance as the beginning of a revolution. But, to them it was gospel. I acted impressed, since I would have to be dealing with these guys. Right now, what I needed most was the safety of numbers. But they didn't seem like a very powerful group. The whole clique numbered about twelve in this dorm, with maybe fifty others spread around the compound. Their strength lay in the group and not the individuals. I was tempted to believe they only had balls because they had backup from each other, that alone none of them were worth a shit. One exception to this impression was Ronnie Sanderss. Ronnie was a big Aryan looking guy with a tattoo of a Klansman holding a noose and a scythe that covered his forearm. He caught me on the side and explained that these other guys were all right, but not to count on them much for anything useful. Ronnie explained how the Klan leader had gone to the box that afternoon for breaking some guys head in the chow hall. Since I'd ended up in the leaders bunk, they were resentful. Ronnie assured that if I did get in a bad situation, he would back me up. Any excuse to fight was good enough for Ronnie. He said I had potential and didn't act like the typical new cock. He liked the way I handled myself. But, he included that until I proved myself he wouldn't have much else to say to me. Walking away, he said. "Don't go anywhere alone until you're settled in."

I spent the weekend hanging out with Church. He kept telling me how great B-Dorm was, and that I should try to get a bunk change. Bunk changes were supposed to be no small feat. Usually people were moved around for a good reason such as going to the box or the hospital. Church pointed out that my age was something to take advantage of. Since I was the youngest on the compound, the hacks were a little concerned with anything happening to me. If they refused my request for a bunk change and I got messed up or killed after they refused it, then they'd be liable. I didn't care too much for the guys in D-Dorm, so what to hell I'll give it a shot when I saw my team officer.

I also had my first visit from my family since my sentencing.

My folks had panicked when my letter reached them and took the long trip up to Lake Butler. They were given the run-around from Butler to BTU and back to Butler again until finally they were told to look for me at Sumpter. They had spent most of the weekend believing I had been lost in the system, as I had written. In spite of this, the visit went well. I brought them up to date on the present happenings, then had normal family conversation... They gave me some cash and put more in my account.

We were limited to fifteen dollars a week that we could draw out of our account. This was for personal items such as shampoo, deodorant, or name brand soap the state didn't provide. The canteen also had convenience store type pies and cakes we referred to as sweetie-goes.

The state did provide its own brand of soap called DC brand, which tended to irritate the skin and leave a bad smell behind. Every dorm had open cases of DC brand cigarettes. They were in a white pack with an orange outline of Florida. Little triangles represented the Institutions locations throughout the state.

The smokes inside were unfiltered with a poignant raw taste to them, I was told the state bought the floor sweepings from the real tobacco companies. Sometimes you'd light one up and hear a strange popping sound, and if you looked at the cigarette fast enough you could see these little brown beetle looking bugs come running through pinholes perforating the length of the smoke. We fondly named these cigarettes RIP for Rest in Peace. RIPs were treated with some chemical to keep them burning, this was to keep the compound clean from the litter of thousands of butts being thrown to the ground daily.

'Kools' were the main cigarette of the astute convict. They had the same value as cash and were traded, gambled with, and used in place of cash as a second currency. Only a few could comfortably afford to smoke real cigarettes all of the time, the majority smoked RIPs in private and saved the tailor-mades for social functions such as ball games in the TV room.

There was an ample amount of drugs for those who could afford it. A five-dollar or nickel bag of reefer was measured by filling a cap from a lip balm stick. Acid and speed were the main chemicals. There were a few speed junkies that sold their ass to pay for their habit. During the movie, especially a good sex flick, you could see their outlines as they jumped from one guy to another drawn to their destination by anyone holding up cash or cigarettes. In here as on the streets, the guys with the most money get the better-looking ones. But in the dark of the movie house the homely were in just as high demand.

Monday came without further incident and my orientation started. My team officer explained how the gain-time system worked. For very month you don't get a disciplinary report you earn time off from your sentence. This was called mandatory gain time. Then there was extra gain time the team could give for exemplary behavior. This meant you did something exceptional or you snitched or maybe the team was just in a good mood. Since gain time only counts off the end of your sentence, I asked what good that would do me. I had life, and a life sentence has no end to it as compared to a ten-year stretch. They said that if I were to get a sentence reduction it could mean a lot. I asked about a bunk change, and was directed to see a Sgt. Woods, so off I went to see Woods.

He was a big country boy with his own office. The first thing he asked when I walked in the door was "What do you have for me?" I answered, "Nothing I'm just here for a bunk change." He asked, "Why should I give you a bunk change, if you don't have anything for me?" "Because I'd like to stay out of trouble, I think I might get into some where I'm at, and I have a friend over in B-Dorm. So can I have a bunk change, please?" I was beginning to feel like "Oliver Twist." He continued, "I know you've got a little trouble over where you're at especially with one particular nigger that threatened to set you on fire." This surprised me. How could he know about such a trivial conversation that I'd more or less forgotten already. I did notice how he kept looking at the book of matches he was playing with. Then I realized that there was some writing inside the matchbook cover.

This is one of the ways the snitches get their messages up to the man. I responded, "Well, some black guy said something like that once, but I figured he was just kidding."

"Do you know his name?" "No, I don't."

"Could you point him out?" "Nope, they all look alike to me."

He went on, "I'm going to write up a report on this incident and you're gonna sign it." "Why? He ain't done nothing to me. Why don't you just have the guy that's feeding you this information do it?" Woods, "No, he's too important to me."

"Look I'm just here for a bunk change, it's no big deal. Just give me the bunk change and when I have something for you, I'll send you some matches. So how about it?" He thought for a moment and said, "OK, just sign this release form for the bunk change and I'll fill it in later." I asked to look at it first. It said "request for dorm change" across the top, which was good enough for me.

Leaving the office, I began to think I shouldn't have had to sign anything. On my way out I saw Crazy George sitting outside the office. He asked what I was doing up here, I told him getting a bunk change. He said, "Maybe you're telling them something! " I paused for a second, "Now how would you know this is the place to do that? ", then walked out.

This little incident had brightened me up on a couple of things. First, you can't trust anyone. Not the people around you, or the guys with notorious reputations. When I'd first started screwing up and doing wrong in my search for something different, I thought that if I ever end up locked up that I could hang out with the convicts, just like in the movies. I'd assumed that everyone kept to there own business and took care of their own problems internally. If I had known this was the level of people I had to deal with I wouldn't be here right now. Woods expected me to rat for him simply because I walked through his door. This meant that most everyone walking in there must be a rat. This was something to keep in mind.

Orientation was a bit strange. We took tests from academic, to seeing how fast we could put washers on a steel pin. They told me I could pick any vocation I wanted but air conditioning was their recommendation, this being a one year class that they were very proud of. I picked auto mechanics instead and practically had to argue for my choice since they knew what was better for me then I did.

On Friday after count time I moved to B-Dorm looking forward to the following Monday when I would start vocational training. Once in B-Dorm, Church introduced me to Fitz and Wilson. They were partners that slept in the same row I was in. I had the top bunk over some jowl-faced boy that hung out

106

with the Hamsters. Enough said about him. Next was a black, then a Mexican, Fitz, and then another black guy nicknamed Black who was the Mexicans' partner, then Wilson, in that order. We were one row away from the rear TV room. "Black" ran the dorm canteen and used to have a partner now referred to as "Face".

I went back to my bunk to get a cigarette and found a candy bar on my pillow. I thought this was kind of cute so I smashed it, put it back on the bunk and announced that people shouldn't leave stuff where it didn't belong or it could get damaged.

Some laughing erupted one row over so I figured I'd gotten my point across. An argument over a card game broke out at the end of my row which escalated into a fight. The two blacks involved really went at it. The bigger one had his mouth split wide open but it didn't stop him from putting the other guys head through one of the plate glass windows that covered the inner wall and trying to saw his throat on the shards of glass poking out from the aluminum frame. The cops came in and broke it up, and then told everyone to stay in their bunks until they ordered otherwise. A half an hour after this the lights flickered a few times. The cops ran out of our wing just as the lights went out completely.

For a long moment there was utter silence, then something whizzed past my head and struck the wall near my bunk. Other sounds of impact were coming from all over the wing. Some struck steel and others concrete. Hollering and laughter accompanied this from all directions. When the lights came back on, batteries were laying everywhere and everyone was climbing into their bunks as if nothing had happened.

Afterwards, Wilson told me to keep a couple of D-cell batteries taped under the edge of my bunk. Whenever the lights flicker locate whoever I don't like, because in half a minute or so the lights would go out. That's my chance to nail my enemies. Of course batteries will be coming my way also. And don't get caught hiding under a bunk when the lights come back on or you're a coward. This explained why the cops ran out when the lights flickered.

Early the next morning I stepped into the latrine to shave my couple of whiskers and brush my teeth. The inner wall of the latrine had widows facing into the courtyard. A couple of these were broken at the bottom and a cold breeze was blowing in. I'd almost hit my head on one of the fixtures that poked out from the wall over the sink. The water handles were cross shaped and extended out a good five inches. The steel soap dish protruded almost as far. These were mounted high enough to easily cause damage if you leaned too far over the sink. There was a shuffling sound near me and I looked next to me to see a medium sized Hamster standing there. "You was in K-Wing thirteen top?" He asked. I asked him to repeat himself as I turned in his direction. I noticed that there were two others with him.

The main one stood directly in front of me, a bigger one behind him about three feet and to his left stood yet another one. The third was a big boy and stood guard by the doors in front of the rows of wooden benches. I looked at the main one who was just a little bit bigger than me and said, "No, I was in twelve top, you've got me messed up with the kid in the next cell." He poked me in the eye, I punched him in the head, he then tried to grab me. We wrestled for a couple of seconds until I flung him backwards into the sink where one of the jagged handles went into his back. The second guy came at me in a half crouch. I grabbed him by his head and shoved him backwards through one of the broken bottom windows where he hesitated to move from fear of getting cut. I was at high speed for the door with only one more obstacle in my path. He grabbed a hold of my jacket and I started spinning him around like a centrifuge about three times before prying his hands loose. I couldn't have done better if I'd planned it, he went tumbling over the benches in the most undignified manner, slamming his head a couple times against the heavy unforgiving wood. Then I was out the door before the first one from the sink could reach me.

Practically flying into the wing I went to where Church and Fitz were and told them what had just happened, "They tried to kick my ass, Come on lets get them!" They said, "You did real good, don't worry about it. They won't fuck with you again. Besides they're probably already gone." And sure enough, when we went back to look there was no trace of them except for some small glass shards on the floor from the window where my second attacker had been lodged. My friends thought this was cause to celebrate but I was annoyed that these guys had disappeared as easily as they had first appeared. Things here were going to take some getting used to.

One example was showering. During classification, I'd showered in the day time when the dorms were almost empty. About eight o'clock Church said, "Come on we're hitting the showers." Wilson added, "If any one so much as touches you, bust him in the mouth and don't let off him. And if some one looks at your ass just look back at his." I had to laugh at this crap they were telling me. But they kept it up all the way to the latrine, even adding the advice to do what everyone else does and never go in the shower without slides (flip-flops) on.

The shower room was about twelve by ten foot with showerheads on three of the walls, stepping in and getting at the water was a real chore since there were about fifteen guys in there before we stepped in. The floor had a slight incline towards the middle where the drain was. I saw one guy getting fucked over in the corner, everyone else just stood around jerking off.

Up until getting locked up I wouldn't even admit to playing with myself. I could now talk about it like everyone else did, but as far as doing it in front of anyone especially an audience, I was still a little on the shy side. Proper shower manners dictated that you walk to the middle of the shower and come as close to the drain as possible when getting off. The wearing of something on your feet made a lot of sense now.

I noticed the Black guy next to me staring at my ass as he played with himself. So I stared back at his ass and soaped up my Willy. I wasn't into this at all and the lack of enthusiasm showed in my lack of an impressive erection. The Hamster asked, "What are you looking at CRACKER?" "Nothing," I replied as I gazed intensely at his ass. He then said, "You better stop looking at my ass like that!" I thought I could hear a little bit of nervousness in his voice as I became aware of my hard on.

He moved over a couple of people muttering something about "Cracker don't know who he's fuckin' with." Church came over by me and said, "We're leaving now so rinse off and let's go." Apparently my friends thought that my actions were riling the natives. Though their advice seemed sound, I was starting to doubt their usefulness as backup.

The Auto mech. class was at the end of the vocational building. A couple of bay doors faced in the direction of the rear gate. This was a large sliding gate on rollers directly overlooked by a guard tower. The shop had some school desks in the middle facing the rear wall towards the instructors' desk. Looking in through the bay doors were an alignment machine to the left and vehicles to the right. Blacks stayed to the left and whites in the right rear corner near the bathroom. This is where I met Bear and Turner.

These two partners were a couple of the biggest weight lifters on the compound. Turner was about 5'8, with arms so big he could barely get his hands in his pockets. Bear looked just like his name. He had enough hair on him to qualify as a pelt. Both of them were in for killing their girlfriends with their bare hands.

From the rumors I heard, Bear actually ripped the head right off of his old lady. My opinion was that if these women were stupid enough to cheat on their old man then they should have picked smaller boyfriends. This was the opening line that made us sort of friends. After the required tests from the auto mechanics book everyday, we'd hang out on the steps by the bathroom and smoke some pot. Sometimes we'd get lit drinking the wine we made in the shop in either gallon jugs or one time in the washer reservoir of a disabled van. Turner was the hustler of the two, always trying to get me to sell pot for extra money. I didn't feel too comfortable with the idea of carrying the stuff around since it invited robbery.

The first time I drew money out in B-Dorm, Fitz had told me the Blacks were waiting in the TV room to jump me when I came back to the dorm. He told me to look at one of the narrow windows in the TV room from the walkway where I could see a bunch of faces leering out. Fitz said to wait until the last second for count time before going in, but I thought this was a bit too cowardly. Fitz insisted that there were too many of them to take on with only the four of us. I told them to watch what I did as I left them standing out front.

I walked in through the main door and across the courtyard using the mob of people in the yard as cover. If they were waiting at the TV room door closest to the main entrance that meant they couldn't see out. Gambling on this, I went through the center wing and into the far TV room at the other end of my wing. I could see the robbery squad crouched on each side of the TV room double door at the normal entrance everyone used. I got a smoke from my bunk, lit it up, and walked up behind them while saying, "Excuse me guys" as I pushed through them and out the door to the inner yard. My balls were in my throat while I did this, but I thought I made the right impression. My friends got a real kick out of it, and complimented my originality. Later that night I made quite a different impression.

My Lawyer met me at the front gate and explained everything to me. The appeal had come through and the state had offered a substantial settlement rather than go to court. I soon found myself at my new home checking out the furniture. Walking out into the backyard, I saw the pool and the most gorgeous brunette sitting on the other side. I asked if she came with the house, my Lawyer just smiled and faded away. I hollered over for her to get naked while I tried to get out of my state blues. I jumped in to swim across to her. Halfway to my destination something like a rope snagged the end of my foot, holding me back so that I could just get my face between her legs. Too impatient to go back and unhook my foot I started jerking off with her barely within sniffing distance.

Just as I came, the pool and the girl disappeared. I found myself Dick in hand, spurting all over the place with my foot hooked on the end rail of my bunk. About forty people sat in their bunks staring at me, as if I was possessed. I'm sure I'd given that impression if my tongue had been going like it was in my dream. I looked around at everyone and said, "Hey, y'all didn't see her!", and started cleaning myself off.

The Set Up

Over a year had passed since I walked through those bank doors. It was now January of 1977 and with the New Year came news that I would be going back to Broward County for an appeal bond hearing. This was the same as being released as far as I was concerned. The winter had been an unusually cold one. Long sheets of ice hung from the roof of the kitchen reaching almost to the ground. The cold damp wind whipped across the compound keeping everyone inside the dorms. The only exceptions being the necessary trips for food or work.

It was on one of these days that we couldn't find Bear. Bear had left an hour before to get some sandwiches from the chow hall and hadn't come back. Turner and myself checked both the chow hall and the gym, but no one had seen him in either place. Walking back into the shop I noticed the bathroom door was shut and banged on it asking if that was Bear inside, repeating myself three times since I couldn't make out the muffled replies. It kind of sounded like him, so I sat down on the wooden steps a few feet away and waited for Bear to come out. A couple of minutes later the door opened and out stepped a Black guy about my size.

He walked up to me and attempted to point a finger in my face. I slapped his hand away, and then eluded a wild swing. My punch connected, he then backed off and said, "Let me get my jacket off." As I started removing mine, he turned and ran off across the shop, towards the other side. Sprinting after him, I reached mid shop near the desks, before Bear and Turner came running in and grabbed me by both arms. "Don't go over there, Man, it's a set-up!" I yelled, "Let me loose, I'm gonna kick that little Shits Ass!" Turner, "That's just what they want you to do, if you go over there we won't back you up. Just trust me, and in a while I'll show you why!"

Twenty minutes later, the Blacks went outside for some kind of a meeting. We went over to their side to see what they had stashed. Turner started pulling out pipes and a couple of boards with nails in them. "This was meant for you, if we hadn't stopped you when we did. A guy from D-Dorm overheard something about it yesterday, and Bear was checking into it this morning. That's why we couldn't find him." We took what obvious weapons we could find and hid them over on our side. Turner said not to go anywhere by myself for a couple of days, and to keep some kind of a weapon on me. I found a long steel bolt and sharpened it just a little on the grinder. This made it look more like an old bolt and not a weapon.

The next morning was the coldest yet, everyone was waiting until the last moment to leave for their work assignments. If the temperature stayed below a certain level, then we could stay in the dorms for the morning. Then the announcement came over the loud speakers to report to our assigned work areas. Fitz and Wilson were strangely reluctant to leave, so I went on by myself. I had my bolt stuffed into the front of my pants and carried my shop book in my left hand, coffee in my right. The compound was almost deserted. As I walked between the kitchen and the rear of the vocational building. I heard some one yell, "Hey Cracker!" And turned to see the same guy from the bathroom incident from day before.

This was a golden opportunity. He had no army to run to that I could see, so if it came down to a fight I had a real good shot at tearing him a new asshole. I responded, "Get out of my face, before you piss me off. You ran away yesterday and I'm not in the mood to chase you around this morning." He picked up a rather large rock and muttered something about Pussy Cracker.

Well for one thing I'm not a pussy, and I already knew better than to turn my back on a rock-wielding coward. We faced off with about three feet between us. Then this really great plan popped into my head. If I can get in a little closer, and throw my book straight up in the air, he'd look up, and I can nail him with my dull spike. Only one thing went wrong with this plan. When I threw the book, he threw the rock! The impact caught me across my left eye and cheek.

I was stunned both by the unforeseen and from the blow to my head. "I'll kill you and your ugly ass mother," I hollered as I went for him. But the bitch ran, and I wasn't moving forward like I'd intended. The feeling that something was very wrong came to me when I noticed that I had no vision or feeling on the left side of my face. I reached up with my left hand and felt it fill with something warm—my blood.

The rock had done more damage than I could have imagined, but revenge was more important than my injury. If it took a week to chase him down one step at a time then so be it. "You're one dead nigger!" I said while forcing one foot in front of the other. "His eyes got big as he kept backing off, with me trudging along after him like some creature from a cheap horror movie. Then a bunch of his buddies showed up. Their set up was a bit more effective this time around. Hands tried to grab hold of me from different directions, trying to hold me so the chicken shit could get another shot in, but he wouldn't come within ten feet of my reach. Remembering the steel in my hand I started swinging.

Fortunately these guys were holding me up so I could swing more accurately. I counted two heads and one shoulder I made contact with before they took off in different directions yelling "Let that teach you," and "it ain't over yet Cracker!"

Suddenly I was very alone, I couldn't tell if I still had my left eye, and my balance was way off. Looking down I saw the blood running down my shirt, and down the front of my left leg, to the shoe where it divided again into two small rivulets that left drops on each side of every bloody footprint made by my left foot.

It took every bit of concentration to put one foot ahead of the other and head towards the infirmary on the other end of the compound. About fifty yards from my destination I asked someone I recognized if I still had my eye. He stared for a long moment shook his head, and told me that he didn't think so. He offered to help me up the stairs but I declined, if I'd made it this far on my own, then let me finish the trip alone.

After an eternity, I made it up the steps to the infirmary where they took me to a small Korean doctor that spoke broken English. "Look like shank," he said. "No, Doc, it was a rock. Hey, do I still have my eye?" "Oh, rock just fly off ground and hit in eye?" "No, Doc, some asshole threw the rock." "Still look like shank to me." After he had sewn me up a nurse put a bandage over one quarter of my head. Still no one had taken the time to tell me how many eyes I had left. Two guards that wanted to take a statement approached me. They also wanted a description of the incident and of the assailant. I told them someone caught me off guard with a rock. For his description, I told them a black guy with brown eyes, curly hair and wearing a blue uniform. And no, I couldn't be much more descriptive than that. I was handcuffed and shackled, then loaded into a sedan to be transported to the hospital at Lake Butler.

There must have been some serious sinus damage on that side of my face, it seemed like every half hour

116

we had to stop so I could vomit up the blood I kept swallowing that filled the back of my throat. Once we reached Butler I was taken to the hospital ward for x-rays where I finally fell asleep on a cot in a hallway.

I awoke the next morning with the mother of all headaches. This was the first time I'd been in the hospital wing and the first time in a long time that I'd slept in a real bed. I was called down to have my stitches checked and eye looked at. They told me the left eye had received quite a shock, and that I may lose some vision in it. Within a few days, my sight had returned to normal. After a week, it was stitch removal time.

The nurse started to remove the stitches, and attempted to make small talk by asking how this had happened. I told her how one guy had nailed me with a rock before the rest of the niggers jumped in. Her whole attitude changed as she said, "I don't like the word nigger, those poor black people are just defending themselves the best way they know how. And from what they have told me, it's the white people that team up on them." I debated, "Ma'am you've been seriously misinformed, they run in packs like mad dogs and should be treated as such. It's just that up here you don't get to see them as they really are."

She said, "I live with a black man and he explained a lot of things to me. You should make friends with some blacks and you'll see what I'm talking about." I felt myself stiffen at hearing this. Just the thought of some fuck bitch putting her hands on me pissed me off, besides she was doing a lousy job of removing the stitches. I said, "Look, why don't I just remove the rest of these stitches myself, I don't think your skills are any better than your social advice". At this she threw down the weird little tweezers she'd been fumbling with and said, "Go ahead see if you can do any better, I don't want to do any favors for a bigot like you anyway." I went back to the room, borrowed some nail clippers and pulled the rest of the stitches out myself.

The Doc had done right by me with the way he stitched my face up. It looked like a chunk of meat had been ripped out by the rock and I could feel something like a crack or a crease on my cheekbone beneath the scar which was about an inch long. This was healing up nicely, in a couple of weeks, I'd be ready to go back and make that nigger wish he'd never been born. The next afternoon I was put on the compound.

The two guys bunking next to me along with some others scattered throughout the dorm were nicknamed the East Unit Mafia. Big John was the leader, a heavyset balding character that looked more like a lawyer than a convict. He warned me that something was going down and that I should make myself scarce. They had some kind of a problem with a gang from another dorm and I had showed up just in time for the rumble.

I had it in my head that if I got myself messed up again in a short period of time, that I might have a shot at a law suit against the state, this could help in my appeal. I told John that my bunk is my house, and anyone coming around my house for any reason had a problem with me.

Our showdown came outside of the oppositions' dorm. The opposing gang was all young guys, both black and white mixed about twenty in all, while we numbered only ten. The two groups squared off and spread out while two people from each side met in the middle. Then the unexpected happened, they apologized.

There is a correct way to back out of a situation without saying the word sorry. To back down or bitch up as we say is admitting weakness. The same goes for saying that the other person is right and that you're wrong. But one side can say that they were mistaken, acted on bad information, or that there is a misunderstanding that must be discussed first. But they had out right apologized. Walking away, I asked John why he let them get away with this, since from my understanding of the situation they were obviously lying about the incident in question.

He said three things, "One: we were outnumbered two to one, Two, it was a no-win situation, since either way we'd all go to the box and you can't make money in the box, and Three, when anyone publicly apologizes you have to accept it. If they are man enough to admit a mistake, you have to be man enough to accept their apology. It's a matter of honor that you always accept someone's humility. Accepting their apology gives us a lot more credibility than if we'd kicked their asses. To attack them after they admitted they're wrong makes us scumbags.

I learned a few good things from Big John before going back to Sumpter a few weeks later. But the concept of honor was something that would always stay with me. Convict honor brings with it the air of respect and esteem that can make a man stand out from the current rash of "inmates" that had infested the prison system.

We celebrated that weekend by staying stoned, John's gang ran most of the dope on the compound and we had a small variety of drugs to choose from. Me and a few other guys got a dime of pot and the rest were doing something called preludes. I could have done the preludes if I wanted but it had to be injected and that's something I won't do.

They were using a big horse spike, like the kind they take blood with. Smashing up the pills and boiling the contents in a spoon with some water, they drew the finished product through a cigarette filter in the bottom of a pill bottle, then poked themselves repeatedly until puncturing a vein with the dull spike.

They gave up after a while and gave me the remains of the pill bottle, which I swallowed at once. John worried I might OD so they kept an eye on me for the rest of the day. This turned out to be in my best interests when I decided to run twenty laps around the rec field. They dragged me back to the dorm and stayed up all night with me, while I chewed gum, smoked and talked simultaneously until morning. I was still speeding when the hacks told me to pack my stuff and put me on the bus back to Sumpter with a bunch of New Cocks.

I hadn't been in long enough to be considered an old cock but at least I wasn't like these guys on the bus. Two of them that could pass for twins, both were young, slim, and a little on the tall side. One of the others, a boy named Earl was a twisted little thing that walked crooked and went by the nickname SideWinder. And then there was Tim Stanley. I'd met Tim once when he was in my Dorm at RMC doing some kind of business with Big John.

He was one year older then me, with dark hair, and kind of girlish looking. Sometimes I don't like someone the first time I see them. It could be the body language, or maybe they remind me of someone else I didn't like before, but most of the time this dislike turns out to be well founded. Tim came from a money family and he wore it well. The boy was pushy and acted like his money could bail him out of anything, which to some degree was true, whether in here, or on the streets. I told the whites the same thing I'd been told before reaching my permanent camp "Don't hang with the Blacks, don't get anything fronted on credit" since their money would be delayed coming from RMC. Tim had some smart-ass remark about what I was telling the guys on the bus.

I looked forward to seeing how well he did at Sumpter.

After we reached the camp I was assigned to A-Dorm in what was known as "Cracker Alley". I had a top front bunk on the TV room wall. Two Tampa boys had the end double bunk at the end of my row in the corner. Across from them was Friar Tuck, the Klan leader in the dorm and an old acquaintance from BTU.

Then Crazy George and some other real crackers along with a punk or two. The majority of us were from Lauderdale or a city adjoining it. So I was now with my Homeboys. Moose was also from Broward County. Originally, Moose was sent to Desoto but he'd chased some guy that pissed him off into the Lieutenants office, stabbing him with a pair of scissors. Because of his size, the Desoto Hacks waited until he vented his anger before telling him he had to go to the box. Once shipped to Sumpter they gave him a job as the dorm barber. I guess because of his familiarity with the tools of the trade.

Bear and Turner welcomed me back to the shop with a small party and filled me in on all of the rumors that had been circulating. Some cracker had seen my little altercation behind the Voc. building, and by the time I had come back, the story had grown into the makings of a legend. The number of hamsters I'd been fighting turned into an army of twenty. And with half of my face missing I had managed to cause damage to more then a few of them. I preferred this version of the incident, to how I remembered it. It had all of the good parts of the real story, while touting me as some kind of an invulnerable hero. Instead of somebody that just had his ass kicked. I now had a reputation and respect. These were the two things that opened a lot of doors. One of the guys from the Thunderbolt click in D-Dorm let me know that I could be a member of their clique, I declined saying I was getting out soon, though the offer was still appreciated.

Except for the couple of dollars in my pocket, I was not financially stable. They'd shipped us off just before a draw day, so the money in my account was delayed coming from RMC. I asked Turner about maybe hustling some reefer to get a few bucks in my pocket. He told me I could have four dime bags up front for five bucks each. Once these were paid off I could have four more. After that I should be stable enough to pay him on delivery. There would be no set time limit on payment, but I had to pay him on the day promised. All of this was agreed upon, now I just needed to find a partner that knew a few more people in A Dorm then I did to get things rolling. I picked Jap.

Jap was Asian of course, and a loner with no real money to speak of. When I ran down the dealing proposal, he seemed genuinely interested. The next afternoon we met with Bear and Turner next to the kitchen. We smoked a fat one and then made the transaction. There was something wrong with the way the deal was rushed, and something else felt wrong about the bags. I handed them to Jap to look at, but he just stuffed them in his pocket to get them out of sight. The one thing Turner did make a point of was not to front anything to a couple of guys out of D-Dorm. He said Jimmy and Dave were a couple of stoners that liked to get high but didn't like to pay for their habit. "Don't deal with them unless they've got cash," Turner insisted.

I told Turner I'd let him know when he'd get paid and we went our different ways to our workstations.

After work, Jap came to the dorm and told me he'd already sold two of them. When I asked for the money, he said we had to wait until after count time. When count was over he told me he'd fronted the reefer to a couple of his friends from over in D-Dorm.

When I asked who they were he assured me not to worry about it, since he knew them so well. I took the other two bags from him and sold them over in B-Dorm. Half the money went to Turner, the other half went in my pocket leaving Jap the responsibility of taking care of the remaining debt.

Turner wouldn't front anything else until the full debt was paid. Wanting to move more product, I asked Jap who he'd fronted to. He told me Jimmy and Dave from D-Dorm, but not to worry since he personally guaranteed that we would be paid.

The next day, Turner told me at the shop that someone saw Jap with these two characters smoking a joint under the tree by the weight pile, and warned me to watch out for my so called partner. I promised at this point to have the rest of his money in two weeks on a Friday regardless of who owed us. My draw money had finally caught up to me, so I could cover the few bucks I owed but it would eventually have to come out of Japs' ass, one way or another. The problem was resolved one afternoon when I was told to pack up my belongings for the trip to Broward County Jail.

The ride home was a long one, and I had plenty of time to let my mind wander over the events of the past year. From the robbery and trial, to seeing that rock come at me, I had emerged from the chaos triumphant. I was now sixteen years old with a GED, and a new future lay ahead of me. I'd been away from the drugs and alcohol long enough to think clearly, and for the first time in my life, I began to think about college, and a career. Maybe the Judge did the right thing when he gave me that life sentence. Had I been sentenced to anything less, I wouldn't have taken any of this so seriously.

By the time we pulled up to the courthouse/jail I was considering how much of a vacation to take before furthering my education. Back in the Broward County jail, my new cell was a bullpen reserved for serious offenders, or guys like myself already convicted. I took a bottom bunk mounted in a corner of the bull-pen. A big guy that bore a strange resemblance to Ben Franklin about twenty years old occupied the upper bunk. I made a big deal about how much he looked like Ben, and after getting the whole cells opinion on the matter my bunk-mate had acquired his new nickname. Walking towards the bullpens entrance that led to the cells, I was stopped by a tall character just a little older than myself, wearing the now very familiar state blues.

He started the conversation with an unnatural amount of bass in his voice, "Oh, I see that you're from prison too!" I responded, "Yea, So?" "I'm from H. C. I., I'm back here for an escape charge," He said this quite proudly as if I was supposed to be impressed. I'd heard about HCI, it was a camp full of young wimps and jitter-bugs. If he'd escaped from there, he was either stupid or one scary white boy. When I told him I was down from Sumpter he deflated, and moved out of my way. I could see now that I was going to have some fun with this boy.

My cell partner (Ben) turned out to be a great partner for playing spades. The jailhouse version took some getting used to, since it used wild cards called by the dealer. Outside of poker, spades was the main form of gambling through out the system. Since Ben didn't smoke, I collected the cigarettes we won. I figured I could surprise him by buying the big guy some extra food with his share. The old guy we were cleaning out had picked the boy from HCI as his partner. Early in the game I started calling the boy "Kid" and "Young Boy." When the kid pointed out that he was two years older than I was, and that I should be the young boy, the cell went quiet. I happened to be dealing at the time. Without slowing down the deal I calmly explained that it was a matter of hormones. Even though he had a few years on me I had more testosterone. That made me a young man and him a young boy!

The guys in the cell howled their approval, until someone told the Kid not to let me get away with that kind of an insult. The Boy stood up from the table and said something to the effect that he was more of a man then I was. I came around the end of the table expecting a fight, what I got instead was a poor excuse for a wrestling match. Some people just don't know how to fight, and this kid was one of them. It only took me a few moments to have his arm pinned behind his back, and his wrist twisted at a rather painful angle. Applying pressure with one hand and patting his ass with the other, I told him to call me Daddy or I'd break his arm. He held out for a while, squealing like a pig while I applied more pressure. It looked like he might have need of a cast, when he suddenly called me Daddy, at which point I let him go.

Looking into the boy's eyes, I could see the shame and embarrassment that he felt. A glimmer of sympathy almost clouded my moment of victory, before I remembered how that could have been me on the losing end, and I would have been awarded no pity had he been the winner. The boys spade partner insisted that the game go on, now that we'd concluded our disagreement. This took the pressure off the boy and distracted me from my mixed feelings. The game ended when the old cock was out of cigarettes, I gave him back a couple of packs to hold him until the store brought him more. Everyone left the game happy except for the now sheepish "Young Boy."

The other guys that stood out in the cell were Ernie, and the Shrink. Ernie was in for killing a couple of guys, and expected to get at least two mandatory 25 year to Life sentences. He mostly stayed to himself in one of the back corner cells that ringed the bullpen. Ben told me that Ernie was a junkie that somehow managed to keep a constant supply of liquid Demerol and a syringe. This seemed to keep him somewhat on the mellow side, which everyone considered a good thing, considering how big and crazy looking Ernie was. The Shrink was the typical stereotype of what a well-educated man in his mid-thirties should look like. He had a medium build, glasses, and was slightly balding in front.

Supposedly, he actually was a psychologist, and he did leave the cell every morning as if going to work. The story was that the cops had him doing some kind of counseling, and paper work for them as part of his sentence. The Shrink had a bad habit of putting his two cents in whenever a dispute erupted between guys in the cell. He did manage to quell a few fights before they started, but his mouth would eventually lead to his own undoing.

They postponed my appeal bond hearing for a couple of weeks and I was beginning to feel a little bit apprehensive about this whole affair. To keep myself occupied, there were always card games, and TV. But it was the Shrink that helped me pass most of the time. The Shrink loved to argue his educated view of society as a whole. And I enjoyed trying to convince him that society was an illusion created by the weak to manipulate the stronger of the species. These discussions would last days and sometimes well into the night. It was during one such debate that the Shrink got a personal example of just how right I was.

Somewhere in Ernie's troubled mind, a plan to escape had evolved. The plan was simple, since almost no one had successfully escaped from the main County jail, his plan was to have the cops take him to an easier place to get away from. That place would be the prison ward at the County Hospital. All he had to do was get injured or sick enough to be taken there. It was common knowledge at the time, that if you inhaled steam while sick with a cold or flu, you could induce pneumonia. So Ernie proceeded to stick his head into the one-gallon coffee pot we had in our cell. The Shrink, not knowing what was going on, started yelling at Ernie, telling him how "Unsanitary that was," and how "We didn't need his germs contaminating the coffee pot!"

Ernie told him, "Mind your own business old man," and stuck his head back into the pot. The Shrink told him, "Get your head out of there now or I'll kick your ass myself!" Ernie lifted his head out of the pot very slowly and looked at his adversary that now stood within fighting distance. He dumped the pot of hot water on the Shrink, punched him in the stomach a few times, and then grasping the back of his head proceeded to smash the Shrink's face against the steel edge of an upper bunk. It took five of us to break them apart, but the damage had already been done. The shrink was unconscious for half an hour, and when he did come out of it, he was blind.

For fear that Ernie wouldn't get his chance to escape the cell decided to keep the Shrink hidden, and I was assigned the job of keeping my now blind associate awake so that he wouldn't fall into a coma. All night he kept chanting one word, "Why?" I explained to him, "Just because some one is not as smart, or rich, or as well spoken as you, they still deserve respect. Not because it's the polite thing to do but, because that poor, ignorant, unappealing bastard might have the ability to rip you apart limb from limb, and they don't appreciate someone physically inferior acting superior. In other words Bull-shit Walks." I only had a few hours sleep that night before going to my bond hearing the next day.

The next afternoon, I was handcuffed and shackled, then taken down the maze of hallways to the hearing room. At one end of a large conference table sat the judge with the prosecutor. At my end sat my lawyer, my father, and myself. The first thing my lawyer asked was that my cuffs and shackles be removed. The prosecutor argued that removing the restraints from a violent convicted Lifer was asking for trouble and had no relevance to the hearing. This sparked a debate with the judge in the middle. Tyson agreed to take the cuffs off, and then reminded the prosecutor that he did have a gun in the event that I try to run away or attack anyone. He said this while pulling up his robe to expose a handgun. That was to be my only victory for the day. No matter what precedent or fact of law my lawyer came up with, Tyson shot them down as quickly as they were presented. I found myself sinking into my own little world of shadows, where all of the voices around me melted into distant murmuring with no meaning. I did catch my lawyer telling the judge that I was little more than a child and how I'd almost lost an eye, and possibly my life while fighting hardened criminals that I was no match for. All of this fell on dead ears.

It had now become obvious that this hearing was little more than a formality. Tyson never had any intention of letting me go, and anything that anyone had to say in my defense served only as an annoyance.

Up to this point, everything had made sense. I had really screwed up, been sent away to learn my lesson, and now that I'd set myself straight, I could get out and lead a normal life. Any moron could see that this was the end of the story. No purpose could be served by persisting on this life in prison thing! The judge and prosecutor were sitting so close together they were practically embracing. They were the cause of my situation, the robbers of my life! You just don't do something this wrong to a person, even I could see that! My Adams apple felt heavy and swollen. I could feel it crushing my windpipe, making it very hard to breathe.

Glaring at them from across the table I weighed my chances of getting Tyson's gun and killing them both. It might be twenty years before another chance to get this close to both of them with a gun would come along. Tyson made some remark about how I had yet to show any sign of remorse, as if crying or begging could alter his decision. He just wanted to bathe in my humiliation. He would never get that satisfaction. The words "bond denied" reached my ears as I was re-cuffed and led away down the hallway, a very disappointed man, with a lot on my mind and a very real life sentence.

Nip It in the Bud

By mid-afternoon the next day, I found myself back at the gates of Sumpter. While waiting in a holding cell at the main entrance, one of the kitchen cooks I'd seen around A-Dorm came up to the bars and tossed a shank into my cell. A shank, or a shiv, is another name for a hand made knife. This one was like a dagger with a cloth grip, and a blade sharpened on both sides. He went on to tell me how after I left, Turner and Bear had paid Jap a visit over some money they were owed. When Jap insisted that he didn't personally owe them anything, he was roughed up a little, and given half a day to cover the debt. This had happened a week ago, and Jap still had a black eye. My ex-partner had vowed to kill me if I ever came back. Now here I was, being assigned to the same Dorm. Thanking the guy in white, I put the shank in the back of my pants, and waited to be released back into the compound.

My new bunk was in the same wing as cracker alley in A-Dorm, but on the other side of the wing and all the way in the back, next to the bathroom. Tallahassee had instituted some kind of population control while I was away and half of the upper bunks were removed to comply with the new regulations. Only the outer most bunks that lined the TV room walls had remained doubled, which allowed for better visibility.

I put my personal property away in the drawer under my bunk and stepped out into the court yard. Sitting on the concrete table facing the entranceway,

I waited for the appearance of my ex-partner. A couple of guys came by to ask what had happened in court and let me know to watch out for Jap. From what I could gather everyone was surprised that I'd come back, and the talk of the Dorm was who would win between Jap and myself. There were quite a few bets on the outcome. Most of the guys warning me were actually protecting their wager by making sure I was prepared and armed. As count time neared, the courtyard emptied and I found myself alone on that concrete table waiting for Jap, quite sure that he'd been armed and advised on the matter the same as I.

The buzzer sounded and after a few moments, people started streaming in through the door. Instead of going into the wings, the majority seemed to be gathering along the outer edges of the courtyard, looking towards my general direction. To pull the shank prematurely seemed like a mistake at this point, I figured to give Jap the first move, making anything I did to him an act of self-defense. I caught a glimpse of him a couple rows back, trying to pile through the door like everyone else. A black eye was an understatement! The whole side of his face was discolored.

If this was how he looked after a week, I could imagine how bad he must have looked the day after my friends had paid him that visit. As he entered the courtyard, Jap stared straight at me with a scowl. Intense hatred seemed to emanate from his eyes. He was about fifteen feet away and closing the distance between us. I raised my arm to wave and smiled at him, as if greeting an old friend. Then I pretended to stare, and changed my expression to one of intense concern. I hollered across the now closing distance between us, "Damn, Partner, what happened to your face?"

Jap answered, "You know damn well what Happened!"

"How would I know? I've been gone a while."

Jap, "Your friends did this to me over the money you owed them!"

"You mean, over the money that you didn't collect."

Jap, "Well don't worry about it, I took care of everything."

"I'm glad that's been taken care of, but what's this I hear that you're gonna kill me?"

Jap, "Oh, I was just pissed off at the time, I didn't really mean it."

"If we have a problem, now is the time for us to settle it. Now, do we have a problem?" I asked as I reached back and pulled out the knife. I saw Jap's eyes get big enough to lose their natural slant as the dagger like shank became visible.

I continued, "We still disagree on whose fault this thing is. Now, if you really believe what happened to your face is my fault, then I think you should kill me." Grabbing the blade of the shank I offered the weapon to my partner. "Now or never, Partner." Jap's total attention rested on the blade as he said, "It was nobody's fault. It's just a misunderstanding, but we are not partners anymore, I think you can understand why." With that said he backed off, turned, and walked into the dorm. I walked over to the guy in white that had been taking bets throughout our conversation and handed him back his knife. "Thanks for the shank," I told him, as I headed towards the dorm for count.

With the change of seasons came the warmer weather. Summer was just around the corner and tempers had begun to flair as hot as the humid air that clung to everyone at Sumpter in '77. It surprised me how many of the new cocks that had come with me from RMC were still on the compound. Tim Stanley had moved into our wing, bringing with him an endless supply of pot and money. He wasn't quite as cocky now as he was on the bus, but he still agitated me with his mere presence. Another New Cock (Ricky) had come to me asking for advice on a problem he'd brought on himself. Rick had gone for the old "I'll be your friend" game that I had warned him about. He told me that he'd gotten himself hooked up with a gang of Blacks.

They were like his best friends at first, sharing things and sticking up for him. Now they had begun to hint at some sexual favors he could do for them. They'd gone as far as offering him a black sissy of his own if he'd just try being a bitch for a day, and if he didn't like it he was assured that he wouldn't have to do it again. I told him to jump one of them before it was too late, any hesitation at this point showed that he had BITCH in him.

The fact that he let them question his manhood and didn't react violently put him in line for a rape. None of the other whites were talking to him, since they figured he already was a punk.   He asked me if I would back him up if he got into a fight. I told him I would if he did it that afternoon right after dinner. But I warned him that if he didn't do something before dark not only would he be on his own, but that I'd make it a point to get myself in line for a piece of his ass.

Come dark he was sitting on the edge of a bunk with a grim expression on his face surrounded by his "partners." After an hour of staying within helping distance, and giving every imaginable signal to do something, I gave up and went to watch some TV. That night I had a very strange dream.

I'd awakened around midnight, walked a few bunks down to the guy that hadn't said a word to me since my first day at Sumpter, and woke him up. My only words were "let's go fuck this white boy up for hanging with niggers." His simple reply was "OK", as we walked over to Rick's bunk. Rick had both arms by his sides under a blanket. We pinned him down by sitting on the blanket on each side of him and started randomly punching him about the head and face. "This-is-for-hanging'-with-niggers!" each word was emphasized by another blow. This continued until our arms grew tired, then we stood up and went back to our bunks.

I woke up in the morning, and looked a couple of bunks down at my dream co-conspirator. I almost thought I saw something in his poker face, something along the lines of an understanding nod. Nah, no way, it was just a really strange dream. I looked across the dorm for our imaginary victim, but Rick wasn't in his bunk. He was probably up early dodging dicks, or maybe he was catching one right at that moment. I'd pretty much forgotten about the strange dream by the end of breakfast, and it was a big day for everybody.

Late that afternoon our ball game was interrupted by someone running into the TV room announcing that someone had just been stabbed outside the cop shop. Piling out the door with everyone else I saw a rather large Black guy holding on to a steel post while his blood poured out of him. From the looks of it he'd been stabbed clean through his back and out the front by something with a wide blade. The blood was foaming up with the escaping air as he slowly slid down the pole and eyed the crowd with an odd look on his face. Once he stopped twitching, I re-entered the TV room to get a better seat, and avoid the questioning that usually accompanied a stabbing.

After dinner while leaving the Chow Hall I ran into Wilson, my friend from B-Dorm, He mentioned the stabbing in our dorm and told me that it was over an incident in the visiting park. Rumor was that the Black guy had made some remarks to a white guys' sister out in the visiting park. Something along the lines of "show me some leg Bitch." The word was that one of the new white guys had done it, and the Blacks were on the war-path for "Get Back." Wilson wanted to know if I'd done it, since I had a couple of sisters and answered the general description.

I did feel a little uneasy that someone who knew me could reach such a conclusion. If a friend could make this mistake, then so could a pack of mad Brothers. He also informed me about a "fine young French boy" that had transferred from his dorm to mine.

The boy was supposed to be 17 years old with dark curly hair, and a real homo from the street. Wilson suggested that even though I had no interest in boys that it would be in my own best interests to consider poking this particular kid, or at least check him out. I told him I'd check the boy out when ever I had a name to go by, and headed back to my dorm. Getting some ass from a chain-gang bitch was really about the last thing on my mind, besides he didn't tell me the kid's name.

After secure count, sitting on the edge of my bunk, that now familiar feeling I'd begun to rely on, fell upon me once again. Something was coming my way, and it was by no means good.

Most folks are domesticated, the same way animals get when raised in captivity. When a dog is raised from a puppy and taught through discipline not to follow his instincts such as snapping when he plays, or marking his territory, we call him trained. When people are taught to ignore their instincts they're called civilized. Any animal that's not fully domesticated can be set loose in the wild, and given the chance will find the instincts to survive.

Humans on the other hand, have been away from the jungle a little bit too long. Very few of us could survive without the most basic of tools, in the very least a knife. Since we've killed off or restrained most of our natural enemies, our worst threat is each other. The rules of civilization have domesticated people by using the fear of discipline to stifle the instincts of the masses.

Being antisocial or 'untrained,' I was well on my way to surviving off my gut feelings, which had proved to be reliable. I could now sense when to attack and when to back off, I could also feel when danger approached or as in this case, when I was being hunted. Looking up from my bunk, I could see a hunting party of about eight Brothers headed my way. I casually looked at them as they approached trying to analyze from body language and expression what this was about.

The headman was Larry from BTU, the guy I used to buy sandwiches from. His first words were, "We've got a problem with you! What's this I heard about you beating up white boys that talk to us Niggers?" My expression of confused amazement didn't have to be feigned, my jaw actually dropped with the realization that my dream from the night before was no dream. Still trying to appear bewildered, I asked him what he was talking about.

Larry answered, "You and some other Cracker busted up one of my white partners because you didn't like him hanging out with us Black People. The Boy couldn't tell us who the other Cracker was, but he recognized you, and you'll soon be telling us who the other one is soon enough!"

"Man, I don't know what you're talking about. I think I'd remember jumping somebody. Seems to me that someone's feeding you a line of bullshit. Who told you this?"

"My partner Ricky told me it was you and some other Cracker, now why would he make this shit up? Or are you gonna tell me he beat up himself!"

"I don't know why this kid decided to cause all of this shit, but before we go any further I suggest that we meet in the court yard and hold court. Bring this kid you're talking about and we'll all find out what's going on."

Chaingang court is held when two sides disagree on an event or a subject before it escalates into a major confrontation. I had about ten people on my side and Larry had maybe twice that number on his. We faced off in a blind spot in front of the latrine with Larry, the kid, and myself in the middle. A Puerto Rican named Chico mediated as an unbiased judge. I started things off with a run down of the accusations-

"Larry came to me tonight telling me that this guy (Rick) told him how me and another guy jumped him in his sleep. Now for one thing I didn't do this, if I had, I would have done it myself. I really don't think I need any help to kick this Kids ass. For another thing I have no reason to cause Larry any problems, this Kid is the problem and that's why we're all here!"

Larry went on to tell everyone what the boy told him. Different guys from both sides asked questions, which both Larry and I answered. This went on for about fifteen minutes with no resolution in sight. Both sides were getting agitated and had begun to focus on me again.

I stated, "We can stand here all night accusing each other of stuff or we can go right to the source. Let me confront the boy myself, he's the one I've got the problem with and I haven't heard him talk yet!" Chico agreed that this was only fair, and told Rick to tell his version.

The boy was visibly shaking, and looked like he was about to cry as he started telling the story of what happened the night before. When he reached the point where he said that I was one of the attackers I interrupted, "There was enough light to see it was me?" "YES" "But you just told everyone that you were pinned under a blanket, how could you see me through a blanket?" "I just knew it was you!" "So now you're saying that you didn't see me because of the blanket, and that you just picked me at random for some unknown reason?" "I don't know for sure, I just thought it was you!"

"So now you think it might have been me, that's a lot different than saying it was me!" "Well, I'm calling you a liar, now do something about it!" "I'm not lying." Squealed Rick.

I continued loudly, "So call me a liar so I can kick your ass in front of everybody, I'm saying that I didn't do it. Now, call me a LIAR!" Rick asked Chico if the two of them could talk alone, away from the group before saying anything else. After a couple of nods from both sides, Chico and the boy walked about twenty feet away and had a private discussion in hushed tones, while blacks and whites stared each other down. Chico walked back up to us and said, "Ricky says that he was scared of the blacks he was hanging with, and that he figured that if he made up this story about getting beat up by whites for hanging out with blacks, then they would leave him alone."

This was by far, one of the worse stories I'd ever heard, but if everyone there went for it, then it sounded good enough for me. Larry told the kid that if he didn't want to be around him and his partners, then all he had to do was say so, they didn't force him to be a partner, he could walk away at anytime. I joined in by asking him 'why he picked me for this little game of his?' Chico said, "It didn't matter, the kid was just scared and this was the only way out he could think of."

Then the boy mentioned that I had told him I wouldn't back him up. Chico asked him what he meant by that. The boy went on to explain to everyone what I said about getting in line to fuck him if he didn't stand up for himself. This brought a very negative response from both the Blacks and the

Whites, even Chico started ranting and raving about turning on my own kind.

Shit. . . I was about to get my ass kicked by both races and a third. "Hey wait a minute, I said, I told the boy I'd back him only if he stood up for himself and that if he didn't then I'd get in line just like the rest of you. Now you see how he returned my offer to back him into this bullshit about a blanket party. If anything he stabbed me in the back after I told him I'd back him.

Small discussions broke out among the warring factions. Larry dissolved the court by saying that he and his group were through with this punk and started to walk away. Court ended with everyone leaving in different directions, only the kid remained standing in front of the latrine. Sometime during the night, Ricky disappeared, never to be seen or heard from again.

During the addition of new bunks my homeboy "Shotgun" took his spot on Cracker Alley and I got the top bunk over him. Since it looked like I was going to be a guest of the state for a while, I'd decided on acquiring a hobby. Both Fitz and Wilson were in the leather shop, and after hanging out with them for a week or so, and seeing how there was money to be made in hand carved leather, I joined the club. Time went by a lot quicker when I was in leather shop. I started with just a couple of tools and a basic pre-cut kit. You lay your stencil out on the leather to etch the pattern, then using a wedge shaped blade mounted on a swivel shaft you cut on the marked lines. Tapping a machined tip tool with a small wooden mallet, you shape the edges to make the picture three-dimensional. This was tedious, time-consuming work; but nothing else existed while creating my projects. This was my escape, my world. Every day there was some other technique to try, or piece to finish, I had something to look forward to. Until the day I had a visit from Tim.

I had an upper bunk along the TV room wall that was towards the rear corner of the dorm. A couple of Tampa boys occupied the double bunk separating Shotgun and myself from the rear wall. These two guys were surfer types from wealthy families. Potheads would be the best description of them, if that could be considered a characterization. Tim claimed know them from the street, which would qualify them as his homeboys. Tim and these other guys seemed to keep out of harms way by buying people off with both cash and pot that they shared freely, with both blacks and whites. It was for this reason that Tim approached me about buying my bunk, so that he could be close to his own kind.

He came to me one night around 8 o'clock and offered me thirty bucks and a radio. This was a very high price at the time, considering that a carton of cigarettes was a good fee to have some one you didn't like beaten up. He was pushy as he always was, but I could understand this, since he wanted to be near the closest thing he could find to real friends. I told him that as soon as another bunk opened up in this predominantly white section of the dorm, he could have my bunk for twenty bucks, and he could keep the radio. He insisted that he wanted it now, and I responded that he'd just have to wait or he wouldn't get it at all.

The next night I was in the small back room in the corner of the TV room that served as a barbershop, with it's single florescent lamp, and lone barber's chair. Homeboy Moose always did a nice job with his scissors, and I tipped him for the extra effort. The haircut was almost finished when a couple of Zambuzi warriors (little Blacks that acted like jitterbugs) walked in. Moose informed them that he wasn't cutting any more hair for the night. One of the

Brothers replied that they weren't there for haircuts; they were there to talk to me about a problem. I felt a tap on my shoulder, and then something metal with two ringlets was slipped into my hand under the barber's cloth. The little tie around my neck was also loosened. Moose had slipped me his favorite weapon, his scissors. I asked them what kind of problem they needed to discuss.

It seemed that they had a friend that was very interested in purchasing my bunk. And since reason had no effect on me, they had been sent to inform me that there might be serious consequences if I didn't give him the bunk immediately. I saw red! Getting up I placed the scissors on the seat and told them I'd take up this discussion directly with their employer. Pushing them to either side of the door, I walked through the T V room and out into the inner yard. From there you could look into every wing the way the cops did if they wanted to locate someone.

Tim had been in the opposing wing watching from a corner window as if it were a box seat. He ducked away from the window when he saw me motion for him to come out. Running into the wing, I caught him trying to blend in with the others watching a game in the TV room. Pulling him upright against the wall, I kneed him in the groin, and then bounced his head off the painted cinder blocks that he was pinned against. I yelled in his face, "You stupid fuck, I was practically giving you that bunk, all you had to do was wait a couple of days. Now I can't give it to you for any price, because I'd look weak. And as far as sending blacks after a white, we'll see how many white friends you've got after I tell the Clan what you did!" Cowering he responded with some feeble excuses that didn't credit my consideration.

Turning my back on him, I went straight to Friar Tuck, the Head of the Dorm Clan, and told him the whole story. The Clan held court and decided that

Tim was no longer one of us or under the clans' protection. Except for business transactions no whites could even be seen holding a conversation with him. This included his Homeboys who quickly agreed to these conditions, rather than run the risk of loosing the protection of the Clan.

Everyone turned their backs as he walked over to his little black warrior friends and tried to act nonplused by his banishment from the white community. There was no rush of victory or satisfaction of revenge in any of this. There are set rules that are not flexible, and he'd broken the most sacred of them all. Never turn on your own!

Late spring of '77 was warmer than usual. Most of the whites believed in the theory that blacks tend to be more violent in the warmer part of the year. My personal observation led me to agree with this, but I had also noticed how the whites grew more aggressive in the cold. The Clan did not welcome this early heat wave, with good reason. Small fights broke out throughout the compound for various reasons. The majority of them were between the different cities. Guys from Miami were fighting other groups from Tampa and Orlando, regardless of race.

The escape attempts were on the increase. Sumpter is located in the middle of Florida surrounded by swamp, deep woods and watermelon patches. The rumored reward for catching an escaped convict was a hundred dollars and a 50 lb. sack of grits.

At first I thought this was a joke they told the new cocks but I was assured this was true by the guards also. Every time the escape alarm sounded you could see the local country folk (some as young as twelve) gather outside the compound with hunting dogs and firearms that varied from shotguns to .22's. This bunch would then disappear into the woods hooting and hollering like a party at a trailer park. Very few escapees actually got away and the ones that did normally died in the process. This will take a moment to explain, but please bear with me.

Eluding the locals was unlikely but not impossible, and convicts as a group aren't stupid. One of the best ways to make an escape from Sumpter was to hide somewhere until count time. After confirming who's missing from a roster check, the guards search the compound. If they still haven't found the missing guys they search the perimeter with the dogs. While this is going on other guards walk the inside of the fence line with long steel spikes poking deep into the ground looking for tunnels. As the dogs are taken further from the camp searching for the scent, the escapee leaves his hiding place, cuts through the fence and heads off in another direction then the present search. As long as the tower doesn't spot him he stands a chance of getting away.

One of the more popular tricks used to throw the dogs off was wearing another cons clothes. Clothes or property from the missing cons bunk would be used to give the dogs a scent to follow. Wearing someone else's clothes and shoes for the escape tended to confuse the trail. But with all of our tricks and clever plans very few escapees made it past the fence, some didn't get that far. Florida's water table is only a few inches below ground throughout most of the state, making tunnels difficult if not impossible to maintain. Building materials from compound construction could be acquired and used to shore up the tunnel ceiling. Most escapes are attempted at night during rainstorms to limit detection from the towers and cover any trails left behind. But the rain also softens already saturated earth that pushes in on the sides of the tunnels filling them in and drowning anyone inside with mud. Twice at Sumpter, the guards found collapsed tunnels with bodies in them.

Once they were searching for someone that had hidden in the ceiling of the school building, and the second time while looking for a guy that had gone to the infirmary. Both times they made groups of us walk by the rotting bodies laid out in a neat row on the ground, while berating us on the dangers of tunneling. Unless one of us received a letter from someone that had escaped, it was a safe assumption that they just hadn't stumbled across the missing mans body yet. As terrible or desperate as this may sound there were more amusing ways of getting out of Sumpter besides escaping.

A Boy on the compound wanted to get back to his Daddy at the Rock, so he paid Crazy George to stab him. The two of them had gone to the weight pile to complete their transaction along with a few of George's friends. The boy gave George the knife and pointed to a point high on his right shoulder where he wanted to get stabbed. George had a nervous twitch, which caused his aim to be about a foot off. Once he'd realized that the boy now had a punctured lung, George and his friends took off, leaving the kid lying across a weight bench, drowning in his own blood. A body builder came along, and carried the kid to the infirmary. George went to the box as the compound bickered about someone from Lauderdale stabbing a Tampa Punk.

Contract

By this time I was spending most of my spare time in the leather shop, where the problems of the compound could be left behind. From dinner to secure count during the workweek and late morning to dinner on weekends, I kept myself busy. If the shop was open, you could find me there, until one Sunday afternoon when I had overslept. During the weekends, the cops left the TVs on until two in the morning. Whatever had been on the tube the night before was worth staying up for but it left me dead tired in the morning.

After breakfast, I'd fallen asleep on my bunk waiting for an unusually long roster count to finish. I had another one of those dreams about the streets that left me disoriented and dazed. I was standing in a line for some reason talking to some guys that I didn't currently know, but in the dream they were good friends. For some reason I had looked over at a plain building that had hundreds of little slots across the front of it. One of these little slots had something that belonged to me in it.

It was at this moment that I awoke to find myself soaked in sweat laying on my top bunk at Sumpter. The jacket that had kept me warm for the walk to breakfast had become unbearable in the early afternoon heat. Taking off the jacket, I looked around to see an almost empty dorm. I checked my watch and saw that it was close to eleven, but the dream had left me sorely dazed and for the life of me, I couldn't remember what time the hobby shop opened on a Sunday.

Being disoriented like this was not a normal condition for me, it numbed my senses, which I was about to have need of... While sitting upright in my bunk trying to regain some sense of reality, I heard one of the TV room doors slammed open. A large Hunting Party of blacks came briskly running through the Dorm. They were obviously looking for someone in particular.

After checking both TV rooms, they walked each row of bunks and then left to check the other wings. I could see them go through the same routine in the opposing wing before coming back into my area. It seemed obvious that someone was in a lot of trouble. When eighteen sets of eyes stared in my direction, I had a bad feeling that the someone they'd been looking for might be me.

They approached as a mob, stopping about ten feet from the end of my bunk. One guy stepped forward. He was about my general size, but wearing a bandanna around his head. This identified him as a karate man. Although a lot of the guys inside studied or even believed that they knew karate, only a handful were actually effective with it. This guy was just a wanna-be Bruce Lee, not a real threat. He probably wanted to make a name for himself by going after someone young like myself. Not having any real balls he'd picked what was in his mind an easy target. He muttered something unintelligible and I asked him to repeat himself.

The second time he was just as hard to understand as the first. So I told him, "I don't know what you're saying, but maybe you should take it to your mother!" He moved forward to grab my legs as I jumped down from the bunk. He landed the first punch, which I returned with two of my own. Then he wanted to wrestle, we were evenly matched at that

146

also. He managed to get a thumb into my eye. I thrust both of my thumbs, each one behind either of his eyes, and began to pull his head around by his retinas. When he tried to pull back I tripped him, and down he went with me on top. He couldn't get out from under me in the narrow space left between the bunks. The advantage was mine.

I began slamming his face into the concrete floor, all the time asking him "Who did you think you were fucking with?" I was about to do some real damage when I remembered how many other people he'd come in with. My experience in this kind of situation was to let him slip away, now that he knew I could beat him. He'd put on a show by running his mouth while backing away. This gave him a dignified way out, rather than being handled twice in the same fight by a Cracker. If I kept beating his face into the floor, then his partners would have to jump in to save his ass. I loosened my grip and he slipped out, I spun to my feet in a half crouch only to see a foot coming at me. For some reason it strangely resembled a rock for a moment.

The foot to my face knocked me back against the wall between the bunks. Now I was pissed, he knew I'd given him a break and in return he took a cheap shot. Bouncing back off the wall swinging I landed a couple of good punches to his face, which now exhibited one eye swollen shut, and the other one about halfway closed.

There was a lot of blood coming from somewhere but I couldn't tell where he was bleeding. He wasted his time trying the open palm thrust to my nose. This move is supposed to force the bridge of the nose into the brain. I concentrated on heart punches, which dropped him to his knees twice. But I had no follow up, it was as if all of the energy was draining out of me. The fight had lasted maybe three to five minutes; it felt more like an hour. I couldn't tell how bad, or where I was hurt, but one thing was for sure, it had to end soon.

I made the time-out signal, "We're making a mess with this blood thing, How about we finish this tomorrow?" He must have been as bad off as I was, because he turned and walked away holding his ribs saying, "We'll finish this tomorrow Cracker!" Then he and his army were gone. I went into the latrine to find a mirror that would give me an idea of where the blood was coming from. The person I saw in my reflection seemed to have an unusually flat nose, with a splinter of bone poking out towards the top. Other than that, I looked pretty good.

Putting a pinky finger up each nostril, I pulled outward while trying to push the bone back in. Except for the swelling my nose was back to normal within a few minutes. I was admiring my work when hands grabbed me from both sides. It was the cops, they dragged me in the office and asked what had happened. "I fell off of my bunk." "How many were there?" "I fell off my bunk once." "What color were they?" "The same color all the bunks are." After about twenty minutes of this they escorted me up to the infirmary where a medical tech. said I was OK. After a couple of more questions they took me through a steel door handed me a pair of shorts and deposited me in the box, Cell 6.

The confinement cells at Sumpter were about Eight foot by ten. Some had a single bunk on the wall but most were just three walls and steel bars. There were four of us in cell #6. Turkey I knew from the escape attempt at BTU, Dave Stevens, who I'd seen around, and the now well known Sidewinder.

It was obvious why I was there, but everyone likes to hear a story. The others told their tales with the exception of SideWinder. Since she was a bitch, no one cared to hear her story. She did repeat a little poem about herself, the last part of it ended with "all night grinding, cock finding fast Eddie." This little bitch had the hots for me because of my age and reputation, and she wasn't shy about asking me to throw her some Dick. As of yet I hadn't messed with any sissies, and in my present condition wasn't interested in starting now. If I were interested, it wouldn't be with this bony, twisted version of Quasimodo.

Turkey said she was cell property and to use her whenever I was up to it. Before falling asleep I had the opportunity to see Turkey and Dave turn her every which way while they sexed her from both ends. Damn, she sure was UGLY!

Early the next morning I woke up unable to breath. It felt like something was caught in my throat, cutting off even the smallest hint of air. Getting up on all fours I tried to cough, it took a couple of tries before I dislodged a golf ball sized clot of congealed blood from the back of my throat. Then my nose started streaming blood, I figured it would stop in a few minutes, but after soaking half a sheet, I started yelling for the guard. The others awoke and started yelling with me. After a few minutes, a guard came and took me to the infirmary where an MT gave me a shot of some vitamin that is supposed to thicken the blood. Whatever the stuff was, it worked. I asked about having my nose x-rayed to see if it was broken. The guard answered that since I hadn't cooperated, by telling them what had happened; there wasn't much else they could do for me.

Back in the cell that afternoon I had another one of my "girl by the pool dreams. " Only this time I got a piece of the girl on the other side. Waking up in the middle of orgasm my eyes came to focus on Ugly Earls head bobbing over my lap. Even with her mouth full she managed to look up and give me one of her crooked smiles. Turkey and Dave were rolling on the floor laughing, they had found my change in expression a little too much to bear. I had to admit that Earl did a real nice job of polishing knobs, but damn that boy was ugly. He would receive no conscious repeat business from me.

The next day around noontime, they released me back to the compound. My new bunk was in C-Dorm. I had the front bottom bunk next to the TV room wall. The guy on the top bunk was the young cop killer I'd known at BTU. The last thing I'd heard about him was that a rape gang had approached him in a TV room his first weekend at Sumpter. He'd pulled a knife out in defense, but made the mistake of not using it. When they were done cornholing him, they shoved his own shiv up his ass. Now standing along side the bunk, I casually asked him why he hadn't been around for a while. Taking his eyes off the Bible he was reading, he turned his face towards me. The boy's face was even gaunter than I had remembered, almost skeletal. His eyes though directed towards me, didn't seem to focus, like he was looking through me. His lips curled back in an unnatural way exposing small crooked teeth, he mouthed a few words but no sound came out, just little puffs of air. He then turned back to his Bible acting as if I'd turned invisible.

As the dorm began to fill up for dinner count, I noticed a guy I knew from hobby craft named Justice. He explained how mostly people that worked in the kitchen occupied C-Dorm, he also included that our wing was almost 50% she-male.

Looking around during count it now became obvious that there was a low level of testosterone in my immediate area. I counted six flamers, and more than a dozen known pressure punks. Justice assured me that his estimate was correct. When asked about the boy in the top bunk over me, my friend replied that no one messed with him. "Why's that, when it's obvious he's an easy fuck?" I asked.

"Have you talked to him? The boy is mindless. No one wants a stupid Fuckboy, there's no satisfaction in it. If you're gonna screw something, you at least want them to appreciate what you're doing to them!" This was a new form of logic to me, but the concept did make sense. There's no conquest in screwing the dead, and that includes the brain dead.

The swelling in my face had mostly dissipated during my brief stay in the box. You'd never know I had a broken nose except for the two slightly blackened eyes I was sporting. Sunglasses could have hidden this easily, but the top of my nose couldn't handle the pressure. Besides, it was a war wound, it was better to show off the fact that I hadn't been seriously hurt in a fight that was still a topic of conversation around the compound. It helped fuel the idea that I was invincible. More than a few blacks made comments such as "What does the other guy look like" and "Hey, Rocky Raccoon!" But no one seemed to know who my adversary had been, except that he was from another dorm.

I came back from breakfast my first morning in C-Dorm to find my bunk had been made and my clothes folded. Justice had said something about the boys in the dorm taking care of the men, but this was an unexpected perk. If I'd known that C-Dorm was like this, I'd never have wasted my time in the other dorms. This was paradise in Prison, but paradise was lost on my third day out of the box, when I was called up to the Majors office.

I stepped into a room full of guards, the lowest ranking was a sergeant. After sitting down the lieutenant seated across from me said, "Someone doesn't like you." "What makes you say that?" I asked. "Someone paid a lot of money to have that done to your face, and now they've paid a lot more to have you stabbed in your sleep before tomorrow morning!" "How much is the contract?" I asked. "Thirty for the first fight, and seventy-five for whoever stabs you." "We think the best thing for you right now is protective custody until you are transferred."

"I'm not going to PC. And if you know all of that, then you know who's paying the money, so just tell me who it is, and I'll take care of our little problem myself."

"We can't do that, the best thing for everyone involved is to transfer you to Desoto. You'll like DCI a lot more than Sumpter anyway."

"I earned my respect the hard way, and there's no way that I'm going anywhere. You can't ship everyone this moneyman doesn't like, it would be wiser just to tell me who he is. Just give me a name and I'll go on about my business."

"The only way you go back on the compound is if you sign a release stating that the state is not responsible for anything that happens to you." "I'm not signing shit, I'll just go back to the dorm and stay awake tonight. As long as you know about it, it'll be self defense on my part."

"Damn boy, you actually think that you're a real convict, don't you? But you aren't going anywhere until you sign this release. I'm giving you a direct order to sign it. If you disobey my order than you're going to the box..."

This time I was deposited in cell 1. Dave from cell 6, Ed, and Popcorn were my present cell-mates. In cell 2 next to us, was Ronny Sanderss from D-dorm, along with Paul Limbaugh. I knew someone in about every cell, even the assholes from D-Dorm down in #4. Ed and Popcorn were having a heated religious debate. Ed was a Satanist and Popcorn believed in meditation. At the height of the argument, Popcorn started puking blood, they took him from the cell and we never saw him again. So much for the powers of meditation over Evil.

After midnight count Ronnie Adams was taken from cell #4 and put in with us. The guys from #4 sent word that this kid was a punk. Dave's eyes lit up upon hearing this. Ronnie was fifteen years old and kind of on the pretty side. Until this point I had little interest in fags, but this one looked a lot like a girl to me. Dave wasted no time in confronting him about his feminine usefulness to the cell.

The kid said that the guys in #4 had raped him and that he didn't give it up easily. This created a conflict in our own cell. Ed didn't want any sex going on in the cell, while Dave's desires were obvious. And I took the middle ground by saying that only if the kid submitted willfully in a previous situation could he be considered open game. Crazy George from #4 filled us in during shower time. He said that the kid was slapped once, and did what ever he was told to do after that. By the rules, that counts as a turning out and not a rape, but Ed still wanted to give the kid a chance.

The boy said that he simply didn't know how to fight. His first day on the compound at RMC he walked up to a big guy and asked him to be his Daddy, and he'd been a bitch ever since. This enraged me, it was because of little weak shits like him that real Crackers that were young like myself had such a hard time in the chaingang. I immediately voted that we fuck him. But Ed who was bigger than Dave and myself put together, said the kid never had a chance, and that we should give him one.

Besides, the thought of Ed's MOJO making us puke blood wasn't too appealing. I asked the kid if he wanted to give Dave some sex. The answer was "No." If he knew how to fight, would he fight Dave, instead of being his bitch? The boy answered "Yes." So, I proposed that we give the boy twenty-four hours to learn how to fight.

Ed would teach him whatever he needed to know. At the end of this time, Dave would try the kid out. If the boy really fought back then Ed and myself would stop the fight before the kid was hurt in any way. And Dave couldn't mess with him after that. If the boy didn't fight back, then it was open house on his ass. Everyone agreed, and the training commenced.

Ed had the kid hitting him for a while, but the punches were little wimpy things, something like what a girl would throw. Dave took the kid's watch in payment for a few karate lessons, telling the boy it was only fair that he knew some of Dave's own fighting techniques. This was all a bunch of crap, Dave knew less of that stuff than I did. In fact, Dave wasn't much of a fighter at all. If it weren't for how fast he could run he'd probably be a bitch himself.

Finally, the twenty-four hours were up, and the game began. The bunks had been removed from the cell wall; this left quite an open area to move around. We placed the mattresses against the bars and counted down the last seconds before Ronnie's big debut on what was once the boy's watch. Dave made the first move. Dave: "I'm gonna make you my boy!" Ron: "Well you're going to have to take it!" With these words Ronnie put his fists up. Ronnie ducked

154

Dave's first swing, and then caught a backhand slap to his face. No response. Dave slapped him again as the kid took up a karate stance.

Dave told him, "The master never teaches the student everything" and bitch slapped the kid again. Ronnie dropped his hands and ignored Ed's coaching to fight back. Dave took Ronnie to the back of the cell and corn-holed him. Ed was pissed, since he'd bet me three days of lunch desert that the boy would fight. I personally felt deprived of entertainment; it was hard to believe that the kid put up no fight at all. Later that night Ed made the kid ask for another cell change. Dave strongly protested until Ed explained that he'd kill the boy himself if they were in the same cell come morning. So off the boy went to service some other cells needs, maybe the next guys wouldn't be as friendly as we were.

My buddy Ronny Sanders was in the cell next to ours. Somehow he'd learned the name of one of the brothers down at the end of the tier. All night long Ronny hollered for Willie B. Whenever Willie answered, Ronny would reply with "Lay down Nigger." After a day and a half of this, Willie was foaming at the mouth with hatred. Ronny had made a zip-gun that he planned to use on Willie when he came by for showers. The box version of a gun was fairly simple to make. Wrap the shell of a toothpaste tube tightly around a pencil, set the enclosed end on a grooved bar of soap, and wrap the handle (soap) and the barrel (tube) with layers of T-shirt strips saturated with dampened soap. We had matches for our state cigarettes, so the match heads served as a form of black powder. Any stone or hard object served as the projectile. These guns couldn't kill anyone, but they could easily put an eye out. Ronny had made his with two barrels, he also said something about a back-up plan.

At shower time Willie came down the tier and stopped in front of Ronny's cell long enough to shoot into it with his own zip gun. Ronny returned fire with both barrels. The bullets went to either side of their intended target knocking small chips out of the wall. Willie threw his gun into the cell and told the Bossman that cell two had zip guns and was shooting at him.

When the Boss came, Ronny was standing up by the bars, denying any accusations directed at him. Willie B was jumping up and down, demanding they search #2 cell. Willie was so busy trying to snitch on Ronny that he hadn't noticed how close he had come to the bars. Ronny pulled Willie's arm through the bars and hit him full in the face with his surprise, shaving powder!

This stuff was a hair remover the brothers used instead of shaving with a razor. Ronny had grabbed some when he was taking his shower, made a paste, and was presently rubbing it into the eyes of Willie B, who now stood screaming with his shoulder wedged halfway into cell #2. After Ronny let go of his arm, Willie ran around screaming trying to rub the paste from his eyes. The Bossman got him into the shower where the stream of water helped, but the other damage had already been done. Willie had no eyebrows or lashes.

An hour later Ronny started all over again, "Willie B! Where's your eyebrows Nigger?" This went on for another day and late into the night until Ronny grew bored with Willie B. Cell #2 was searched and one of the zip guns were found. Although the guards liked Ronny for their own reasons, they had to make a report on him. This meant that he'd have to go to disciplinary court. The row of cells that we were in, served as administrative confinement.

Disciplinary confinement was located directly behind us across a narrow service alley. Depending on what the DR court decided, Ronny could get up to ninety days on the disciplinary side. The meals are smaller with no dessert or smoking. In some cases they would order a restricted diet that consisted of Instant mashed potatoes, stirred with cold water, blended with uncooked carrot cubes. This is served in a small plastic bowl twice a day, and was referred to as P's & C's. By law anyone on restricted diet had to have one real meal a week, usually this would be on a Sunday. Thirty days was established as the maximum anyone could be on this diet, but after one day of three complete meals the 30 day restricted diet could be reinstated.

Another disciplinary tactic they liked was the isolation tanks. These were two steel chambers with steel hatches that resembled something from a submarine complete with a small glass porthole. Both tanks were air conditioned to 45 degrees. If you really screwed up they'd put you on restricted diet in the tank.

Left naked in the cold, you'd be sprayed with mace then with a fire hose through the porthole, then left to freeze. This cycle was repeated every few hours, never allowing the inmate to sleep. After a couple of days pneumonia would set in.

That was how some inmates met a natural death. But, you had to do something pretty severe such as attack a guard or start a riot before such extreme measures were taken. Of course we were never allowed to witness any of the actual disciplinary techniques practiced in the tanks. But we knew, and we could hear the process taking place.

Ronny Sanders and Paul had made the decision that they didn't want to leave cell #2.When the guard came to get them for disciplinary court they both refused to leave the cell. The guard warned them that they could leave under their own power, or be dragged to court by the goon squad. Ronny responded by throwing a cup of water at the guard. A few minutes later, five of the biggest hacks we'd ever seen came stomping down the hallway. Ronny and Paul held them off at the open cell door for all of thirty seconds before Paul was yanked into the hallway, and subdued with a few blows from their metal flashlights.

Ronnie fought like a demon out into the hallway and down towards the far end of the tier. It seemed as if he could hold them off indefinitely until one of the hacks said, "Go for the feet." They started stomping Ronny's bare feet with their hard sole shoes, smashing his toes. He went down and was dragged unceremoniously from the cellblock by his ankles to one of the tanks. It would be a couple of weeks before we learned anything else about my friend Ronnie.

When I was down in A-Dorm after returning from court a few months before, I had noticed an old man in the dorm that was said to be a punk. He was an older white guy, big and burly, he didn't have the appearance of the typical bitch. But I saw him acting like a slave to four little black guys. He did their laundry, gave them his money, and performed whatever sexual acts they asked of him. I found this very repulsive as did a lot of the other whites.

He had come from the Rock, and was supposed to have been a mean character to cross. But here he was just a sissy. When they brought him into the cellblock his arm was in a cast, which he waved about wildly when he found out that he was going into an all white cell. As a rule, Sumpter never mixed whites and blacks in confinement, and this furry punk was no exception. They dumped him in cell #4 with the D-Dorm clique.

Later that night his cellmates held him down and chipped the cast off his arm. They then twisted his broken arm to make him hum songs while holding their balls in his mouth. The white population of the cellblock participated by naming requests for songs he could give hum jobs to.

Periodically during the night, he'd protest to some degree but a little twist of his arm would send him right back to work. Cell #4 eventually grew bored with this and started twisting his arm into different positions while calling him Gumby. In the morning the guards allowed him to stay in a black cell after recasting his arm.

Sometimes the whole cellblock would get into debates about various subjects. These could range anywhere from rumors to accusations. One particular subject was how many ways you could kill someone. We were arguing over something we had all seen on TV, where the army guys break someone's neck by placing an arm around the throat, and the palm of the other hand at the base of the skull, then pulling upward. Cell #4 asked if anyone knew a particular guy that was in their cell. When no one could identify him or even remember meeting him, the guy panicked. He said he was from A-Dorm and had been in a fight with half a dozen Blacks the first week he arrived at Sumpter, and that he knew me from the ride down from RMC. Since I was from A-Dorm, #4 asked if I remembered him. The rest of the cell block wanted blood and started making accusations that the guy was a snitch and should be treated like one.

I let it be known that I just couldn't remember who he was, but if anyone had seen the fight than he should be given a chance. Down in #4 one of the guys had put the neck breaking hold on their unknown cellmate, and damn if it didn't kill the boy just like in the movies. Not sure how to explain a dead body in their cell, they proceeded to rip narrow strips from the dead guys sheets. These were tied to the top of the bars and then wrapped around the corpse's neck to give the appearance that he'd hung himself. The cell then pretended to be asleep while they waited for the guard to come through at count time, once discovered they would feign surprise at the demise of their cellmate.

Count time came and went with no sign of any guards. Convicts tend to rely on their instincts for survival. From astrology to lucky talismans, animal instincts take precedence over reason. This is particularly true in an overcrowded cell with no outside stimulation. They had become tribal by bonding together and expelling an outsider by killing him. Now, in the dark, they weighed the consequences of their actions while the shadowy symbol of death hung motionless just inches above their heads.

This went on for a couple of hours until the body moved, (or appeared to). One of them whispered, "He moved." "No he didn't, shut up!" One of the others added, "I saw him move, too!" "That's it, lets call for the guard, we can say we found him like this."

Their cries for help had a realistic hint of panic in them. The guard came and pushed the body with his flashlight. Assuming that the cell was playing a joke, he ordered them to cut the body down. They refused, no one was about to touch the corpse in any way, shape, or form. A sergeant came down and told the guard not to touch anything until they could investigate the scene and take pictures. Once the others in the cell realized that they'd have to share their living space with the dead for a few more hours they panicked. For an unknown period of time they demanded, begged, and pleaded to have the corpse removed. I could swear that it sounded like one of them was almost crying.

Come morning the guards took some pictures and dragged the body out of the cell and into the hallway. The coroner pronounced him dead on the cold concrete floor. As they carried him by my cell, I caught a glimpse of his face. I recognized him as one of the two new guys that rode down on the bus with me many months before. The reason he was in the box wasn't because of anything he did. He just happened to look like another new-cock that had stabbed the Black guy in A-Dorm. This was the guy that the blacks jumped by mistake. Damn that boy had bad luck. In a small way we all envied him, at least he didn't have to wake up here anymore.

A couple of weeks later, they brought Ronny Sanders back, and put him in #2 next door to us. We had heard through the grape vine that he'd refused to eat the P's & C's they served him in the tank. Another rumor was that he was close to death. Judging by his appearance as he passed our cell, I'd say that both stories were true.

After his last great act of defiance, they'd cuffed his hands behind his back and used his face for a battering ram against the tank walls. After being maced and hosed off a few times, he was placed on Restricted Diet for thirty days. Starving himself was actually a smart move on Ronny's behalf. They kept records of our weight going into and coming out of the box, there were separate records for the tank. Ronny had gone from being a good-sized weight lifter to resembling Gandhi on a bad day.

His face was still black and blue from the initial beatings, and starving himself had slowed down the healing process. When he started coughing the cops realized that they couldn't let him die looking like he'd been starved and beaten to death. They placed him in the infirmary, packed him full of vitamins, antibiotics, and all of the real food he could eat. Then they brought him back to administrative confinement. Ronny told me the story in his now weak and raspy voice, he included that he was now a "Good Cracker" and would do anything the Boss Man said. I didn't pursue his last statement, it sounded too much like he meant it.

Another Sanders, (first name Dan) was brought into confinement and placed in cell #4. Almost immediately the group we now called the hangmen started calling down the hall for anyone that knew him. Someone yelled out that this New Sanders was a snitch, he had to be, since he only had a three year sentence.

Court was now being held in the cellblock. Everyone told stories how Dan didn't associate with anyone, but always seemed to be watching everything going on. I was the only one to stand up for him. I swore on my reputation that Dan was good people. "How do you know him?" someone asked.

"He asked me for a light one time on the rec. field, we smoked a joint and just bullshitted about things in general. He mentioned at the time that he didn't want to mess with anybody, just do his time and get out." "So, you don't really know him, he's just some guy you talked to once on the rec. field for a couple of minutes?"

"I can tell that he's good people, leave him alone." "That's not good enough, we say he's a snitch and we're gonna fuck him after we kick his ass!"

The cellblock started chanting "Fuck 'em up" repeatedly, drowning out any other words I yelled out in his defense. The fighting started with the sound of bodies hitting the concrete walls and floor. I was thinking how this guy was a big boy, but what kind of a chance did he have against those four maniacs. Suddenly the sounds stopped. Sanderss voice rang down the hallway, "Get up and fight me you Pussy Mother Fuckers!" I heard no response from the hangmen. "You want a piece of me come and get it!" Still no response. The guards came running, worried that another hanging was taking place. They opened the cell door, and told Sanders to

come out. "No, I won this cell, you take them out!"
They warned him about the Goon Squad, and after
a few moments of silence he decided to come out.

They put him in next door and told Ronny to make
sure that nothing happened to him. As soon as the
guards had left the tier, the hangmen started telling
Ronny how the guards were the only thing that had
saved Sanderss ass. And that it was now up to
Ronny to finish the job they'd started. I asked, "If all
four of you guys couldn't handle him, what makes
you think Ronny can?" "We were kicking his ass, he
didn't start running his mouth until after the man
was standing at the cell door!" I responded,
"BULLSHIT! He ran his mouth way before the man
came, and ya'll didn't get no straightening."   " Who
are you to talk about straightening? You get your ass
kicked by a bunch of niggers and you think that
makes you bad?"   " Bad enough to kick your ass, if
you and an army can't handle someone you call a
snitch!" At this point Ronny hollered out, "Ain't no
one getting their ass kicked in this cell!"
Crackers told me not to mess with him, and I do
what ever the Boss Man says, so just forget about it!"
Nobody was about to argue with Clansman Ronny.
No one was sure, if the Goon Squad had actually
broken his spirit or if he was putting on an act.
Either way the debate ended, and the hangmen were
a little less aggressive from then on.

My father had taken it upon himself to write to the
Lt. Governor about the fights I'd been in. This
resulted in my move to K-Dorm. This was where the
PCs stayed. PC stands for protective custody or
Pussy Cracker. I strongly argued against this, since
it was a disgrace to be locked up for protection. My
situation had been forced on me, where as everyone
else in the wing had "checked in" or asked to be
protected.

PC had one man cells on the second floor of one of the new dorms. They were well lit and air-conditioned. Although I was more comfortable, there wasn't much to do by myself for weeks on end accept play with myself.

And there are only so many ways to do that, even with different food products for hand lubricant. Butter worked the best but left the cell smelling like popcorn. Apple butter had to be re-wetted with just the right amount of water, too much and your hand slides right off. Too little and the whole plan skids to a halt, not to mention it leaves permanent stains.

This nervous habit would remain with me the rest of my life, and a few times it would lead to trouble at my next camp. Just before leaving for my new camp, Crazy George informed me of who paid for the contract. It was during shower time and George was talking about the fight I had in A-Dorm. He went on to say that a few people besides himself were surprised that Tim had the balls to send someone after me a second time.

So it was Tim that had caused my present situation. It all added up. Tim had the money and the reason. There was some satisfaction in knowing that he didn't get the bunk he so sorely wanted. But I would never be content until I paid that punk back for causing me to loose face. I became obsessed with thoughts of revenge. Sleep and food became secondary, signing the release and going after him would make me the bad guy. And it seemed as if the cops preferred his presence on the compound to mine. Either way he'd be pre-warned, making it very hard to get him before he paid someone else to get me. He'd won this little battle, but one day I would win the war. And that war would be fought on my ground by my rules. I was still planning his demise as we approached the front gates of DeSoto.

DeSoto

D.C.I. is located in the center of Florida on Highway #70, seven miles from the town of Arcadia. In both World wars, this compound had served as a training camp for Air Force pilots. The perimeter of the main camp is diamond shaped, running lengthwise with the highway. The main buildings start from the inner perimeter of the diamond and end at the crosswalk, which runs the center length of the compound. At the points of the diamond were the chow hall at the West tip, and the library to the East. Behind the Library, a small squat building housed the infirmary. For years, DeSoto served as a medium/ minimum custody camp. Built on low-lying heavily saturated marshland, the ground wasn't sturdy enough to support guard towers. Without towers, the camp couldn't house close custody inmates.

This changed when a new discovery called Paraguard was installed around the perimeter of the camp.

This system consisted of hydraulic lines buried in a six foot space between the outer fences. Upon entering DeSoto every inmate was informed how the Paraguard system was infallible and given a quick glance at the control panel in the front gatehouse. This wooden plaque had lights laid out in a diamond pattern representing the perimeter of the compound. Depending on the degree of sensitivity, the Paraguard system was set at; the mere weight of a rabbit could be detected and located at any point between the two barbed wire topped fences. In the event of an escape, an alarm would go off and two blinking lights would indicate the area of the system breach. The gatehouse would then radio the gun trucks that lay in wait outside of the compound, instructing them where to go. Usually, at least one cop would be waiting for the escapee before he cleared the outer fence.

At this time the system was new and prone to failure. Lightning, the main cause of malfunctions, had a tendency to knock the system off line for days at a time. Thunderstorms were quite common, as were lightning strikes. Most escape attempts were made during heavy storms, when the inmates knew the system would be shut down to protect it from lightning damage.

The dormitories were rectangular, the longest in the middle of the compound, and the shorter towards the ends. These drab cinder block edifices were old and tattered, with hinged shutter type windows and very few screens. The front door (located in the center of the broadside) led into the TV room, adorned with tattered wooden benches facing a single TV mounted at head level. DeSotos' version of a cop-shop was a single telephone mounted on a shelf at hip height, from which the dorm cop could see both ends of the dorm through the doorways that marked each cubicle. Every cubicle has it's own latrine and housed ten bunks. Full and half-length wooden lockers lined the walkway of each cubicle. I was assigned to G-Dorm, affectionately referred to as "the Getto".

My bunk was just inside of the first cube south of the TV room. To my right in the back corner was a tall lean American Indian called "Chief," then myself. To my left was a stocky, blond, cherub faced guy named Jeff, he and Chief were partners. My first conversation with Chief was going well until the subject of age came up. He made the comment. "Shit, another Youngin". "What's that supposed to mean"? I asked. "Nothing, it's just that these two other two guys in our cube are Juvies and they both turned out to be wussies." I snapped back, "I know you ain't calling me no wuss." Dude, I don't even know you, but I know those two youngins in our cube are a couple of weak assed snitches." "The one on the other side of my partner is a little pussy, he'll tell on anything he sees. We were looking out for the boy on the other side of the doorway, until he crossed us." It was at this point that Jeff butted in on the conversation to explain how the one boy had been "bought."

According to Jeff, everyone has a price. In this particular case, the boys' price was a sandwich. They had been paying the kid to run for coffee and cigarettes during the poker games they ran in the dorm. In return for these services, they looked out for the kid and paid him in coffee and cigarettes. One afternoon Chief decided to gnaw on a sandwich he'd bought from a guy in the kitchen. When he couldn't find it in the locker he asked Jeff if he'd taken it. Jeff said no; the kid must have grabbed it. When Chief asked the kid if he'd taken the sandwich from their locker he lied and said he saw Jeff eating it. Now if the kid had admitted to the theft it wouldn't have been a problem, but to tell somebody that their partner had lied to them is a serious mistake.

Had the boy intended to rip them off, he could have waited until they trusted him to hold surplus money, then he could have gotten away with fifty bucks or maybe a couple of hundred. Had he admitted he took the food it wouldn't have been a big deal either; they would have given it to him anyway. To lie about it meant that his word had a value of one prison sandwich. To make matters worse the kid left a note on Jeff's bunk during lunch apologizing for his crime. This had enraged my new neighbors even more, since only Bitches write notes instead of facing their accuser. This gross betrayal of trust would require punishment, not so much for its severity but for its flagrant disrespect.

My first dinner at Desoto was bad. After commenting that I could have come on a better day, Jeff informed me that this was one of the better meals. They served mostly starch here and very little meat. The real meals were served at lunchtime. They keep us hungry throughout the night; feed us enough in the morning to make it through lunch then serve the largest meal at noon so we can finish the day's work. The evening meal was just a legal requirement. The logic behind this was to improve work habits. Why feed someone that's not working? It became clear why Desoto was classified a hard labor camp.

That evening, during secure count Chief and Jeff developed a plan to set fire to the Sandwich boy. During the unusually long count, the Kid had fallen sound asleep. Both partners took turns running over and squirting cans of lighter fluid on his blanket. While the Bossman was at the other end of the dorm they flicked matches at him, but for some reason couldn't get him lit. They were about ready to give up, when suddenly the Boy woke up, pulled out a cigarette and lit it. The boy's own match ignited the fumes. "Houston we have ignition"!

The flame hit the ceiling with a ball of heat that seemed to suck the air from our cubicle. After the initial flash, the fire settled back into a few small patches of flame on the blanket. Sandwich boy sat there in a daze still holding the cigarette in his mouth while the remains of his eyebrows and hair smoldered. Chief brought him back to reality by commenting," Looks to me like you should maybe give up smoking." An expression of realization crossed the kids' face, then fear. The Boy pounced out of his bunk and ran outside the dorm, refusing to come back in. The Bossman managed to convince him to sit in the TV room while he checked out the Kid's story.

The fumes from the lighter fluid had either burned off or evaporated by this time, leaving little evidence of arson except for the singed ceiling. Chief and Jeff played the (I didn't see nothing, did you?) game. While I added that they shouldn't let kids with emotional problems play with matches. That's when the boy to Jeff's left walked into the TV room and refused to be left alone with us. We could overhear him telling the dorm cop what had happened. When the little snitch was sent back to his bunk, one of the guys from the other side of our cube ran over and knocked the taste out of his mouth for snitching. This time the guard caught what was going on and called the sergeants. They reassigned the two Juvies to other dorms and the assailant was taken to the box for a night.

The one thing I'd become accustomed to in my few weeks in solitary was some degree of privacy. This meaning that I could just lay back in my bunk, and think undisturbed or practice what had become my new nervous habit, playing with myself. Now that I was back in a dorm I would have to devise a new way of accomplishing a familiar goal while maintaining some degree of discretion.

The mosquitoes were so thick that hand-held foggers were brought into the dorms spewing a mixture of half-burnt diesel fuel and Malithion into the air three times a night. In spite of these precautions, the mosquitoes still managed to invade our rather dismal housing, leaving giant welts on anyone careless enough to leave any exposed flesh or sleep only covered by the thin sheets. Although the temperature inside the dorms reached the upper nineties during the night, everyone covered themselves up with sheets and blankets. Doing the same myself, I could make a tent with my knee and carry on about my business without being noticed. Rather than leave my bunk to dispose of the byproduct, and risk being attacked by the droves of bloodsuckers visibly covering the ceiling, I would inseminate some toilet paper. This I would throw towards the bathroom doorway sometimes getting them to stick on the doorframe. It became sort of a game my first night to see how many times I could secretly do this unobserved until falling asleep. As bad as this may sound at least I wasn't corn-holing boys.

I was startled from a deep trance-like sleep my first morning in DeSoto by the sound of strange music coming from the TV room. Nearing semi consciousness, I awoke to the sound of someone singing a country song "My Wife, She Got a Blue ribbon for callin' Hogs, She Runs Barefoot through the Fields." It took a few minutes to realize where I was until Chief said, "You should see the look on your face when you're jerkin off"! He then went on to make a very strained face for me including sound effects. Imitation is not always another form of flattery.

This was my first Saturday at DeSoto, as we went down to the chow hall for our weekend brunch, Chief and Jeff explained how after the riot (which was more like a sit-down strike), the kitchen had been serving weekend breakfast from Nine to Two. You could eat as many times as you wanted until 2:00 in the afternoon, but the dinners that followed these brunch meals usually consisted of little more than a spoon of greasy noodles and a roll. Though this sounded like a good deal, Chief was convinced that some sinister plot lay behind the brunch system. As corny as this sounded at the time in later years his theory would turn out to be true.

Standing in the chow line, I noticed a square white building to our right with multiple little slots facing our direction. They told me this was our mailroom, for some reason it looked strangely familiar. It appears that the longer you're locked up the more finely tuned your instincts become towards future survival. I had seen this particular moment in a dream a few months before.

What some might call De's JA Vu is little more than remembering a part of a dream that is presently occurring. After mentioning this, Chief responded with, "So what? Everyone in here does it. Tell me when it's something more important than a mail room, like a football score."

I had seen quite a few guys at Sumpter that would concentrate on a single thought for days at a time, trying to will a certain event or thought into reality. At the time, it was considered an acceptable practice comparable to cursing someone by using the power of will alone. This psychic attack would often produce results, but by the same token convicts are sensitive to bad vibes. If you catch someone giving you the eye, it's best to jump him now, rather than wait for the bad luck to come your way.

I'd once read a book that explained the evolution of psychology and the different theories that had been collected and then discarded by the fathers of modern mental health. One of these discards referred to the six levels of consciousness. The shallowest level is present thought or what you are currently concentrating on; the next level is your short-term goal. This means what you plan to accomplish within the next few days or weeks. Then there's your long term or life goal, which serves as the deepest form of conscious thought. Your drive or "Id" as Freud referred to it. Only in this context, Id and ego combine as one to form the base of someone's personality.

Bordering but not sharing this Drive is the first level of subconscious. This level reacts to the conscious mind in the form of dreams, and to some degree interacts with conscious thought. It is also unique to each individual, and is commonly called the soul by theologists. The middle level of the unconscious is the Communal mind. At this level everyone is an open link to anyone else. An example would be to know when someone is thinking about you, or being aware of something tragic happening to a family member. This is the level where witchcraft and hypnosis takes place. My friend Ed from the box at Sumpter had explained: "That to cause some one injury, you simply had to will someone into seeing something different than it actually is." Such as making a busy street appear barren and safe to cross.

I had found that keeping a particular forced thought in the back of my mind could project a subconscious impression on someone. Body language and voice could be used to extract and implant thoughts directly to and from someone's subconscious without mentioning the true topic of conversation. My projection was one of honesty with a hint of menace. This "first impression" tended to make people tell me things they normally wouldn't remember or recall on their own. The menace kept them truthful and curious. Once I knew the secrets that made a person tick, I could figure out their drive, the thing that makes them what they are, the core of their being. But unlike a psychoanalyst, I kept this key to their subconscious to myself, using it as a trigger to inspire loyalty, or attacking the drive directly if I were screwed over. Take away someone's reason for being, and they really don't have a reason to live. Though still in the development stage, this talent served as a line of defense and a hobby so to speak.

After secure count on my second night, some of the guys from G-Dorm began milling about. I could sense that something was up by the hurried way they were moving from place to place with stuffed pillowcases in their hands. Piling out the window in single file like paratroopers also gave some indication of an unusual event taking place. Three of them headed towards the back fence, while two others ran towards the front, carrying pillowcases laden with sand. When everyone was in place, the pillowcases were thrown between the front fences, setting off the Paraguard in that sector. The gun trucks were radioed about the breach and immediately sped to the front of the compound. The guards left their trucks and dash mounted radios to search between the fences with flashlights for footprints, the five guys had figured this would give them the longest amount of time to hit the back fence and get a head start. What they hadn't counted on was the high visibility of a white pillowcase.

After the rear perimeter alarm went off, the cops figured out what was going on and sped to the opposite side of the camp where the newest breach had been detected. As the trucks rounded the end corners of the compound their lights illuminated the fields in the rear of the camp along with the silhouettes of the running escapees. Two trucks ran down one escapee each, while the three other runners disappeared into the woods.

DeSoto was reputed to have the best dogs in the state. Worked in teams of three, two dogs would sniff the ground while the third sniffs the air. The dogs picked up the scent of the two brothers that had masterminded the escape, but their trail disappeared at a road. The third had simply vanished once out of view.

The next day I was walking around the rec. field, which was located along side of the vocational area

173

in a large, fenced area behind the compound. Jeff was explaining that because of my age I would never get the opportunity to grow up socially. Finishing high school, working as an adult with responsibilities, interacting with others, and relationships with women were important stages of my teen-age years that I would never experience. Even if I were to get out within a year's time, the damage would have already been done.

Time stops in here, the same way a young kid's childhood stops when their parents break up or some other harsh reality slams them out of emotional development. That's the real reason guys become institutionalized. They can't relate to anyone on the outside, they sense their loss when confronted with normal people, people that are all there. It's easier to come back to the chaingang where we can be with our own kind and not have to confront our emotional inadequacies. There is no place for emotion in here, it's despised and rejected as much, if not more so than we are by society.

Jeff was in his thirties and I respected his opinions, but this recent bit of information startled me. I was not about to let myself become institutionalized. I wouldn't let it happen! What Jeff had just told me seemed very real and made a lot of sense. He also said there was no way around it, and no exceptions to the rule that he knew of, Jeff should know . . . He was speaking from personal experience. Then it dawned on me. What if I developed through other people? I was only seventeen now, if I talked with seventeen-year-olds now, and collected their stories, I could play their stories out in my head. Substituting my personality and reactions for theirs, I could live out my "Lost Years" in something along the lines of a psychic simulator. This could work, even if I spent more time here then I expected. Jeff thought on this awhile, apparently it had never occurred to him that there might be a solution to the problem that had plagued him the larger part of his life. There was only one small problem with my theory. The people I'd be gathering my stories from were already damaged themselves. But what to hell, sometimes you just have to work with what you've got.

Monday my orientation started along with about a dozen others. There was Grider from Lauderdale; a guy from Indian River called Chicago with a rather obvious scar from the corner of his eye to the bottom of his chin. Then, there was Skull and his bunch. Skull was a very Aryan looking character, with blonde hair, and a weight lifters build. He was supposed to be one of the more notorious "Killer Fags" from the East Unit that Chaingang stories were made from.

Word was that he'd been run down by one of the most vicious guys in the Unit and promptly stabbed in the chest. Skull had then pulled the shank out and stabbed his attacker to death. In the short time he'd been at DeSoto, Skull had already managed to surround himself with some Pretty boys. Rumor was that he planned to convert these cute little youngsters into La Femme Fatals'. This would prove interesting to see a true Booty Bandit at work in his element. I would have to make it a Pointe to get to know him on a very casual basis; this would make it easier to observe the whole turn out game through its different stages.

After orientation, my assignments were eight hours kitchen duty a day, and four hours Vocational Auto Mechanics. Depending on how the weekly schedule was planned, I could go weeks without a whole day off. The kitchen in any institution is the worst possible job assignment, and this kitchen was like a scene from one of Dante's nightmares. My first morning at work we had two fights in the dining

175

room before the doors were opened for breakfast. The floors were forever slippery from the dampness that seemed to sweat from the walls throughout the night and early morning hours. This grease bearing moisture clung to everything but the food. This wasn't surprising since even the flies seemed uncertain about landing on some of the items we were serving.

I was trapped on the serving line handing out some rather nasty looking sausage patties. After the first pan ran out, I started throwing one sausage into the old pan underneath the serving line for every two I dished out. Within an hour I had a large amount of meat stashed with no way of moving it to a more secure area. When Chicago came up for the empty pans, I brought this to his attention and told him to take care of it for me.

With just a momentary stare he caught on and carried them back to the pot sink, where he bagged the meat and carried it back to the Getto. This was the beginning of our partnership and our business. Within a few days we had so much food coming out of the kitchen that a roaming locker had to be set up to hide all of the contraband. As long as we moved the locker every other day, no one could stake it out and rob its contents while both of us were absent from the dorm. We had meat we could sell to the guys that ran canteens for sandwiches, and of course the sugar and yeast that we procured would be used to make buck (wine).

It was about this time; Jeff mentioned that my partner and I should house a poker game. The house had to keep a player in the game to boost the pots; this player could be Chicago. We would take five percent off every pot. Some of the profits would be used to keep the players supplied with coffee and cigarettes during the game. I got a boy to perform the service of a waiter named Mike. Mike was one of

Skulls potential Boys; of course he wasn't allowed to linger during actual playing, since fags are notorious for bringing bad luck, and convicts take their gambling seriously. Things couldn't get much better until one afternoon when Chicago dropped off a large bread bag full of powdered chocolate, sugar and liquid yeast in a steel capped jar.

Being half-awake I walked over to the stash locker in my cube and opened it, leaving the lock hanging on the clasp. Picking up the bag and only half-assed covering it with my shirt, I had almost reached the locker when the thought of checking for the man suddenly occurred to me. Sure enough, the dorm cop was standing a foot from me staring at the shirt hanging off my arm. Instead of leading him to the locker, I casually turned and walked towards my personal locker that contained no contraband.

This particular cop had only been on the job a few days. He kept his uniform starched and tucked in like he was a marine or something. Yet for all of his, "by the book" attitude he was a very naive and unsure young boy that shouldn't have been left alone in the dorm we called the Getto.

Any other cop would have just taken the sugar for his own coffee, poured the yeast out, and let me go. Instead he grabbed the bag and asked, "What's this"? With my best look of miscomprehension I replied, "There is nothing there, if you really think that there is something there, and you believe that you want it, I suggest that you take this thing you think you see and keep it"! He led me outside between G and H dorms where a small crowd gathered around us. Shaking the bag in my face he went on to ask what was in it.

"Sir I don't see anything in your hand. Now you're the Bossman and a lot smarter than I'll ever be, but I think we should get out of the sun before you start seeing pink elephants or something." Sticking his finger into the bag and then into his mouth he said, "This is sugar isn't it? And this tastes like.... Chocolate"? Then he opened the jar, stuck his nose in it, and squealed, "Oh God what to hell is that"?

"It's what ever you say it is Bossman. If you say it's sugar, then it's sugar. If you think it's chocolate, then that's what it is. But I really think that we should get out of the sun until you make up your mind about what is real and what isn't"!

The crowd standing around us started picking up the act by adding comments like, "Bossman don't look too good", "He really thinks there's something in his hand", and "Maybe we should call a doctor or something"! He escorted me into the dorm and up to the phone where he called the Lieutenants office. They didn't take it very seriously, telling him to write me up and put the bag into the storage locker until a Sergeant could come down and check it out. I walked back into my cube to re-lock the stash locker when Clyde (the dorm hustler) approached me with a deal.

For half of what was in the bag he'd steal it back, but I had to get the cop as far away from the storage locker as possible. Knowing what that amount of yeast was worth, I at first argued the price, then the means of getting the cop far enough away from the storage locker. Clyde reminded me that I had about ten minutes before the sergeant got here to come up with a way. Then it hit me, telling Clyde to get ready I walked towards the TV room doorway. Waiting until the cop looked at me in the doorway of my cube, I stopped and let my eyes get big with guilt. Then I took one step back. He moved foreword a step, and I moved back another, on his next move I turned and ran to the farthest end of the dorm with Super Cop hot on my heels.

Turning at the end of the dorm and ducking into the bathroom, I immediately assumed the hands against the wall position. The cop seized this opportunity to

178

begin searching me, just like in the book. That's when a sound like an explosion could be heard from the other side of the dorm. The cop grabbed my shirt and quite forcefully dragged me back towards the TV room.

The storage Locker door lay split in two and shattered on the floor. There were traces of white and brown powder everywhere, a cloud of it hung suspended in the air like dirty snow. A zigzag trail of it seemed to lead all over the far side of the dorm as if some maniac with a sieve and a poor sense of direction was on a rampage. For a moment it looked as though the cop was gonna cry on me. He tried to call the office again, but someone had pulled the phone cord from the wall during my distraction. Frustrated, he stammered, "You're gonna pay for this you son of a bitch! We'll see how smart you are when the sergeants get here. You think that you're so smart stealing that contraband back, Don't you?"

"But Sir I couldn't have done this, you were shaking me down in the end of the dorm when this happened, and I told you before that I never saw any contraband in the first place"! That's when the Sergeants came and took me to the Office, Where Lieutenant Yomans was waiting for me. "So you think you're slick stealing back the bag huh"? "Sir, there never was a bag".

"Don't try that SHIT ON ME! Officer Hays may be a Little green, But I'm not! This would have been a little contraband charge, but now it's destruction of state property, that's serious, and your ass is mine"!

"Sir, I wasn't anywhere near that locker when it was broken into and I have Mr. Hays as a witness. And as far as contraband goes; if you ain't Got No Body, then you Ain't Got No Murder"!

Yomans pounced across the room and pinned me up against the wall. "I will beat your ass so bad you'll never pull anything else like this again"! "Yes Sir, But

179

before you start with the beating thing, I think you should know that I am a juvenile, and I bruise easily. Now how will I explain that to my rather wealthy parents when they come to see me"? "You'll be in the box for a couple of weeks, by the time they get to see you all the bruises will be gone." "My folks aren't stupid; they'll just send my Lawyer. And you have to let my lawyer in."

He seemed to think about this for a few moments before backing off. Then in a shaky voice he said, "OK Smart Ass, we have ways of dealing with people like you. Someday you'll want a favor, and guess whom you'll need it from? I shrugged my response. "From me that's who! And I promise that I'll remember our little conversation we had today. Now go on back to your Dorm. If I hear your name come up again on my shift I'll have your ass"! Yomans transferred to the midnight shift soon after that. It would be a couple of years before I would have to deal with him again but true to his word, he did have a good memory. In the mean time there were other things to deal with.

Some tall white boy moved in against the far wall, and McDonnell was placed in the empty bunk on the other side of Jeff. Chief informed me that McDonnell was the kinda guy that liked to refer to himself as a "real nigger." He brought nothing but trouble with him, and I was advised to keep an eye on him.

The Buzz

Someone had managed to steal twenty-eight cans of wood putty from one of the shops. Put a small gob of this in a bread bag, cover your face with the open end, and you could see God! I'd always looked down at huffing as the lowest form of high but Chicago insisted I at least try it. The whole Dorm was sharing about eight bags in small groups of three or four guys. One group was taking five-minute turns in one of the stand up lockers. When the allotted time was up they'd remove the lock and the next guy would get in. There were ten guys in the bathroom in my cube, which was also where the bulk of the stash lay hidden behind the mirror over the sink.

This stuff really left you disoriented. So much so, that when the Goon Squad came and started grabbing people, no one paid much attention to them. It took the cops forever to get Brisket out of the stand up locker. Each time the cops pulled the flimsy door open, He'd yell it ain't been five minutes yet and pull the door shut. The story we heard later was that they had to let him keep his bag to get him up to the box. Somehow they managed to overlook a lot of us. The truth of the matter was that they didn't have enough room in the box for thirty people, instead they told everyone in the Dorm to stay in their bunks for the night. Since I couldn't sleep, I'd been left with only one form of self-entertainment.

Chief had named my little inseminated wads of toilet paper (Skeet Rags). By two o'clock in the morning, there were five of them stuck at various points around the bathroom doorway. A fresh one hadn't stuck and had fallen on the floor of the opening. Calling it a night I turned on my side to go to sleep. A few moments later, I could hear someone getting up to use the bathroom. From the sound of the dragging feet, it had to be McDonnell. After the flush, there were a couple of steps and then a hesitation at the doorway, a few more shuffled steps, then he kicked my bunk. "Hey Man, What the Fuck is this"? Recognizing McDonnell's voice my response was, "What's what"?

"This," He said raising his leg to show me a wad of toilet paper stuck to his toe! "That's a skeet rag, what else would it be"?

"Hey Man, Get it off"! "I ain't touching that shit, it's been on the floor"!

"How am I supposed to get it off then"? "I don't know, shake your foot or something"! Shaking it from his foot, he shuffled back to his bed and fell asleep. (That should teach him about dragging his feet).

The next afternoon at lunch count, Chief told me that McDonnell was pissed-off about something from the night before and that he was out to kick my ass. At that moment the Nubian Berserker rounded the corner saying that he had "something to talk to me about"!

"Man I'm gonna kick your ass for that shit you pulled last night"! "What shit is that"?

"You know, that skeet rag thing, you disrespected me"!

"I told you what it was when you asked, if you're going to cop an attitude then you should have done something then, why wait until the next day"? "I didn't believe you last night, then Chief told me you was for real"! "Did I lie to you?" " No" " Did I put that on your foot on purpose?" " No"" Do you realize how many people are wondering what we're talking about? And that the longer we stay on the subject the more will know what you were stomping around in last night?" ...Silence. I continued my argument, "That shit happened last night, its history. It's not my fault you didn't believe what I told you. The next time you think you have a problem with me, just ask and I'll tell you straight. But don't come to me the next day with bullshit"! He turned and walked away saying, "That's one Sick Ass Cracker." Outside of one small incident when I poked him with a kitchen knife, I never had a problem out of McDonnell after that.

Voc. Auto Mechanics had a morning and an afternoon class. Anyone working in the kitchen that also had a shop class was condemned to the morning shift at the chow hall. This meant getting up at five in the morning, working until twelve-thirty, and then running to the back gate for school. The auto class served as the nearest thing to a break from work. There was an older guy that worked as the Vocational Aide. He was the one that worked on the vehicles brought in from the outside while the rest of us watched on. With of the amount of people in the class only a few of us ever had the chance to lay our hands on an actual vehicle.

It was common knowledge that the vocational courses were little more than a formality. This was an attempt on the part of the state to show the public the wide range of opportunities made available to us for learning a trade. In theory it was a good idea, but in practice, a dismal failure. Most of the guys like myself were too tired from our jobs to pay attention, others that were genuinely interested soon grew distracted after being repeatedly denied any hands on training.

One time they took a few of us "sleepers" to an office and asked us what our problem was. After explaining that weeks at a time without a day off and twelve-hour days during the week tended to exhaust the average person, they responded that school was a privilege. If we couldn't handle both work and school, then we'd be removed from school and only have the kitchen to deal with. It seemed that labor was valued more than education. Either way, my screwing up was about to interfere with even the most immediate of goals.

Everyone was so wasted on party night that nobody remembered where the wood putty was stashed, accept myself. Chicago and I were both off from kitchen duty and decided to spend the morning getting toasted. We were in the end cube huffing away when I noticed the Bossman coming. Stuffing the bag under the bunk I was laying on, we tried to look as casual as possible. The cop walked past us to the window and grabbed another bag from the ground outside. After denying that we knew it was there, we were escorted up to the Lt. Office where we were presented with disciplinary reports (DRs)

Returning to the Dorm we sat discussing how well they'd managed to blow our high when the same cop came back, reached under the bunk I was sitting on and pulled out the bag we'd been using previously. We were then put through the whole process a second time.

The next day I had to go to DR court over the invisible bag thing. If all three DR's came before DR court on the same day, they would have a field day on my ass. Either way I'd have to put an end to my huffing fumes and find another way of getting off. Pot was expensive, and although we had the money for it neither Chicago nor myself cared to stay stoned. The chain-gang wine or buck as we called it wasn't always available. It took three days to make, and the smell of the fermentation process often betrayed its whereabouts to the cops. Then we discovered Senequan.

During the development stage of a new drug, they'd give it to us in varying quantities to figure out dosage, and or side effects. To get Senequan you simply had to see the psychologist.

The camp shrink was a rather large Latin woman, who spoke little English. She seemed very nice, almost normal until sometime during the conversation her one hand would try to attack her. Of course, the other hand would prevent this from happening by pinning the wrist of the evil hand to the arm of her chair. Through out this process she'd try to distract you by making you explain yourself in plain enough English for her to understand. But without proper hand signals from the Doc herself, communication was minimal at best.

Chicago walked in there speaking Spanish and got himself all kinds of scripts, including Senequan. When asked where he learned the language he explained that he lived with the Indians of New Mexico using peyote to experience a higher sense of reality. As we walked outside, we ran into some friends of ours from G-Dorm discussing a mission.

It seems that a new Fat Boy on the compound was a known child molester. The guys from G-Dorm were hard pressed to do a number on him. But they couldn't come up with a way to lure him behind the library where they could bang him up. This fat-boy was called Moon Pie. The name came from an incident where he'd blown some guys for a Moon Pie each. Upon seeing me, the crew figured that with me being young, I could probably lure him into the back, where he could be beaten, fucked and whatever other things that might come to mind. I did my best to coax him behind the Library, but Moon Pie either knew something was up or had better sense, then to wander behind the library with me. After hiding behind the library for twenty minutes, the guys grew tired of waiting and came around the front to find out what was taking so long.

Seeing the approaching mob, he turned to run, but the gang was too fast for him. They simultaneously began pounding a mud-hole in his ass. When he cried out through his tear stained bloody face "Why are you doing this to me"? One of the guys replied, "You're a child molester and you have to die"!

"But I didn't know she was sixteen!"

"Liar, you fuck with little kids, now you get to know what it's like to be handled by someone bigger than you"! For some strange reason I tended to believe him, but to feel sympathetic towards a child molester was totally out of character for a convict. Personal opinion, right or wrong, these things didn't matter at the moment. I was now part of the group acting as a mob. I thought for a moment that the same thing was going on in the other guys' minds from some of their expressions. He was down and semi-conscious when the cops came running and pulled us off him.

Finding myself once again in the Lt. Office, we used the excuse that Fatboy had approached me and that the gang from G-Dorm had come to my rescue. The cops didn't believe this for a moment. They explained that Moonpie was a school counselor that had made the mistake of banging one of the sixteen year olds he worked with, and that if anything else happened to him we'd be charged with assault. We all knew that this was bullshit.

The local county courts didn't like to be bothered with the going-ons inside of a prison. And out here in the woods no one would convict us for what we did. If anything, we'd get a standing ovation. They let us go after we promised to leave Moonpie alone.

My first visit to DR court was a real joke. Back in the box, behind the Lt's Office there is a little room where three officer's sat waiting behind a small table. They would read the charges, ask for a plea, then tell you to wait outside while they figured out what to do with you. The options are taking away gain time, disciplinary confinement, weekends in the box, or disciplinary squad. Disciplinary court was only a formality, no one is ever found innocent, if you're there, you're guilty. They called me back in and told me that they were undecided on how to handle me. Since my sentence was life, loss of gain time had no immediate effect on me. We all knew this but they didn't know that I knew. So I begged them to put me in the box, because I really didn't want to lose any gain time. That's when they all smiled and agreed to take thirty days. I signed some papers and walked out laughing. What Morons!

My partner and I had become obsessed with thieving food from the kitchen. Besides the extra income it brought in, we both enjoyed the challenge. Imagine an antiquated chow hall with tiled walls and floor and no obstructions to obscure view accept in the rear where the ovens are. At any time there are three to five guards watching us and the doors are all locked.

One day they were making chicken in the back and closely monitoring every piece of chicken put into the oven. Six feet from the rear door there is a chest high tiled wall creating a walkway in the very rear of the kitchen. On the inside of this wall was the pot sink. Between the pot sink and the ovens were steel tables were the food was placed on bake pans before being placed in the ovens. As the raw chicken was removed from the top of the tables the cooked ones were placed on the lower shelves of these tables. Three guards stood in the walkway monitoring this process.

Chicago was working the pot sink and saw an opportunity to nab some bird. For half of the take, two Cubans would create a distraction. When the guards turned he would grab a tray of chicken, dump the bird into a pan, then stick the sheet pan into the sink as if it had already been cleared by the cooks. My job was to bone the chicken in the bathroom out in the main dining hall, place it in empty bread bags and smuggle it out the door when they opened up for lunch. I had Peabody (he resembled his nickname) sit outside the bathroom with a broom in his hand. In the event anyone was coming he'd let the broom slip and hit the door as a warning.

The Cubans started an argument which evolved into one chasing the other with a kitchen knife. The distraction was long enough for Chicago to grab two sheet pans of chicken, and duck out into the dining hall with a deep pan of steaming bird. I took this along with a fork and three bread bags into the bathroom where I immediately began to shred the flesh from the bones. The chicken had come straight from the oven and the grease was unbearably hot in the closed bathroom. It scolded and stuck to my forearms as I feverishly worked to make our cache transportable, then the broom hit the door.

I hadn't really planned to be interrupted, the bathroom was very small with two sinks and two commodes with nowhere to hide anything. The one shitter was in a boxed in area which is where I was currently working. I put the bags into the pan, scraped the chicken chunks from my now redden forearms, dropped my pants and sat on the commode while sliding the pan sideways between the wall and my throne just as the Bossman entered.

He walked by me and wandered around the bathroom sniffing the air like a dog. He stood over me applying the same sniffing technique. I gave him my best inquisitive look and asked if he wanted me to get up. Feeling awkward, he turned and left the room.

Later that night while we ate our chicken salad sandwiches, Grider was telling us how he got screwed by our mutual supervisor. Kline our kitchen manager was supposed to help Grider beat some minor charge in return for taking on one of the cooking positions. Grider had started the cooking job but the charges hadn't been dropped. In fact he was supposed to go to court the next afternoon. Once you are a cook you never get out of the kitchen, this infuriated my homeboy. I managed to dissuade him from using poison or razor blades on the bosses chair by offering a more psychological solution.

We gathered some old magazines and cut out various words to form the sentences we wanted, gluing these to a piece of notebook paper with toothpaste we formed the message "Kline we know you're fuckin and we want ours signed the men in the kitchen". To top it off we found a picture that looked just like the Bossman. The original ad had this heavy set guy sunk heavily into a beach chair with a drink in one hand and the other hand gaily slung upward. "Come to sunny south Florida" was the original caption.

The plan was for Grider to put it on the bosses' desk sometime in the morning but Grider was busy cooking breakfast and handed the note to me. I was called out to the second serving line so I'd handed it to Chicago since his position at the pot sink left him closer to Kline's office. Just before lunch Chicago slipped the note onto the desk pulled me from the serving line to watch Kline's reaction to the contents of the letter.

He picked it up, read it, and turned bright red. The cussing could be heard through the glass above the noise in the kitchen. He wrote something on the front of the paper and started to tape it to the glass that surrounded his office then changed his mind and laid it face down on his desk. Me and Chicago were laughing our asses off as we took turns peering over the wall when I noticed Grider walking into the office.

He figured that Kline had simply forgotten to pull the D.R. and that maybe the Bossman would make a call to the DR board to find him not guilty. He was unaware that we'd already deposited the note. Kline had picked up the note again and was studying it intently when he looked up to ask what Grider wanted. The toothpaste used to produce the note had soaked through the paper causing an outline to appear on the back. Grider recognized it and stifled a laugh. Kline went nuts. "You son of a bitch, you know something about this"! Grider tried to act convincing but to no avail. Kline said, "You have DR court today don't you? Well guess what, you're going to the box and after that we'll see how much Disciplinary squad time you do". True to his word Grider was sentenced to a month in the box and indefinite Disco squad. He rarely talked to me all the way up to the time of Skull and Heads big fight.

About a week after the ransom note incident Ronny Adams had showed up at Desoto, and I did my best to get him to transfer to G-Dorm. The boy we had running for us during the poker games had been "turned out" by Skull. The story I'd heard was that someone had slapped our errand boy Mike. When he refused to defend himself Skull gave him the ultimatum to either hit the guy with a pick-ax, or give Skull a blowjob. Apparently, Mike would rather suck a Dick than fight. Of course, after he blew one he had to service a few more. The sixth one to have him was MacDonell. After laying the boy on his back, throwing the feet over his shoulders and corn holin him, Mike fell in love. We needed another boy to run errands during the games. I was still trying to bag Ronnie when everything fell apart on my next trip to DR court.

After walking into court, the DR team read the charges. Possession, and under the influence of aromatic stimulants. They went on to read how

Chicago and I both exhibited a flushed face and glassy eyes. The fact that a bag of the stuff had been found in our vicinity seemed to slam the lid on any defense. Still I presented the argument that the flushed face, glassy eyes, and incoherence were the result of long hours in the kitchen and then being awakened suddenly. And the truth of the matter was that the bag of wood putty really did belong to someone else.

After a short wait in the hallway, they found me guilty and took another thirty days of gain time. As I turned to leave the room, they discovered the second DR. At first they thought it was an accidental copy, until one of them noticed that the reported times were one hour apart. After reading off the same charges as the last time, they were actually interested to hear what story I had for them now. "Well, the glassy eyes, flushed face and attitude were still there because I was still stoned from the last time."

"But you plead not guilty the last time"?

"Yeah, But since you found me guilty I might as well admit to it. The bag they found during the second search was from the first time they wrote me up. One of those bags, belonged to some one else, I swear it"! They told me how convincing the story was, but when in doubt the verdict is still guilty. Thirty days in the box!

DeSotos' version of the box was a bit different from Sumpters'. This hole had the same painted over windows, but the cells were much smaller with poorer lighting. Greasy filth clung to the walls and ceiling. No one bothered trying to kill any of the variety of bugs parading through the cells. To add to our discomfort, they'd run the fans when it was cold out, and leave them off when it was hot. The rations were a lot smaller on the disciplinary side. The last cell was reserved for the guys on Ps & Cs.

Chicago was brought back that same afternoon. The cops put us in the same cell to keep us from yelling down the cellblock to each other. Later that night the guards came through to take our pillows, blankets, and sheets. The guards claimed that someone had head lice. Everyone in the box on both sides had to go two days naked, covered with quell lotion, with no showers. Our third day in, the inspection team took a tour of the box. We called this new patrol the Dick watching squad. As they passed our cell, we started singing, "Tie me Kangaroo Down" while Chicago showered them in cereal saved over from breakfast.

He was put on Ps & Cs later that afternoon. Every morning I'd send him half of my meager meal so he wouldn't starve, but after ten days, I was let out, and Chicago was on his own. Usually the guys would send something down to the end cell. But some wouldn't do this; either out of personal hunger or the fear that if they were caught they'd wind up on Ps&Cs also.

Someone in the Lt.s Office had decided that the Getto had been a bad influence on me. They thought it would be in the best interest of the compound to break up the G-Dorm click starting with Chicago and me. I went to the largest, nastiest dorm on the compound.

Shades of Grey

F-Dorm was one of the two largest dorms on the compound. One half was mostly Black and the other end mostly white. To teach me a lesson I was placed on the black end. The dorm was so long that the cops couldn't see into the end cubes from the central TV room. My bunk was in the doorway of the next to the last cube. This was a good thing as far as visibility, but bad because of how many people walked by while you were sleeping. Big Lou was across the doorway from me, Larry to my right, and the rest were assorted Blacks known to be amongst the worst rogues on the compound. It was almost Christmas of 77, and the games were about to begin.

The first play was a version of the "We're gonna mess you up and then some one-steps in game". About five blacks from the end cube came by the end of my bunk and started running some crap about how they didn't like White people and that I had to either leave or pay them. I casually explained to them that they were much better off having me in the cube instead of some asshole. Also that I worked in the kitchen. If they persisted in their bullshit then I'd make sure they never saw full portions when they came through the chow line. It was a well-known fact that you didn't want an enemy on the serving line. My spitting on the floor at this point in the conversation emphasized my meaning. It was at this time that Larry remembered his Queue, and put on the act of sticking up for me. I announced thanks, but that his help wasn't needed. Unsure if their game had worked or not, they followed the script and told me how lucky I was that they respected Larry as they walked away. When I mentioned that, I'd see them in the chow hall. Two of them came back and said, "Don't Fuck with our food Man"! "Then don't Fuck with ME"! I said, baring my teeth. Turning my attention to the main player, it seemed the right time for a conversation with Larry.

As he tried to feel me out, I filled his head with small subliminal warnings. One of these was that a friend of mine from the kitchen had told me to look up a couple of guys named Scooter and Lucifer at the other end of the dorm. These two were supposedly Bikers that hung with the stronghold of Whites that fancied themselves as Clansmen. As I'd suspected, Larry and his clique were at war with the Clan, and from what I could gather actually feared them to some extent. It occurred to me that it might be a good time to look up these guys in case I was ever in need of back up.

As great white warriors, they weren't very impressive. Mid twenties, short and wiry, they gave the appearance of simple white trash. The other Whites in their gang were all big boys, mindless weight lifters that had banded together to share a common brain, with the exception of one guy that reminded me of Ronny Sanderss. Also named Ronny he never said much. For the most part, he seemed to tag along and watch the rest of them wander around in their mindlessness, interjecting thoughts to steer them in a more productive path from time to time.

They numbered about twenty in all; the leader was a huge toothless character that claimed to run F-Dorm. His inability to speak clearly mirrored his lack of mental ability. Look him directly in the eyes and all you could see was vacuum. But he was dangerous, and a hell of a fighter when pissed off. I did notice that he didn't go after anyone close to his own size, but that might have been because no one else was that big. Either way the three-week rule was not going to apply to the mind games played at DeSoto. And the shit was about to hit the fan.

It was football season and everyone had gone to their bunks for count time. After count, most of the guys had gone back to the TV room to finish watching the game. I had set up my pup tent with my blanket and was having a good old time with myself and a girl I'd seen in a sex mag. Being self-absorbed in thought, I hadn't noticed that more than a few others had also stayed behind in the last two cubes on my end. My goal was only a few strokes away when a tall slim Black guy came around the corner of my Bunk and started running a reel on me.

I could never recall everything he said, but it was the smoothest line of bullshit I'd ever heard. It was actually a pleasure to hear some one so well spoken with the English language. Then he screwed it all up by using the word "BITCH." With my free hand, I pointed at him and said, "You know, you've got a really good rap. When I'm playing with myself, I take it very seriously. Normally we'd have to fight for an interruption like this, but what you said was so well put that I'm going to forgive it this time. The next time you run a reel like that don't use the word Bitch, it ruins the whole thing. Now go on down the line and run Your Bull-shit on someone that will go for it."

"Cracker I'll bust you up! You don't talk to me like that"! He replied. I continued," Look Man, I already told you that I'd let this slide, now let me finish what I started so I can go watch the game, don't make me get up out of this bunk"! He walked around the corner only to reappear a moment later. He started by telling me to get up out of the bed. Jumping to my feet it became apparent that this was a set-up. There were at least half a dozen in on this either hiding in the shadows or pretending to be asleep. "What'cha gonna do now, I'm out of my bunk, my dicks not hard no more, and I'm missing the game, I hope it's worth it to you, cause it ain't to me!"

"Don't stick that white chicken chest out at me or I'll cave it in." He hissed. Pissed off at this point I continued, "Well go on and do it, or are you all talk and no fight? Maybe you got bitch in you, if you're too scared to hit some skinny little white boy! I see the two in the dark, and I know your partners aren't asleep. Now do what you gotta do or get The Fuck out of my face." After a long moment of silence, he mumbled something about how lucky I was that he didn't want to jamb his time and strutted away into the end cube. Larry asked if I actually thought I could fight all of them. I asked him what he would do if I came down with a bunch of whites. Would he suck all of our dicks? He responded that we'd have to kill him. "Well Larry maybe we do have a little something in common after all".

Although this minor crisis had gone better than expected, it was only a matter of time before the Brothers tried another move. With the way things were going this might be a good time to hang out with my own kind, sort of build an alliance with the clan in the other end of the dorm.

Scooter and Lucifer tended to tell the same tales over and over. It wasn't that they had short memories; they simply lacked original thought. Their stories didn't impress me much, but they were company. They said that the rest of the Clan had something to talk to me about and to come down after secure count.

That night after count, I found myself cornered by this malignant group that called themselves the Clan. I was down on their end of the dorm on their turf. Scooter and Lucifer were the obvious instigators of this plot, but they were insignificant compared to the Bulk of the gang that presently resembled a Pro football defensive line planning a blitz. Scooter started the dialogue.... "We've been discussing this for a little while with the clan and we've decided that you're gonna be our boy"!

I replied, "This ain't funny guys, and I really don't care much for your sense of humor"!

"We ain't kidding, you're about to get your ass took, and don't even think about yelling for the man"!

"The man's on the other end of the dorm, besides I don't need him." (This was the best I could come up with on short notice).

"Don't think you can run away either, we'll just run you down and take that ass." He was right in that respect, where could I run too. So I backed into a corner, sealing off my only escape route. "I guess I can't run now"!

Doing this surprised them a little bit; they hesitated long enough for me to come up with a plan. If I got a hold of one of the two shorties behind this thing, I could cause him grave physical damage while using him as a shield between the more dangerous ones and myself. If the plan worked, I wouldn't get hurt too bad before the cops came to check out the commotion. If things didn't go well then I was in for a real ass whooping. Either way I had to piss them off enough to forget about the fucking part of their plan. If I'm gonna, catch an ass kicking then I might as well run my mouth...

"You all are some sorry Mother Fuckers. I'll bet when you first got here you hit the weight pile because you were scared. Then when you got big, you found other guys your size to hang out with because you were still scared. Then you were so frightened by a skinny little Cracker still weak from the box, that you had to gather an army to come and try to scare him. And you know what? I'm not scared; Hell I'm not even impressed. You all must think I'm bad or something"!

"We ain't scared of nothing, everyone's afraid of us and we're gonna show you why"!

"Now wait a minute! What's all of this "WE" shit? You got a mouse in your pocket. I'll fight all of you one at a time, if you promise not to hurt each other trying to get to the back of the line." The last thing they expected was a verbal barrage of insults, but this was only a temporary condition. It was like dealing with a swarm of bees. Once someone on either side made any fast movement, the shit would hit the fan. I could see Ronnie in the rear of the pack with an unpleasant expression on his face trying to put a word in for me, but they were pretty pissed off.

A good-sized crowd had gathered to watch this event and sure enough, it attracted the cop's attention. Someone yelled "fire in the hole". When everyone turned their head, I used the opportunity to push through them. "Where do you think you're going"? One of them asked. "I'm going to my bunk, come get me after you all see the Wizard about getting some Heart"!

Fighting my urges of self-preservation, I slowly walked away without looking back. I don't think I took a breath until I was back in my own bunk on the other end of the dorm.

This whole incident had really bummed me out. The people that I thought were friends had turned on me. I felt more hurt than afraid. In fact I was getting pissed off. Maybe the things I'd said down there were true. But that's all the more reason for them to get really pissed off once they figured out how I handled them. These thoughts were still juggling in my head when Ronnie came down to talk to me.

"Look man, I just wanted you to know that I had nothing to do with what happened down there. The only reason I was with them was because I'm one of them. They're really good guys; they sent me to let you know that everything is cool, and that they were only acting on what Scooter told them. In fact Scooter and Lucifer are terrified that you're gonna come down there tonight and stab them in their sleep. They'll be down later to apologize personally. If you ever need any back up, we'll be there for you. I shook his hand and told him that I wouldn't have anything to do with people that turned on their own kind. But I appreciated the way he had tried to stick up for me.

After Ronnie left, Larry asked me about what had happened with the Clan. He'd heard how the clan tried to run a rough off game, and that I'd bitched them all up. This was of special interest to him since this same group had been keeping him and his Homies in check. I told him it was no big deal, they were just some assholes running some bullshit that I wasn't about to go for. It crossed my mind that now everyone would know that I was not connected to the Clan. This meant that I had no back up.

It became noticeable during the last twenty minutes or so that the blacks were swarming back towards the end cubes, one of which was mine. I could tell that this was somehow connected to me. It didn't take a psychic to notice people sticking their heads around the corner to look at me and then go back to talking in hushed voices. First, it was all the Whites, now it was all the Blacks. Hell, do I have to fight everyone? To top things off along came Scooter and Lucifer.

"Where do you get off coping an attitude like that? We were only playing, and you acted all crazy. You're lucky you didn't get your ass kicked with some of the shit you were saying to us down there"!

"You all weren't playing, and I really don't care for what you tried to do. If you're smart you'll just turn around and go back to where you came from and I'll let the whole thing slide." "Don't cop an attitude with us or we'll kick your ass right here and now"! Scooter yelped.

I'd noticed the Blacks had been filtering in through the various doorways during this exchange of words; I counted about a dozen, maybe more. "Now there you go with that WE shit again. I don't want no trouble with you guys. I'll stay in my end of the dorm and you stay in yours. But right now, I'm telling you to get out of my cube. Just do that and every things cool."

"No one tells us what to do, we run this dorm. You can't tell us to "GIT" like some kind of dog. Make us leave"! Suddenly they took notice of the large number of blacks that had surrounded us. Larry said, "You heard the man get out of his cube"! Then some of Larry's partners repeated the request. The two scruffy Aryans turned pale and seemed to shrink into little boys as they looked around in fear. Slowly they began to walk backwards from the cube while informing us that we didn't know who we were messing with, and that they'd be back.

As the duo sped away, Larry said that the brothers had my back if I wanted to go down to the other end and put a hurtin on these Pussy Crackers. I told him thanks but no, let them worry about when I'm coming. The unknown is a lot scarier than any ass whooping. The Clan didn't come back until several days later and then it wasn't to visit me.

An Arian had some dope fronted to him from the Brothers and figured that he didn't have to pay his bill. Larry had slapped the kid, then informed him he had an hour to either pay his bill or settle the debt with sex. The Clan waited until Larry was alone and came down on him in full force. Larry talked his way out of it explaining that the whole thing was just a misunderstanding. The Clan turned and left with the belief that they had reasserted their Authority in F-Dorm.

Within an hour, the Brothers went down to the white end of the dorm for a final conflict. The two armies squared off with both sides numbering about fifteen each. They exchanged a few words then Donald the brave White leader said, "Fuck this shit" and proceeded to jump out of a window to get away. Without a leader, the rest of them scattered to the far ends of the dorm leaving only my buddy Ronny to stand there alone, yelling after his partners to come back and fight.

Now all alone, Ronnie told them to come on with it, he didn't need those pussies anyway. Larry told him he could walk away; they'd already made their point. So ended the reign of the almighty Clan in F-Dorm. I enjoyed a few months of peace during this period. I'd managed to gain respect from both ends of the dorm and started to get comfortable in F-Dorm. Every day I'd come in from work, light up menthol, and read something while listening to my radio with the headphones on. Tuesdays I'd get the Lauderdale paper and read what was going on at home.

One article had caught my attention. A convict escaped after he'd been handcuffed to the bed in an outside hospital. They'd left him unguarded for 20 minutes, long enough for him to use his homemade key to escape. His name was John Edgar.

Conflict of Interest

Two new white guys moved into my end of F-Dorm. Sparky was an ex-golden glove boxer from NY. Short and stocky, his face looked just like Dondi from the newspaper comic. Never being out of his home state, he'd gone on a drinking spree with some guys he met up with while vacationing down here in Florida. It was the first time he'd ever been drunk and his new friends thought it might be funny to send him on a mission.

Handing him a gun and pulling up to a convenience store, they told him what to do and promised to wait for him. Once inside he asked for the money at gunpoint. The storeowner maced him, then jumped over the counter pinning the drunken Sparky to the floor and proceeded to beat him in about the head and shoulders with a wine bottle. Blinded by the mace and somewhat disoriented Sparky shot upward at his victim turned assailant. The manager dropped dead just as the New Yorker passed out. After going through the courts, he'd landed at DeSoto with a twenty-five year to life sentence.

The other new cock was Tim, a big clumsy character from Tampa. Not being very bright, he tended to remind me of an oversized Jethro Clampit. Tim moved into the other side of my cube while Sparky went to the end cube. Both of them partnered up with blacks in spite of my initial warnings.

As a rule, interfering with someone's game is a serious trespass, and I originally had no interest in getting involved with Tim outside of watching the game from both points of view. Tim's so-called partner was Blister Head, whom I had very little personal knowledge of. He was a short stocky guy that seemed pretty mellow, but over a period of a couple of weeks, I had the opportunity to see his rather devious game take shape.

Blister had Tim sharing a locker so that no one would mess with his stuff. Every night at lights out, his partner sent Tim to the locker for one thing or another. Blister would tell him not to lock it so he could get something out of it later. This gave Tim the habit of leaving it unlocked until asking his partner if he needed anything. On one of these nights, Blister pretended not to hear Tim and let one of the other brothers insist that it was OK to leave the locker open.

Later that night I saw Blister in the locker moving stuff around and putting a couple of things in another locker nearby. The next morning Blister was raising hell about how some one had been in the locker and stolen a ring he was holding for collateral on some fronted pot. Tim felt really bad about this and offered to pay the four hundred dollars back to his partner, to cover the value of the ring. It was a creative game and would have been acceptable if not for how they pursued it.

The following night Tim came up to the TV room with his lip split open. He went on to tell me that the Brothers had jumped him. After the ass whooping, they told him he now owed one thousand dollars, because of interest. When he complained that his parents were bringing the four hundred but couldn't swing a grand on short notice, they beat him up a little bit.

Tim was no Sissy; this boy was big, and cock-strong. If he ever lost his temper, he could easily cause major damage to the small army that was playing him. Nevertheless, they had him believing that he was wrong, so he wouldn't fight back. It was at this point that I tried telling him that since he didn't know about the ring being in the locker then he wasn't responsible for it. Unless he lost it after it had been handed to him for safekeeping, it really wasn't his problem. If they wouldn't take the four hundred and be happy with that then screw them.

However, for each of these legitimate arguments he just mumbled for me not to worry about it. After another walk to the end cube, he re-emerged with a black eye. That was what did it for me. I told him how the game worked and what I'd seen. Now all he had to do was fight for himself. If he still wanted to give them the money that was on its way fine, but that was all they should get. He stayed back there talking to them until count time.

Laying on my bunk at midnight count, I noticed that the bulb in the bathroom was out, leaving the cube almost totally in darkness. It only figured that they were gonna do another number on Tim once the Bossman had passed through our cube for count. I sat up to watch the boss walk down towards the other end of the dorm when out of the corner of my eye a shadow moved oddly out of sync with the rest of the wall. Without a sound Blister had landed one good swing on me.

Grasping the edge of my bunk, I kicked upward to what should have been my attacker's face. Because of either misjudgment or his forward momentum, the heel of my boot caught him in his nuts, hoisting him a good foot off the ground. Though surprised by this move he had the presence of mind to grab my foot, preventing me from getting off the bunk. A few more punches were exchanged, but he had the advantage of swinging from a standing position. Trying to pull him down onto the bunk didn't work; it only left me with pieces of his shirt and a hand full of slinkies.

Some one yelled recount and everyone returned to their bunks as the Bossman came back through our cube.

As the Man walked past I could feel something warm on my face, wiping it off I found blood. It didn't feel like he'd nailed me well enough to split the skin under my eye. Blister must have used a razor blade. Getting out a blade of my own, I waited for the cop to finish our end so I could charge through the bathroom to slice that niggers face.

Blister met me halfway through the bathroom with his hands out saying, "Man I made a serious mistake, I misunderstood something Tim had told me and I want to apologize." He then held his hand out for me to shake it. His partners had surrounded us, I'd screwed up their game and he was apologizing to me. If I made a move on him now, I'd be dead wrong, giving his army the right to jump me in numbers. Even the cops would consider me dirt for jumping someone after admitting they were wrong. There was no other option but to shake his hand and share a joint in an offering of peace. I told him that I would have to go to the infirmary for some kind of stitches and he agreed to wait until morning to go for his recently acquired inability to walk properly.

The cops escorted me from the infirmary to the Lt. Office were I explained that I'd slipped on the wet bathroom floor while brushing my teeth and managed to hit my eye on the sink. They didn't accept my explanation of how the injury had occurred; I was ordered to sit outside in the cold wearing just a pair of blue pants until I decided to tell them what had really happened. At sun-up they sent me back to my dorm.

A few days later while removing the butterfly stitches the MT made some comment that my eye might be damaged. Normally this wouldn't be too upsetting but for some reason, I had a minor flashback. The two eye incidents melted together and I saw Blister as the Zambuzi that had thrown that rock at Sumpter a year before. Getting Blister was the same as getting them both. But this time I knew where and how to get him.

Hopping off the Doctors table, I told the MT there were a few things I had to take care of and that I'd be right back. Going to G-Dorm, every one of my so-called friends refused to give me a shank. I asked what good it served having one if it was never going to get used. Their argument was that they didn't want to see me blow my appeal or jamb my time on an act of revenge. So, I went to Skull. He said that his weapons were hidden and that he'd be right back with one. Within a few minutes, they called my name over the loud speaker to report to the Lt. Office. Skull had ratted me out.

Lt. William's was the king of the snitches, although I'd never talked to him personally, his reputation was well known to everyone on the compound. He started out by telling me how he had been made aware of a problem between some Blister character and myself. In addition to that, he wouldn't tolerate any stabbings on his shift. I countered that I had never heard of any such person and that he'd been seriously misinformed.

They brought in Blister and placed him in a chair next to mine. He acted both surprised and nervous. The nervousness was caused by the fact that he was in the hands of the Crackers now. In his mind, he was powerless once they got a hold of a brother alone. We both pretended to act as if we hardly knew each other and insisted that we didn't have a problem with each other. Williams told us that he could prove we were lying, and that once he proved it we were both going to the box.

He called in Larry and the Jamaican that had run his rap game on me a while back. The two of them spilled out a story of how a ring was stolen, and that I had interfered with them trying to get it back. Somehow, the game, the dope, and Tims' beatings had been deleted from the story. After the two snitches had left the room, Williams asked what we thought of his informers' statements.

Blister was stunned into silence, he'd been ratted out by what he thought were his partners and left alone to take the heat in the Lt. Office. I started laughing, and told Williams how that was the most ridiculous story I'd ever heard. If he was going to lock us up, then just go ahead and do it, but don't punish us with fairy tales. Then I added, "Presently we don't have a problem. We didn't have a problem before, and we don't have a problem now. But if you lock us up. . . then we'll both have a problem. So do what you gotta do." He thought for a long moment before sending Blister back to the dorm. He then spent the next hour explaining to me how the system had changed over the last few decades and how the inmates now told the cops almost everything going on.

He began, "One inmate is rarely a problem, two can cause quite a bit of damage. But, if I see three or more together, I don't have to worry about it, because one of the three in that group is mine. That's the reason we know everything going on here. Guys you would never suspect come to me and tell me things for favors, or to get their asses out of a sling. The old days are gone this is how it works now. Your convict code only serves your enemies. It gives them an advantage you don't have, police intervention.

I let some of the dealers operate because they feed me information about escapes or other serious infractions that we will not tolerate. Do you really think we care if you guys get drunk or high? For the most part, we don't care if you all killed each other off, as long as state property isn't destroyed and no one makes it outside the fence. I'm telling you all of this for your own good, if you're smart, you'll jump on the bandwagon and use it to your advantage. I can tell the other guards to lay off you, so you can operate that poker game you were doing so well at, maybe even tell you when a shakedown is coming. If you work with me then I'll work with you. We can start by giving you a dorm change back to G-Dorm. Now, what do you say"?

Everything he'd told me made a lot of sense, and the dorm change sounded tempting. To change dorms now would give the appearance that I was running from a problem, so that was out, at least for a few weeks. But, if I was going to tell on someone then I should have done it when it would have done me some real good. I could have dropped the whole robbery thing on Zig back when I'd been busted and been out by now. To tell at this point would make everything that had happened up to now one big joke. I declined the offer. Even if everyone else did it, I guess my standards were just going to be higher then everyone else's. No one could ever say that they bought me.

Williams acted like I was making a big mistake, and went on to threaten me in some very unpleasant ways, he couldn't mask the respect that he held for me at that moment. His odd stare displayed envy for my belief in an idea that didn't benefit me in any way that he could comprehend. After a long moment of staring at me he shook his head and looking away told me to go.

Returning to the dorm Blister was like a best buddy, telling me how no one had ever stuck up for him like that before and that he had told his snitching friends to stay out of his business from now on. He even mentioned a partnership, not one like Tim's but a real partnership where we could make some good money. A true salt & Pepper team could cover a lot of ground acting as a go-between, dealing with both of the races. He actually seemed dismayed when I told him he'd have to settle for friendly associates. Before he could argue his point, the conversation was halted by a commotion in the last cube of F dorm.

Being wrapped up in my own problems for the last few days it wasn't all that surprising to find out that Sparky had been having the exact same game run on him by another group of Blacks in the end cube. Sparky being a little smarter then Tim had told them that the missing item wasn't his problem. Sparkys' partner a (light-skinned black with one blue eye and one brown named Aja) was as much a New Cock as Sparky.

The brothers in the end cube had been filling Aja in on how to play the game. Their real plan from what I could gather was to let the Malloto scam Sparky and then take away anything he got. In other words, this half-breed was being played for a chump himself. When Aja and a few of his new friends approached Sparky to beat him up, they got a little surprise. Sparky pulled out a kitchen knife and plunged it into Ajas' belly up to the hilt.

Actually, the knife had broken off an eighth of an inch from the hilt when the tip contacted his stomach. The remaining fraction of an inch did break the skin and watching the illusion of that much blade disappear into his belly made Aja's eyes roll back in his head and feint. While Ajas' partners stared dumbly at their fallen comrade they now presumed dead, Sparky noticed that his weapon had been neutralized. That left just enough time for Sparky to jump out a window and turn himself in at the Lt. Office. He spent a month in the box for stealing the knife from the kitchen. After he got out, he was assigned to the barbershop, where he always kept scissors nearby.

Over the next couple of months, it seemed as if I'd just plain run out of luck. My partner Chicago's' gambling debts grew so large that they had to transfer him before someone stabbed him over money. In addition, there was so much heat on me that I couldn't walk across the compound without being searched twice. This lead to more than a few DRs. My friends wouldn't have nothing to do with me, from fear of being searched themselves. After DR court took all of my gain time, they realized that sitting in the box was more comfortable to me than working in the kitchen; they sentenced me to an indefinite period of time on Disciplinary Squad.

Disco Squad

Disciplinary, or Disco squad as some called it, was about as close to the old Chaingang as you can get. Every morning at sun-up, they'd gather us at the rear gate and escort us out into the fields under shotgun guard to do the worst manual labor they could find. Most of the work was useless, such as moving earthen embankments a mile long to another location and then back again. We would load three dump trucks with hand shovels.

With five to seven guys to a truck, it took an average of thirty minutes to fill a truck dragging our asses. I soon learned to enjoy this mindless labor. After a week of shoveling, the body gets used to it and follows a routine while the mind wanders off into some other place. Working out in the broiling sun was far better than lingering in the menacing air of the compound. Sometimes, we were out of sight of the camp altogether, but the single dark cloud that hovered over the compound in the distance reminded us, that the lack of barbed wire and steel didn't make us free.

Three guards would station themselves in a triangle around our work area. In the event that anyone should try to run, all three guards could get a clear shot at the runner without hitting each other. The head walkin' Boss was Sgt. Keirce, a seventy-year-old Bossman from the old days. He carried an old six-shooter in a hip holster and liked to brag about how many convicts he had buried at night in his youth.

For the most part, he was a fair Bossman, with his beady eyes and broken smile, he barked out our orders expecting them to be followed without question. One day for a laugh, we followed them a little too well.

A half-mile long hill ran alongside of a canal, ten yards across and about fifteen feet high. This small ridge rose straight up from the ground and then gradually sloped to an even level with the canal bank. The rain had been washing the sand into the canal, slowing drainage enough for them to decide to move the hill for a legitimate reason. The trucks were spread across the end of the hill. As we filled them, they became spaced further apart. Since each truck covered one third of the mound, it only figured that the highest point took twice as many loads to reach level ground as the truck on the edge of the canal bank. It became a game to see how fast we could fill a truck. If we filled one in five minutes we could rest for fifteen while the truck left to dump its load.

We'd noticed the canal bank crumbling from the weight of the truck as it repeatedly rolled only inches from the edge of the dirt bank now lacking the support of the grass we'd removed. Our plan was to overfill this truck on one side, with the weight of the dirt towards the canal side. This would shift its center of gravity to the outside wheels. When the truck tried to drive off, the bank would crumble. The vehicle would go in the canal, and we'd be left with only two trucks to fill. Less work, more break time.

It looked like a good plan until Keirce figured out what we were doing and drove the truck out himself. Ignoring his yells to stop, we kept loading dirt into the back, as the bank crumbled. Some how he managed to get the Dump truck out of its predicament.

Sitting in the dirt enjoying our break we discussed our next strategy as two white vans approached from the compound. They backed up to where we sat as Keirce called out our names and told us to load up for a surprise. Once back on the compound it came as no great surprise to find ourselves escorted to the box.

The box was crowded that day and I found myself in a cell with a couple of pussy white boys and a black. It was unusual for them to mix races in the box for obvious reasons, but I didn't care, the cell was nice and cool compared with the sun outside, so I tied a shirt over my eyes and went to sleep.

This was a strange place I'd found myself in this time. Like something out of the caveman days. Large fires raged, with the shadows of men dancing around them set against an opaque sky that absorbed all light and sound. A thick tapestry of impending doom draped over this world of undefined borders where I found myself alone facing an angry army of blacks. The fight had already started as I was hit from behind with something heavy that knocked me blind but not unconscious. Swinging wildly I made contact a few times before noticing that something was covering my eyes.

Pulling the T-shirt from my head, I found myself standing in the confinement cell with my cellmates facing me with their backs pinned against the bars. The black guy said, "I don't even know you, and you jump up swinging and talking about how your gonna kill all the niggers! Man you crazy"! I apologized by explaining that it must have been a bad dream, but at my cellmates complaining the cops moved me down to another cell, were I met my new buddy, Tennessee.

Short, round faced and round bellied; I'd seen Tenn. around the compound always hanging out with blacks. It was for this reason that everyone assumed he was a fuckboy. Once I talked to him a bit I discovered that he was more or less the gamekeeper for a small herd of fuckboys that he kept in line for the blacks. A white slaver would be his best job description.

There were four of us in the cell; two were on the bunks, Tenn. on the floor beneath the bottom bunk, and my mattress on the floor in the open part of the cell. We got along pretty good with the exception of the boy on the bottom bunk. We figured that he was a bitch. I told Tennessee how the kid had only lasted one night in F-Dorm before bailing out a window and refusing to come back in. Tenn. said he didn't know for sure, but if the kid wasn't fucking, now then he should be. When we tested him, the kid put up a little bit of a fight so we regrouped not wanting to make too serious a move on him until we were sure of his gender.

One afternoon the kid had pulled back the corner of his mattress to write a letter home. Tennessee held a conversation with the kid while he got himself a hard on. Steering his woody through one of the holes in the bottom of the steel bunk, he started pushing up the top left corner of the kids' letter (just under "Dear Mom"). When the kid moved the paper to see what was beneath it, Tenn. thrust himself upward trying to poke the kid in the eye. The boy slammed his hand down on the fleshy intrusion as if he were squashing a bug. Before Tenn. could make a dignified retreat, the mattress was slammed back in place trapping his Dick between the mattress and bunk frame. Tennessee was trying to lean out from under the bunk and grab the kid, but his reach was limited to how far he could stretch the appendage that suspended his ass a few inches from the ground. Grabbing a cup of water, I made the kid pull the mattress back and threw the water on the offending bunk figuring that if it worked for dogs then maybe it would help set my buddy free. After a brief self-inspection, Tenn. slapped the kid around

214

for a while. The kid was ready to submit, but no one was about to let him near his crotch, least of all Tennessee.

After leaving the box, I took the time to learn some things from Tenn. about how to handle boys. With the exemption of the "worm in the whole incident," he seemed to show good judgment concerning the subject. He explained how they can tell when you look down at them. After all, they're not men, just a tool to use for sex. The trick is to make them think that you're a friend.

Having landed back in Back in G-Dorm after my release from the box, I had acquired a boy named Jimmy. Listening to my buddies' advice, I befriended the boy first and took an interest in the things he said. The problem with this was that the kid considered me a friend and didn't want to perform the duties assigned to him when the time came. Not being the bullying type it was hard for me to kick his ass just to get some ass.

Before the situation developed into a messy one, they changed H-Dorm to a Juvenile and orientation dorm. Jimmy was seventeen like me, and he was the first one placed there. In fact, every juvy on the compound was placed there overnight with the exception of myself. When I asked why I'd been left out, they responded that whatever my age was, I was the kind of person they were trying to protect the juveniles from. These words were good for my ego, but a serious impediment to my plans for little Jimmy.

Pay Back

A few weeks later while standing in the chow line, a familiar voice appeared behind me that made the hair on my neck stand up. I turned to put a face to the voice only to find Tim Stanley from Sumpter. If an ice cube could be shoved into the center of my heart jamming one of the valves, then maybe I could simulate the feeling I had at that moment. My mind froze with hatred as I watched my hands reaching for his throat. Suddenly the noise of the chow hall reached my brain and common sense took over. Fights in the chow hall never get very far. Even when forks were shoved into eyes it was never a fatal attack, and a fight in the chow hall is an instant "inciting a riot" charge, half the time followed with a transfer.

To my astonishment he smiled and said to me, "Hey, I know you from Sumpter, How you doin' Man"? This cordial greeting threw me for a loop. For the moment I was left with three options; He really didn't remember, He was playing a game, or who cares lets kill him. The best way to handle this would be pretend not to hate him. If he let his guard down it would be a lot easier to lure him somewhere more secluded later, and have the full advantage of surprise.

It took a few moments of conversation to see that he was starting to remember who I was. I watched his eyes betray his thoughts as he wondered how much I knew about his involvement in my transfer from Sumpter. By the time, we left the serving line he was attempting to put as much space between us as possible. Watching him from a few tables away, he barely ate before dumping his tray and running out the door. I finished eating and headed over to the orientation dorm. Halfway there I came up with a plan, it wasn't my style, but in this particular case, style and rules were all thrown out the window.

During his few weeks in H-Dorm, my ex-boy Jimmy had decided to come out of the closet and become what we commonly refer to as a Dick Monster. Picture the cookie monster from the kid show shoving something other then cookies down his throat and you get an idea of how Jimmy behaved in a crowd. I hadn't been talking to him because of this, after all, he wouldn't gobble me up, but he now regularly serviced five Blacks.

Jimmy was upset that I wouldn't even look his way, unless it was to sneer. The boy had the biggest smile on his face when I walked up to the window he was sitting in and asked him to talk for a minute. He was a little gun shy at first, but his ears picked up when I said he could do me a big favor. "Look I know what your situation is over here and that's OK with me". He lowered his eyes at this point and started apologizing until I interrupted, "Hey, I looked out for you, now you can do me a little favor. There's a new kid at the orientation end of your dorm from Sumpter. I want you to tell your Big Black Daddies about him being a big time 'Fuck Boy'. Let them know that even if he puts up a little bit of a fight it's just an act, he likes having it taken! Can you do that for me"? He said no problem, I was thrilled.

At that moment, I saw Tim watching me from a window at the other end of the dorm, so I went down to have the friendliest conversation with him I could muster. It's an old family rule that you can't hurt an enemy, but you can hurt a friend. I wanted to be his friend so that sometime in the near future he could share his tale of the upcoming night with me in the strictest of confidence. That way I could gloat on my achievement while feigning sympathy.

It was hard to sleep that night as I stared across at the windows of H-Dorm hoping to get a glimpse of Tim's demise. After what seemed like an eternal night, it was morning. Nothing was said during breakfast and there was no sign of Jimmy anywhere. That afternoon disciplinary squad ate lunch in the field, so I had no way of getting any new information until after dinner, when I could run down Jimmy on the compound. Finally, just before secure count I spied Jimmy sitting in his window over at H-Dorm. As I approached with my shit-eating grin Jimmy looked up and said, "You were right about that boy, he's a real Dick-monster"! Losing my grin, I asked what he meant by that.

Jimmy said, "I did what you asked. My partners went down there expecting to have to take it. But he likes doing it; in fact, he did all four at one time. Then he was asking everyone else in the dorm if they wanted any, he sucked and fucked over a dozen guys last night, and my partners really like him"!

I couldn't believe it. He must have been the tall young street fag my friends had told me about back at Sumpter! Reviewing old conversations from the past, suddenly things began to make sense. It wasn't just the money that bought him protection, he was a bitch! And his Daddies back at Sumpter came after me to impress him. Under different circumstances, you could say that they were fighting for the hand of the fair maiden. Now I had given him new protectors and to top things off Jimmy was worried that he might be replaced as Top Boy.

A Top Boy is highly valued compared to a second or third-rate boy. The less desirable a kid is the worse his treatment will be at the hands of his man or men.

At the moment, Jimmies problems were at the bottom of my priority list.

After causing the most horrible violation I could think of to happen to Tim, I'd exacted no revenge. What else can you do after your best shot at someone makes them happy or cum drunk? If I kill him, I'd get more time added to my sentence. And killing a boy is not the same as killing a man; there's no respect to be gained. The same goes for kicking his ass; this is sometimes viewed along the lines of hitting a woman. Fight him or any boy like a man and if by some stroke of bad luck you lose the fight, and you'll never regain respect.

There must be a way to destroy his security, something that would eat up his insides. Until that could be found, I'd have to keep him off his guard, get to know him a little bit better. Then make my move once his weaknesses became apparent. It would take everything I'd learned in here and then some, but one thing was certain. There would be no peace in my life until Tim's destruction was complete. As this laid heavily on my mind a new kind of attitude emerged, I'd become obsessed with the game.

My partner was gone, and without access to the kitchen, it was hard to keep any kind of moneymaking hustle going. I had to resort for monetary relief from my family. Once a month the old man had been driving up to see me and as of late, I had to ask him for money. The feeling of being dependent on someone else coupled with disciplinary squad and constant searches of my locker and person had left me in a constant state of agitation. One week Disco squad stayed in the canal, pulling mangrove roots off the bottom with swamp forks. These forks were about the length of a shovel with three long steel spikes bent at a ninety-degree angle. Water moccasins lived in the canal, and these water bound beasts didn't take kindly to our disturbing their home.

A couple of times an hour someone would yell snake and stand absolutely still until someone else could come up and spear the reptile with a swamp fork. Moccasins are very poisonous, and being a water snake one of the most vicious. They bite out of reflex, attacking anything that moves. If they bite an animal in the water, they lose the air bubble they hold in their mouth causing them to drown. But even in death they hold on, continuously pumping their venom into their unlucky victim. Just before biting, they raise their head out of the water like a small sea serpent. If you stand absolutely still they'll hesitate long enough for someone to get over and spear them before striking.

Blacks as a whole, being somewhat scared of snakes, were very friendly with us white folks out on Disco squad. Personally, I enjoyed killing the scaly bastards and grabbed every opportunity to nail one, even if it was out of the way. The silt on the canal bottom was so thick that standing in one spot for more then a few moments left our rubber boots caught in the muck, sometimes requiring great effort to break them free. One furry little guy named Ruben had a hard time keeping his boots on and on his first day. One time he jumped right out of them when a small head emerged from the water a few feet from him. After that first incident, he swung at everything that moved in the water whether it be animal or vegetable, including sticks.

One day after wandering off to the far bank, I saw something scurrying down the bank at a high rate of speed. At first, I thought it was some kind of a lizard, but as it came closer, it took on the identity of a huge water moccasin. With my fork raised and standing very still, I watched as it turned suddenly to enter the water a few feet from me. Realizing that I was no longer "the great white hunter" but a potential victim, I swung in panic. My swing missed, as did the next couple. The snake showed his animosity by striking at the fork itself before continuing his track in my direction.

During this brief period of time, my boots had sunk into the silt, leaving me with no way to exit this predicament. Ruben appeared next to me but his swings only served to keep me from getting a clear shot at the reptile now only a foot from my leg. By luck, one of the tines from my fork pierced a little piece of skin half way down the snake's body. Trying to rip itself free the snake lunged in my direction. Sergeant Keirce walked up and placed the head of a shovel behind the Moccasins head, twice it squirmed loose, breaking its sharp fangs against the steel shovel blade. This thing was pissed! The Boss finally finished off the scaly beast and told me to get back to work.

Turning around I faced a very pissed off looking black guy. Did I mention that he was big too? When I asked what his problem was, he pointed to a spot on his shirt that now sported a rather nasty looking piece of swamp slime. The squad at this time was an even mix of blacks and whites. While most of us didn't wear shirts, there were a few that seemed to dress up for the occasion.

My new adversary was one of these. His state blue shirt was tailored and meticulously pressed. The tail of the shirt had been rolled up at the bottom so that the waist high water couldn't dampen his appearance.

"Get it off me," he said, as if I'd thrown a bug in his hair. Walking up to him, I put on a show of examining his shirt. Then pulling out a state cigarette I asked, "You think it might be better to use this"? While holding up the cheaply made smoke for his examination. "Yeah, that should do it." He responded. I handed it to him and said, "Good, there's no charge for the cigarette, just consider it a gift".

He raised his fork and told me I was a dead man. I raised my own weapon knowing that his boots were stuck in the muck where he was standing. I'd kept my own feet moving during our exchange, this gave me the advantage of mobility. Split seconds away from battle, someone yelled out, "That was Ruben that got that on you, not him"! A couple of the guys joined in to agree on this new development. Mr. Fancy shirt decided to take the easy way out by bullying Ruben into walking over and removing the slime. The cops watched this spectacle with great amusement, then told us to get back to work once they were satisfied the show was over.

That weekend a friend of mine came over to G-Dorm to ask if I knew Tim Stanly. He said that Tim had been running his mouth about how he'd put a contract on me at Sumpter and that he should go over to G-Dorm and finish the job himself. My friend Kenny told the kid that he'd be more than happy to escort him over to the Getto where all his wishes could come true. When the kid declined the offer Kenny tried dragging him over, but Tim held onto a bunk while my friend pulled him by the feet towards the window, swearing that he was kidding, the kid started crying.

Kenny thought that I should know about this and wanted to know why he was so scared of me. It served no purpose to explain the whole story. But I saw a new angle. If the boy is that scared, I could build on this fear by letting him know I had something horrible planned for him. Kenny could start this rumor for me and let it spread throughout the compound. By the time I did actually corner him, the simplest ass whooping would have the same emotional effect as getting his foot stuck in the tracks as a train approaches. In the meantime, I'd pretend to be his buddy to monitor the games progress.

Whenever we crossed paths on the compound, I'd ask Tim to watch the movie with me or go behind the rec. hall to smoke a joint. Each time he refused by coming up with some lame excuse. At every encounter, his stutter worsened until towards the end of the game he couldn't speak to me at all. To my disappointment, he ended my little mind game by checking in.

DeSoto didn't have a separate unit for the check-ins at this time so I went to the service door at the end of the box to find out who he was sharing a cell with. Kenny hollered back that they were in the same cell and that he'd been regularly corn-holing the kid and then making the boy clean off the mess with his mouth. (Good thing they didn't share a toothbrush). I'd never see Tim again, which was sort of anti-climatic, in the sense that he'd become my hobby. Now it was time to find a worthier adversary to play with. Someone a little more dangerous but well versed in the game. From my last visit to the box I'd ended up in the end cube of G-Dorm a few bunks down from Skull, how convenient.

Skull

I found Skull to be very intelligent; well read, and very well spoken. He just happened to be queer as a three-dollar bill and defended that fact quite persistently. His story started in one of the Carolina prisons that were well known throughout the states as being some of the worst in the country. Having been thrown into the adult system at age sixteen it took less than a day for a rather large rape gang to take his ass.

He never had a chance to get a hold of a weapon, and there was no checking in for him. They kept him totally under their control for weeks until he chose the meanest guy as a Daddy to take care of him. This way he had just one guy to worry about servicing in return for protection. People adapt to almost anything and it seems that he accepted his new role with great pleasure. Under the protection of his new Daddy he could foolishly run around and mess with anyone he wanted to, knowing that his Man would be there to protect him if things went sour.

On the streets he'd sleep with men or women, one time even scoring a brother and sister team. If he was ever short on cash he'd hook into a fag and rip him off. At the East Unit he once again had a well-respected Daddy that he counted on to bail him out of trouble. But when he broke into a mans locker he found himself being chased down and stabbed in the yard, far from the reach of any help. The instinct to survive took over when he pulled the knife out and killed his attacker with it. It was deemed self defense at the time, and he was shipped to Desoto after his wounds healed.

Being a Killer Fag at a wimpy camp gave him the opportunity to be independent for the first time in his life. To some degree you could say that he ruled that end of G-Dorm. With his little army of boys he ran a canteen and sold dope, generating a lot of commerce for the dorm. Of course after turning the boys out, he would teach them how to fight and stand up for themselves. You could say that he was trying to duplicate himself. Every time we talked he'd offer to do something for me along the lines of a blowjob. I'd just laugh and tell him that he was too old and unattractive for me. These talks with Skull had given me quite a few new theories to work with.

To convince himself that his life style was normal, he theorized that everyone was gay. He just happened to be honest with himself while everyone else was living a lie. He sited many examples and more than a few personal experiments both on the street and in the chaingang to prove his theory. To some extent he was correct, but from personal experience I knew that his percentiles were exaggerated just a tad.

I had a personal theory that once a man submits to another man, especially sexually, that he will submit again to the authority of another mans will, recognizing a real mans superiority. Skull didn't like this theory of mine, little did he know that he would soon become my test subject.

There had been quite a turnover of people at DeSoto. As guys were released new people would suddenly appear. They included Teardrop and Head from Sumpter, Tinsie and Jeff from ACI, and a few other Newcocks. Head was a black guy I knew from Sumpter. His original nickname was Horse Head because of the enormous size of his head. Tinsie was a friend of my partner Zig from ACI, and Jeff was the younger brother of the Tim I had helped out in F-Dorm.

Also in this group was Sunshine. He / She was a 6'4 240 pound muscle bound Sissy. Although intimidating at first glance, she emanated a deep effeminate voice that didn't fit her stature. Sunshine had hooked up with a Daddy one-third her size, which proved very entertaining.

One evening she was bugging her man for some sex. When he declined, she picked him up by the neck with one hand and held him at arms length while she carried him into the bathroom. Kicking and swinging at her he gasped, "Put me down you Godzilla looking Bitch", While the rest of us in the cube were laughing our asses off. Horse Head commented that the Daddy should be glad that all she wanted was to give him a blowjob.

Within a few weeks of his arrival, Head had begun to acquire some of the more desirable boys in G-Dorm. Running the free protection game, he offered the boys a much more lucrative option than getting buggered and learning to like it. This caused a major conflict with Skull. It was only a matter of time before war would break out between these two.

TearDrop was a member of the gang at Sumpter that had tattooed a single TearDrop under one eye. He'd moved in and immediately began acting as if he was some kind of a bad ass, but I'd pegged him as a coward that needed the power of numbers before making any move beyond mouth running. For some reason Skull was impressed by this big wimp and took him on as an equal partner.

While we were all sitting around talking one day, TearDrop mentioned a few names I knew from Sumpter. The stories he told didn't match the people he was talking about. Also he had their dorm assignments all wrong. I asked him at what month and year these things were supposed to have happened and he responded that it was during the time I was in A-Dorm. He was obviously lying. I didn't remember seeing him anywhere at Sumpter and his stories were tainted as if he'd heard them second hand. After giving him a chance to recant his remarks he became more persistent.

This almost escalated into a fight that left me wary, and him very aware that I knew he was full of shit. I had now become a threat to TearDrop. Being both cowardly and a liar it was a fair assumption he had to be the one that put Skull up to his next move.

A Theory

March twenty-first, 1978 marked both my eighteenth birthday and one of the least memorable days of my life. For one thing I don't work on my birthday, but Florida's prison system refused to recognize this as a personal holiday. I dawdled at the infirmary early in the morning hoping to miss disciplinary squads' early trip out. The plan worked with the exception that I wasn't sick. They wrote me up for faking illness but refused to put me in the box. As I walked away from the infirmary, I heard Sunshine arguing that she couldn't work because she was pregnant, and that she knew who the Daddy was. They gave her a work pass.

At lunch, they caught me eating in the chow hall before my dorm was released, that was DR number two. Leaving the chow hall I retrieved a letter from the mailroom from my appeal attorney explaining that the courts had shot down my last chance for a new trial. By the time secure count rolled around I was not a happy camper. It was my eighteenth birthday, what else could possibly go wrong.

The laundry at DeSoto wouldn't do personal clothing. This left no alternative but for us to wash our socks and shorts while we were taking a shower. I was finished with my laundry and was rinsing off, when in hopped Skull. He started to play with my crotch and asked if I liked that. I told him; "Thanks a lot, but I already jacked off." Then the bastard hit me! I nailed him in the jaw one good time and we started wrestling.

He was stronger and bigger then me. He had me in headlock while he bitched about me calling him too old and ugly. I bit a chunk out of his arm as we both slipped on the tiles. Squaring off I told him, "You stupid bastard, you dare come in here and swing on me? I ain't one of your boys; I'm a real cracker! Now I'm gonna have to do something to you, so you'd best go get your shit"! Picking up my shorts from the floor I was enraged, "Look at this, I just washed these and now they've been on the floor! Now who's gonna wash them"? I yelled as I threw the boxers in his face. He said, "I'm sorry man, I made a mistake, I thought...."

Still yelling I continued, "Damn right you made a mistake! It's not your job to think about me! Now what do I do about this laundry"? He then took the shorts and sheepishly walked over to the sink to wash them off. I tossed the socks in as I walked by.

Skulls little gang including TearDrop huddled in the shadows stunned at the outcome of our confrontation. They normally did his laundry, now they saw their fearless leader acting like my bitch. I didn't view this as a great triumph, actually I felt bummed out that this was how I'd always remember my eighteenth birthday. Most guys my age were getting drunk with their friends on the street or preparing to graduate, instead of dominating Killer Fags with unproven theories.

I was going to have to re-evaluate my situation and make some major adjustments. The death of my appeal in the courts meant that I had a life sentence, and the only way out was parole. Today this place had become my home for an indefinite period of time.

The streets no longer existed as far as I was concerned, to think about them only weakened me. I would have to live in the here and now. It was just a matter of taking a long hard look at everything around me and using everything I'd learned these past few years to my advantage. Getting out and living a normal life was for someone else; I couldn't afford the luxury of such thoughts. It was time to start dealing with the immediate problems at hand. The first thing on the list would be Skull.

I came home from work one afternoon to find the lock broken on my locker. My first thought was that either Teardrop or Head had something to do it. Before I had a chance to approach Teardrop, Head came to me and said that Skull and his boys had broken into my house and stashed some of the stuff above the lockers in the ceiling.

We pulled the lockers away from the wall and found the larger things hidden in a crawl space that joined the ceiling. Then Head went a step further and started breaking the locks off every locker owned by Skull and his gang. We didn't find anything that belonged to me in any of their lockers, only the few things stashed in the crawl space. I thought it was somewhat peculiar that Head knew right where to go, and nothing of mine was found in any of the lockers that he was so anxious to violate.

Nothing goes unnoticed in G-Dorm. I was now associated with a multiple break-in, and that meant a show down between Skull and us within a matter of a few hours. The thought occurred to me that Head might have been the one that took my stuff and stashed it, then put on a show to pull me over to his side. I'd never seen Skull break into anyone's house, but I just saw head go through a half dozen without hesitating.

Since I was the only one known to back Skull down, Head may be forcing a move using me as a weapon. I asked, "Why are you getting involved in this, you have nothing to gain"? Head answered, "I'm tired of Skulls shit, he's a snitch and a punk. I'm sticking my neck out for you because you're good people, and it's the right thing to do. The Bitch stole your shit, and I wasn't about to pretend that I didn't know who did it. Are you with me or not"?

It took a few moments to respond, "Man, I appreciate everything you did, but I'll take care of this myself. It was my stuff that was stolen and I'll get my own straightening. The best thing for you to do is stay hidden somewhere until I do my thing at dinner count." He shook that big head of his and said, "Make sure you get him first, he doesn't give second chances"!

Now I was committed. Once you say you're gonna do something to someone, the word gets back to your opponent. It had come down to who makes the first move. There was no way that I could just try to hurt Skull. If he wasn't down for the count on the first swing, he might just kill me like he did the guy at the Unit. I had to try to kill him, and hope that I could stop before it went that far. He seemed to hold up pretty good to shanks, and the idea of us stabbing each other until one of us dropped didn't have much appeal. I needed something with reach and weight; a weight bar would do the job nicely.

It would be nice to think that breaking his arms would suffice, but I couldn't afford to take that chance. "Kill the head and the body dies" is one of the most popular sayings in the chaingang, and my motto for the up coming afternoon.

It was a slow afternoon at the weight pile, this made it easy for me to grab a lighter steel bar and place it by the edge of the Rec. hall. The plan was simple enough, Skull had to pass by the edge of the rec. building to return to the Getto along with the rest of the afternoon Vocational guys. I could come up behind him and say his name, then nail him as he turned.

They called Skull back to G-Dorm just about the time I acquired my weapon, One of Heads boys came to tell me that the cops had informed my target about what had happened to the lockers. This would make the attack a lot harder knowing that Skull would be armed, and have his guard up. I told the kid to let Skull know where I was at, that way he could come to me, making anything I did an act of self-defense. A few minutes later the kid came running back telling me to hurry back to G-Dorm.

Turning the corner of G-dorm, I saw an n army of cops trying to break up several different fights. Each fight contained four or five people, in the middle of this was Skull. I wasn't about to club him in front of the cops. Throwing down the weight bar; I deliberately began walking towards him. I didn't get within twenty feet before one of his boys got in my face, almost simultaneously Skull was jumped by one of Heads gang.

It didn't take much to put down my minor diversion, but the cops had now surrounded Skull and began backing away from the dorm with him. Sporadic fighting kept breaking out, but I couldn't tell whose side I was on. Homeboys were fighting friends, friends were fighting partners, it seemed as if everyone had picked a side at random. There was no logical way to figure it out. Since my target had left the building, I went to my bunk as the second wave of cops came and started grabbing anyone still fighting. It wasn't until later that I heard the whole story.

Head heard Skull being called to the dorm on the PA system, and decided to keep an eye on him to find out what weapons Skull planned to use. Instead of entering the front door, Skull came up the backside of the dorm where Head was watching through a window. Grabbing a swing blade he took a shot at Head that would have decapitated him if not for someone yelling a warning from F-Dorm. The blade missed its mark and the shaft broke as it struck

Head on his trademark. Skulls boys piled out the window along with Heads gang while Teardrop ran to the Lt. Office to tell. Skull now found himself facing a very pissed off Black that easily outsized him, and his only weapon was broken. Knowing the cops were coming he tried to make it to the crosswalk, but instead ended up being chased around to the front of G-Dorm. About ten people were hurt in the first few minutes before the cops got there to break it up.

All of this happened in the few minutes it took for me to walk the hundred yards from the weight pile. Because of this skirmish both Head and Skull were transferred, along with Teardrop and some of Skulls boys. I would get one more opportunity to see them in the box before they left.

G-Dorm was mellow after the two warring factions were removed. This break gave me a chance to work on some self improvement. The weekends I'd been serving in the box for refusing to work on my birthday came to an end. As a rule the State cannot force you to work in conditions that are hazardous to your physical health. Remembering that as a child I'd been tested for allergies, I had my folks send the paperwork that stated I was allergic to dust. Since Disco squad usually involved working in a lot of dust, my indefinite sentence to disciplinary squad was dismissed. But instead of going back to work in the kitchen I was placed on Motivation Squad.

This squad was started for people like myself, that had ducked out of disciplinary squad for medical reasons. It started out as a twelve-hour workday doing menial crappy jobs around the compound, such as picking up trash or running a swing blade. The cops grew tired of using extra men to baby sit us for the extra four hours every day and dropped our work hours to eight. They also gave us some sweet jobs near the Lt. Office where they could keep an eye on us. I was assigned the job of sweeping and mopping the inside visiting-park along with my old pal Jeff.

Twice a day we would clean the floor and play cards until count time. Until that one afternoon, that Jeff had a brilliant idea. On the compound end of the building that housed the visiting park, we had a canteen that only opened on the weekends. It was also the main entrance to the compound canteens. The steel door had an unbeatable lock and the only window had a steel mesh something like chicken wire cast into the glass itself.

Jeff figured that we could make a one-inch hole in the glass with a screwdriver and then push over the latch that held the window shut. We could then take the cash, which should amount to a few hundred bucks. I mentioned that we would be the obvious suspects and that we should think about it over night so that our plan would be a little less impulsive, and a lot more professional. That night I tried to talk him out of it but the challenge of pulling off a job like this was too big a temptation for Jeff.

Early the next morning I was surprised to find out that the plot no longer involved just Jeff and me, but almost everyone in G-Dorm. The new plan was to empty out everything in all four canteens. We had ground squad that would move the stuff across the compound in wheel barrows to the dorms, a couple of guys in the dorm to stash the loot in the ceilings, and half of motivation squad to both look out and do the actual burglary.

The Lieutenants words were ringing strongly in my ears, "If there's three or more involved, then one of them's mine." I knew this was going to be a total bust. If I walked away now I'd still catch the blame of doing the crime by the cops and be accused of being a snitch by my friends when the bust goes down. If I stay involved then I'll go down as a ringleader since this was my work area. Damned if I do, and damned if I don't. I might as well be in on this thing and get a little something out of it.

Not wanting to be one of the guys to actually go into the canteen, I elected to be a look out and set some one up from out side of our group. Jeff and I both had a cover story for when they came after us. We'd tell them that we did our final cleaning and left the door unlocked for our Bossman like we always did. If some one went in there after we left, then it was beyond our control and had to have happened after we left. My little addition to this plan was a boy named Paul.

Paul was a dumpy country boy that tried so hard to be one of us that we couldn't shake him. Almost every day he'd come by and try to hold a conversation with Jeff and me as we waited outside the canteen to leave. His one peculiarity was that he always wore some one-of-a-kind tennis shoes that his Momma sent him.

We'd heard some rumor that his uncle was a lieutenant but we found that very hard to believe at the time. Besides if he was the nephew of one of the cops I had an idea that his involvement might be advantageous to us later on if things went sour.

The Perfect Heist

At zero hour, I walked to the front to keep a look out while a small army proceeded as planned with socks on their hands in the place of gloves. I counted over ten wheelbarrows filled with loot, the contents covered with blankets with dirt thrown on top. The burglars then piled out the window and onto the compound, leaving Jeff and myself to finish the job. We wiped down everything and then mopped behind us as we left. I made sure to use extra soapy water to delay the drying time. Sitting in a couple of chairs out front of the visiting area, less than five minutes passed before Paul came along.

Jeff started, "Hey Paul, some Black guys broke into the canteen and left it wide open. Why don't you go in there and see if you can get something they might have missed"? Paul asked, "Why are you telling me and not getting any stuff for yourselves"? I answered, "I'm a robber and Jeff is an embezzler, we don't do break-ins. That doesn't mean that we won't turn a friend onto a good thing. The place is wide open, if you don't need cigarettes or a new watch, then just forget about it. Let the brothers be the only ones to get something out of this." He thought for a moment before creeping inside the doorway. As he walked towards the canteen window I could clearly see the distinct mark of his tennis shoes on the heavily coated floor. We told him to shut the outer door when he was done, and went back to the Getto where we found our coconspirators celebrating.

After dinner, Jeff and I were waiting outside the Lt. Office in the phone line trying to guess at how long it would take before they came to get us. We watched through the chain link fence as the head canteen orderly went into the visiting park to open the store. A few moments later he came running out and into the Lt. Office. A crew of cops went back in carrying their fingerprint box and some other items we didn't recognize. When they emerged fifteen minutes later, Paul was paged to the office. I smiled at Jeff and said, "Told You!" Ten minutes after that, they called me and Jeff.

For half an hour, we sat in a hallway while they rounded up the other three main guys in our scheme. They brought Paul out for a minute. He was handcuffed and crying while two cops escorted him towards the box. A third cop followed, carrying a pair of odd tennis shoes, laces tied together and hanging from a ruler he held at arms' length. Jeff gave me a look as if he was surprised that my set up worked. Keeping our voices low, Jeff and I went over our story, making sure that our times for the last cleaning and leaving the work area would match when they questioned us. We were each others alibi, everyone else was on their own. Jeff was the first one they called in.

Every Sergeant and Lieutenant had been called in for the investigation, including the Major. The investigating Lt. was a big rough looking guy in his mid forties. One side of his face was twice the size of the other from chewing tobacco since childhood. On rare occasions, when he didn't have a whole pouch of the stuff jammed into his mouth, his right cheek would sag like that of a bulldog. With beady eyes and hawk like features, this Bossman was butt ugly. The only thing uglier then him was his attitude, which was now being directed towards Jeff.

The door had been left halfway open so we could hear them break Jeff down. They figured that taking down an old convict in our presence would weaken the rest of us. But good old Jeff true to his nature, stuck to our story without a flaw. After half an hour of questioning the Investigating Lt. yelled into Jeff's face, "BOY, I WILL KICK YOU SO HARD IN THE ASS THAT I'll HAVE TO DRAG YOU BACK INTO THE BOX AND SHAKE YOU OFF MY LEG"! Like a line out of Oliver, Jeff responded with his best innocent little boy voice, "OH PLEASE SIR, Don't kick me so hard in the ass that you have to shake me off your leg." It was so perfectly executed, that I had to force myself not to laugh. Jeff came out and I was called in next.

The interrogation lasted about forty-five minutes. Standard questions were asked with a lot of intimidation, but these guys were no comparison to the cops at RMC. I'd become accustomed to being questioned over the last few years, or maybe I'd changed without realizing it. The average person under these conditions would be a nervous wreck, but it was just another routine ceremony to me.

Sticking to the story we'd agreed on, their questions were answered without a flaw. What it came down to was whether they actually believed that we were involved or not. When asked about the other guys, I told them I had no idea of their where abouts, and as far as Paul went, we did see him before we left, but I never saw him enter the building.

About midnight they released us to the dorm only to find that our home had been ripped apart and ransacked. They had called in the off duty dorm cops to search every inch of G-Dorm. Every locker in the Dorm had been emptied onto the floor, then ripped away from the walls to look for hiding places in the walls and ceilings they adjoined. The cops had discovered and confiscated the bulk of the loot. Anything remotely resembling contraband had been taken; leaving more than a few of the guys in G-Dorm pissed off at us. Of course we categorically denied having anything to do with it. It wasn't my fault that a burglary happened at our job assignment.

Every day for a week the five of us were kept at the Lt. Office for questioning. They seemed to rotate the order in which we were interrogated, but other than this one discrepancy, we viewed it as a daily routine. It was the following Friday and after everyone had been inside for a round of questioning, that they pulled me back inside.

They told me that they would have to lock all of us up, and that it would be better to tell them what happened to save my own ass. Since the amount of property stolen exceeded five hundred dollars this was a felony charge of Grand Theft, which meant that we'd be formally charged and taken to outside court. I was fingerprinted, and told that if any of my prints were found inside the canteen, then I was screwed. Wiping the ink from my hands, I headed towards the exit. They told me I was going the wrong way. "What do you mean the wrong way, I'm going back outside." The Lt. said, "You're not going outside for a long time, you're going to the box. We've got you now!" They roughly dragged me back to the box where I was deposited in a cell with who else but Teardrop. Soon after, they began bringing back the other four of our group at a rate of one person every hour.

They placed us in separate cells for what I thought were obvious reasons. Once we had a full house, the other guys started recanting facts about the burglary by yelling down the hallway.

"Hey Jeff, this was all your idea", "Yeah, well you were the one that actually broke in". "No, I held the screwdriver while you hit it with the fire extinguisher." "Hey Gagnon why ain't you saying nothing, you were the spook, and the one that set Paul up"! At this point Paul joined in, "Set me up? You asshole I knew something was wrong when you were nice to me, I'll kill you when we get out"! I yelled down the hallway, "I don't know any of you guys, and I had nothing to do with this canteen thing.

Now if you were smart, and had nothing to do with it, then you should keep your mouth shut too. You know that the man is at the end of the hallway listening to everything we say, so shut up and leave me out of your conversations"!

Instead of getting smart, they blatted out every little event that they could remember, including some things that I wasn't aware of. Either way I refused to discuss anything down the hallway and kept insisting that they do the same.

We were kept locked down in the box for a couple of weeks. Everyday they'd pull us out one at a time for the same monotonous questions. Until one day when they seemed to have given up and placed us all back in G-Dorm.

I was back in the kitchen for mornings and Voc. Small Engines for afternoons. This shop was a lot more hands on than the auto shop, and the instructor was cool. Within a couple of weeks, I was their main guy, fixing the mowers and sod-cutters that they used in and around the compound. If it wasn't for the kitchen, I could be the Voc. Aid for the shop. The rumor on the compound was that they planed to eliminate split classes and that I'd be put back in the kitchen full time. I had about a month to see if I could come up with a plan that would get me out of the kitchen and into the shop full time. A new path of thought had been developing as far as my future plans were concerned. The appeal was a washout, leaving me no way out of prison except for parole or death. My first parole hearing was just about a year off and in my mind there was a possibility that I might get released once the three year minimum was met.

In the event that I did make it back to the streets, I'd need to have some kind of a trade. This small engine thing seemed like a good way to make a living. It paid almost as much as auto mechanics, and was a lot easier and cheaper to start up your own business. A new long term plan would have to be implemented. I would become the best at this trade, get out and start my own business, then get married, have some kids, and forget this whole bank thing ever happened. The old thoughts of making my mark in life and becoming famous through crime were now replaced with the desire for responsibility and obscurity.

I never seemed to get away with anything I did wrong anyway. I had a very even Karma. Using my spare time (which there was still a lot of), and reviewing the actions and reactions of every event that could be remembered in my life, it became obvious that every wrong thing I'd ever done had come back to me. The most recent example was sending those Hamsters after Tim. Almost immediately afterward, my conflict with Skull had taken place. It was time to make myself a better person, or spend the rest of my life in and out of prison. Of course there were still a few old problems to be taken care of.

My name was the first one to come up for DR court over the canteen burglary. It had turned out that Paul really was the Majors nephew. Since he had confessed to his involvement, they couldn't send us to outside court without also prosecuting Paul. He never saw any of us take anything so he had no value as a witness for the state. There was no way that the Major could send his sisters' kid up for more charges. That meant there'd be no outside charges for the rest of us. My little plan was the only thing that had saved our asses.

Walking into the hearing room, they asked me what I had to say and I told them the same old rehearsed story. "We cleaned the floor like we always did and then left for the dorm. The canteen was intact when we left. Sometime between the time we left, and the time of discovery an hour later someone else must have broke in. But Jeff and I had nothing to do with it." The D.R. team pretended to listen then instructed me to wait outside for their verdict. The most gain time they could take for B&E was ninety days, so if they did find me guilty it wasn't a big deal. A few moments later they called me back in to hear their decision.

"We find you guilty of burglary and conspiracy, and we're taking 175 days future gain time. " Wait a Minute," I said, "You can't take 175 days. Burglary is only ninety"!

"We took ninety for the B&E, and eighty-five days for the conspiracy." Puzzled I asked, "What conspiracy?"

"You and Jeff planned to do it the day before but changed your minds. That made it a conspiracy." That was it, someone really went out of their way to tell the cops the whole story! This wasn't cool at all. This only proved that it was time to get out and away from these assholes. My image of convicts laying low and getting over on the man had been thoroughly shattered this time. Simply put, I didn't belong here with these people, and I never would. But for now, the slight problem of a life sentence tended to limit the amount of say I had in the company I would keep for the next few years. Guess it's time to get real.

Putting all of my efforts into the small engine class made me feel like I had something to look forward to. The thought that I'd miss a single day in the shop kept me from screwing up. Energy previously spent on schemes and plots that were destructive were now redirected to projects that are more constructive. Not being greedy, I shared whatever I learned with the shop, and tried to make the whole thing a learning process for all of us. In return I got respect and some appreciation from the other guys. This was a high point in my life; even the kitchen had become more tolerable, especially with my new assignment.

Scott, the professor and myself worked together in the salad room. Of the three of us, Scott had been in the kitchen the longest. This meant that he was next in line for the best job assignment in the kitchen, the can room. But Scott had been pissed off about the outcome of a progress report. In his opinion he deserved more gain-time than they awarded him. To retaliate he caught about twenty tree frogs that were attracted by the slimy kitchen walls. With surgical precision, he sliced off the upper part of their heads from the top lip up, then arranged the little heads in the staff salad with all forty eyes looking in one direction. He then placed the bowl on the guards serving line where he could face his accusers as he served them the reptile-laced salad. The salad was half eaten before anyone noticed.

Scott was transferred that night, the professor was placed on the serving line, and I was made the new Can Man.

There stood behind the kitchen, a small building about twelve by twelve. The lower halves of the walls were cinder block for the first five feet. This was topped by a three-foot section of screen on every wall. "The can room" as we called it, was easily the best job in the chow hall. All I had to do was take the big tin cans the kitchen used, peel the labels off and then wash them out. They'd use these cans out at the nursery for planters. When the plants were mature enough they could be moved easily.

On a busy day the actual work might take twenty minutes, but after my third day on the job some one broke the can opener. I saw no reason to inform my Boss that the cans were so badly damaged by the cooks sawing on the lids with kitchen knives that they couldn't be used. So every morning I'd walk out to my room, books in hand to read or sleep. This worked out quite nicely until the state inspectors came along one particular day.

There are more than a few strange sex stories that float around the chaingang. I'd personally seen guys hollow out a cucumber and use it as a "pocket pussy." One guy out in the field was caught screwing a hog, Red was caught humping a rotted watermelon in the cooler, and everyone had heard about the "Mad Chicken Fucker of ACI." When they finally caught that guy, he had a chicken foot in each pocket, and was holding onto the wings while he screwed them to death. Word had it, that they couldn't pry the last chicken off him until he was done.

One day a baker made a set of boobs out of grits using red food dye for the nipples. Below the congealed bust, he sculpted a pussy out of dough and added shredded coconut for pubes. Most of us watched his creation take shape and applauded his talent, until overwhelmed by the moment he jumped on the table and copulated with the dough. We did not to eat the rolls that day.

The one story that had caught my interest was about the liver. Rumor had it that pounding a calf's liver was just like sex with a real woman. Since working in the kitchen I'd bragged that if a whole liver ever became available, I'd treat it like the bitch it is.

One day my friend Jim was working on the grill. Holding up a slab of meat he told me that he had just the girl for me. Stabbing it lengthwise produced the main entrance, and then smaller stabs through the sides created the little flaps on the inside to

244

duplicate muscle action. Wrapped in butcher paper I toted my new bride out to the can room. Jim had warned me to wash it out good in warm water, both for the feel and to get all of the blood out of it, but being anxious, I worked it in the hot water until I figured it was warm enough for lovin.

Out in my barren can room; my prize was tied to one milk crate stacked on top of another. After preparing myself for the moment I entered this lump of love and was pleasantly surprised to find that all of the rumors were true. Damn this is good, a little gooey, but very good!

Then someone rattled my door. "Ok," I said, "Quit messin with me guys"! "Who's in there? Open this door now"! Came a voice from outside. Breaking stride I hollered back, "Who the hell is out there"? "We're State inspectors, open this door right now"! "Yeah, Right, State inspectors. You gotta come up with a better one then that"! Who ever these assholes were, they had ruined the moment. Pushing against the rickety door held only with an eyehook, I peered outside to get a look at this violator of my special moment, only to see two guys dressed in suits.

Oh Shit, They were State Inspectors, I told them I'd be there in a minute. I scanned the room for a possible way out of my situation. Concrete walls and floor, Two milk crates, one piece of rope, two books, myself (dressed in whites), and one large piece of liver, (recently violated). With only a few moments to act, I untied the liver and threw it into the corner, pulled up my fly, and opened the door. In my calmest voice I asked, "What can I do for you gentlemen"?

With suspicion in their voices they asked, "Who are you, and what are you doing out here"? "I'm the can man. I take all of the opened cans from the kitchen, peel the labels off and wash them out. Then they plant seeds in the cans that grow into big trees that are used to enhance the esthetic beauty of the world around us." In spite of their suspicions, I felt that there was no way that they could figure out what I was doing. Keeping constant eye contact, and staying between them and the liver now lying lifeless in the corner, I felt sure that they'd never figure out what I was up to.

"Does the kitchen supervisor know that you're out here"? "Yes Sir, He put me out here himself." They kept looking at the front of my whites, as if some tell tale evidence of my sin was staring them in the face. "Where are the cans"? They asked. "Oh, The can opener broke and the nursery can't use cans with jagged edges". "Well, we're going to have a little talk with your supervisor about this"! Then they headed back towards the main kitchen.

Once they were out of sight, I looked down to see if there was anything out of the ordinary, only to find the whole front of my pants coated in blood. The next time I'd have to make sure the liver was washed out better. Walking over to the corner, I found that my bloody victim now had dirt in her. So much for my kosher lover, and so ended my job in the can room.

The day came when I didn't have to wear kitchen whites anymore. Vocational classes went to full time and my classification officer called me up front. It seemed that my GED, of which they had a copy, was from the federal government. He went on to explain that Florida had much higher standards than the Feds, making my Diploma void. I was placed in school for three weeks until the next State GED test would be given.

Class was a joke. In the most advanced class, it was surprising what degree of illiteracy most of the guys displayed. It was easy for me to pass the classroom tests without studying. I figured what the hell; I'll just breeze through this and in a couple of weeks be the proud owner of two GEDs. When the day of the test came, I was called up front and told that they had changed their minds. My original GED was valid and to report to small engines in the morning.

Small engine shop had a small room where the tools and books were kept. When there was little or no work in the shop, I would study the wall of books, which included about eight Seabee manuals. Armed with the info from these books I had managed to bring a few retired pieces of equipment back to life. The more important I could make myself to them, the better chance I had of becoming a vocational aide. A few weeks into my new job, an argument between the Superintendent and the instructor broke out over a sod cutter. My boss quit and the shop was closed down, but they let me stay to maintain the equipment. This more or less guaranteed my reprieve from full time kitchen duty.

Smoke and Meds

Over eighty percent of the compound smoked. And since store bought cigarettes were a little too expensive for the average person, the majority of us supplemented this habit by smoking the cigarettes supplied by the state. Although these were a sorry excuse for a cigarette, there was always a sufficient quantity.

A private company became interested in the state cigarette machine and made a cash offer to buy it. The person originally approached needed approval from some kind of state board before selling such an expensive piece of equipment. A meeting was called to see if they were going to eliminate this "unnecessary expense" to the state.

After the vote it was decided to keep the program, since inmates without cigarettes were more likely to get excited and cause damage to state property. After this had already been decided by a majority vote, the instigator of the plan told the others that he'd already sold the cigarette machine to the private company. Once the panel was informed of this, they voted a second time and reversed their previous decision. The next matter for discussion concerned the method of informing forty thousand inmates that they couldn't smoke anymore.

The amount of state cigarettes already manufactured filled a large warehouse that could supply Florida's institutions for two years. The story fed to the public was that they were eliminating property damage caused by careless inmates with lit cigarettes. They publicly announced that the State was implementing an anti-smoking campaign to help ease the transition. This program would be voluntary and made easily available to everyone in the system. At DeSoto they told us to either take the program voluntarily, or be assigned the worse jobs they could find. I was in the second group to be volunteered.

The quit smoking class had all of the standard stuff, with pictures of good and bad lungs, and lengthy sermons about how smoking wasn't good for you in general. We were taken for two fresh air walks in the morning and two more in the afternoon. Conveniently, they allowed us to smoke on these walks, which in reality were smoke breaks. Everyone that participated received a certificate of achievement and the state boasted to the media how the turn out was over ninety percent. The State added that they couldn't guarantee how many would start smoking again, but that was to be expected, considering the convict mentality.

During this time, the compound had been undergoing a reconstruction of the dorms. G-Dorm was supposed to be the next one on their list. We were informed that the majority of us would be moved to the newly rebuilt B-Dorm. Simultaneously, in the center of the compound, they were putting up the new Dorm design of the future. This new Style would be a two story T-shaped buildings, with two-man rooms. Each room was made with the specified cubic feet of space required by the government for the minimum amount of living area two people required. This new dorm would house administrative confinement, the check-ins, juveniles, and the honor guys.

Because of the construction, the compound had been operating below its intended capacity. The population sometimes went as low as 350, while at other times climbing to as high as 600. The quality of the food while already dismal at best would deteriorate even more during the high population periods. Rumor had it that we were running on the same budget per inmate for the past three years. This made us a model institution in the eyes of the state. I'm quite sure that someone was collecting a nice bonus to keep the costs down at our expense. Most of us wondered what would happen when the construction ended and the compound operated at peak capacity. If they didn't re-budget for the forty-percent increase when the time came, they would have a lot of hungry, irritable, inmates without cigarettes. I hoped to be gone before that time came.

At the very end of 1978, my name came up on the call out sheet for a parole hearing. It had been three years since my arrest. My three-year mandatory sentence had been met, making me now eligible for parole. I felt confident that they'd take my age into consideration. In the event, the state didn't release me this time; they would most likely let me go next year, since everyone was reviewed once a year. The rule of thumb for parole hearings was to "hope for the best and expect the worse." After the first hearing, this advice was taken to heart.

In Florida you don't confront a panel of experts for a parole hearing, instead they send a probation officer from the city closest to you. This one person sits down on the other side of a desk, and after reviewing your records and asking a couple of questions makes his recommendation. There was a list of reasons why you were being denied a parole with little boxes that they could check off. The reasons they used for me were: 1. has not adjusted to institutional life. 2. Release at this time would show disregard for the criminal justice system. 3. Has not attended counseling groups, etc.

When asked how much time I would have to serve he responded, "The average person with a life sentence serves between seven and nine years, if you keep getting in trouble you will do nine years or more." He said that at the next hearing, the parole board officers would be using new guidelines. This new system would take into account age and prior convictions. This would probably work in my favor, but he couldn't say for sure until the final paper work was out. This meant that I had at least one more year to serve before seeing him again. Once the new system was implemented, I would see him every two years.

I was a little let down to hear that it would take another year, but things didn't sound too bad considering my record. I asked to be put in the dorm group, and set about getting into some other required activities. After all I only had a year to get this small engine thing down. I also paid a visit to the infirmary to have a couple of little bumps checked out on my nuts. The Doctor said that they wanted to do a biopsy, and that it would have to be done at Lake Butler. Whether it was cancerous or not, I wouldn't let them castrate me, but a trip to RMC would kinda be like a vacation, so I agreed to the biopsy only.

A couple of weeks after G-Dorms exodus to B-Dorm my name came up for transfer to Lake Butler. I made sure they understood that I wanted my same job back upon my return. They assured me that it would be no problem. So off I went to RMC, but it was no vacation.

My first day in RMC, a dozen of us were taken to the hospital section and lined up for whatever minor operation they had planned for us. Some guys were getting old bullets removed, and one guy was getting a hand removed for infection. A nurse walked by as we lined both sides of a hallway, inspiring two of our group to stare at her ass in passing. They were grabbed by the Bossman escorting us, and dragged off to K-wing for "reckless eyeballing". The surgical assembly line procedure was interrupted again when a busload of casualties rolled in from a new camp called Hendry.

I recognized one of the guys I had known from BTU. He told me how great the camp was, but since it was new they'd filled it up by shipping in all of the problem inmates from a variety of camps. A riot had broken out on the second week of operation as the blacks and whites fought to gain control over the money and the individual dormitories. He'd had his leg broken with a weight bar and was anxious to get back to the fighting, after setting his leg they sent him hobbling back the same day to get his wish.

Through all this, the nurses kept walking up to a cardboard box and reaching into it like it had some kind of a toy inside. As they were preparing me for my minor operation, the box was brought in and placed on the gurney next to mine.

Some guy in a lab coat had shaved all of my pubes and started rubbing some brown gooey stuff all over my crotch. He went on to tell me how cool and soothing this was going to feel. It was more like cold and gooey.

A doctor walked up to the box on the gurney next to mine, pulled out a kitten, petted it for a moment and then brandishing a scalpel, sawed its head off. Still stunned I watched as he removed three other kittens and repeated this aberrant behavior, using a new scalpel for each beheading. I was told that the guys before me had left out of the back door, but the concern that maybe no one left here had begun to cross my mind.

The weirdo was still stroking me with the gooey stuff while the Doctor wrapped the detached "cat heads" in wax paper and stuffed them into envelopes.

252

Finding my voice I asked, "What did the cats do to you"? He threw me a dirty look and replied, "For your information, one of these cats scratched a nurses daughter and we are having them checked for rabies." Then the same Doctor came over to me and asked what was going on.

I told him just to remove the two little bumps on my nuts and to stay away from the head. Since they had used the last of the real scalpels on the kittens, the doctor used something that resembled an X-acto knife on me. I told him that I could still feel the blade, so he used a little more of the local anesthetic, when I complained again he said, "Too bad, we can't be here all day." He then completed the job and handed me some strange little cup, with instructions to wear it for three days. When the back door opened, I got the hell out of there. Fortunately, the stitches were the dissolving type that required no second visit.

A few days after the "operation," a guy about my age plopped himself next to me on my bunk asked how it was going. He looked a little familiar with his swollen eyes and shaky voice. He asked if I remembered him and then looked away as if embarrassed. Then I noticed the marks on his forearms. There were scars on top of scars, probably self-inflicted. It was Kenny from the juvenile detention center!

For the last couple of years he'd spent his life in and out of institutions until landing in the adult prison system for B&E. He'd become comfortable with the idea of being taken care of by the state. "After all," he said, "There's a roof over my head and three hot meals a day, why should I be out there, where I go hungry and have to steal for a living"? "Besides no one will hire me with how many different medications they have me on."

He then went on to give me the list of drugs they'd been pumping into him over the years. It occurred to me that he was the perfect person to try some of my new rehab ideas on. Instead of using my mind games to screw someone up, I could get into his head and give him something to look forward to. The thorazene and other drugs would have to go, along with his defeatist attitude. The first drug to be eliminated was his asthma medication.

Telling him that most asthma was psychological, the best thing for him to do was start smoking, and lay off the asthma meds. To his surprise, my system actually worked, but weaning him off the heavy downers was going to be a little tougher. Once the state decides that you have to be medicated, they make sure that you stay that way. It was common knowledge that people existed in the system for years doped up to the point of not knowing who or where they were for the length of their sentence. To make sure these patients stayed passive, and to prevent them from selling their medications, the infirmary strictly supervised the dopers while dispensing the Meds. This meant that Kenny had to hide the pills inside of his mouth three times a day, and then spit them out at the first opportunity. If he were caught doing this, they would tie him down and force-feed him his prescriptions.

For the most part he became drug free with the exception of the few times when they checked him so closely that he had to swallow the pills. Within a few days, the change in his personality was obvious. The bags beneath his eyes were gone and he smiled a lot. The boy never stopped talking about all of the things he would like to do if he ever got the chance. I felt that it was time to build up his self-esteem.

There was a plumbing class at his institution that he'd taken a liking to. I suggested to him that he approach this new interest with everything he had, using plumbing as a career and a way to support himself on the outside. Most people don't look at the future of being a shit chaser as a very bright one.

But for someone that spent seventeen years of his life being blown this way and that way by the winds of chance, this was a golden opportunity to control his own life. I personally felt really good about doing this for him. He would serve as a sort of pilot program. If this worked for him then it would work for me when my time came. We both shared an enthusiasm for a bright future, until the day he stopped coming around.

It wasn't unusual for RMC to transfer guys early in the morning, so it was a safe assumption that this was the reason for his disappearance before breakfast. The probable reason for his absence would be that he'd been shipped back to his permanent camp where he could start out on the new road he'd chosen.

Later in the day a rumor started circulating about some kid that had refused to take his dope over at the hospital. Supposedly he'd been dragged away kicking and screaming to some dark corner of the hospital where they could deal with him in their own special way. The story had no special meaning to me, until a couple of Old Cocks approached me a few days later.

Sitting on my bunk playing solitaire, two rather large guys came and stood within a few feet of my bunk. "You know that kid you were hanging with is dead." "What are you talking about"?

"That boy Kenny wouldn't take his meds, when they ordered him to take them he refused. So they tied him to a gurney and force-fed him. The first time they left him alone and untied, he hung himself. And it's all your fault"!

"How is it my fault? That dope they were feeding him made him a zombie. I showed him how to be a human being without it, I gave him hope"!

"You didn't give him SHIT! He'd be alive right now if it weren't for you and your mind games. We catch you running your bullshit on any one else and we'll be back to kill your ass"! With that final statement, they turned and left.

This really sucked. For once, I try to do something good for someone and it ends up killing him. Maybe he would have killed himself anyway. His arms were littered with the evidence of his many attempts to do just that. Then again, maybe after seeing what kind of person he could become, the thought of going back to the numb life of drug induced euphoria was just too much for him. Either way my friend was dead, along with his dream of a better life.

In reality, none of this had been his idea. That was my dream that they had murdered along with Kenny. Call it paranoia, but this was taken as a personal attack directed towards me by the state, to show me the hopelessness of my situation. If Kenny could have made it on the streets after spending years incarcerated, it would prove that I stood a chance of making it on the outside myself. I needed to know that there was something to look forward to once my time was served. Instead of being beaten by this chain of events I would make it a point to make my plans come true, not because of my situation but in spite of it.

Returning to Desoto was comparable to coming home. All of my friends inquired if I still had my balls, and to ask who I'd run into up at RMC. G dorm was still under construction, so I was placed in B-Dorm, not far from my previous bunk. Getting a pass the next morning, I went to the small engine shop to check on my old job, only to find that it no longer existed. There were two guys sitting out in the shop with all of the equipment piled around them in pieces.

In my absence, they'd managed to bullshit their way into the shop claiming to be small engine mechanics from the street. Before my trip, there were six mowers and three Gravleys. Now they were down to one Gravely. The Vocational coordinator was convinced that they were doing a wonderful job and had decided that I was better off in the welding shop next door.

Welding was a six-month course taught by one of the best welders in the state. The instructor was a wiry old guy that spoke with a harsh country accent. Very opinionated, he had a talent for always being right. When nothing at all worked next door, he'd let me go over to small engines for an afternoon so that the camp would have something other then swing-blades to mow with. After being told that at the end of the welding course, I'd be sent back to the kitchen, the necessity of a plan became apparent.

The two so-called mechanics would take turns operating the gravely out on the compound. Now a Gravely 7.6 was originally designed in 1912. It weighs a little over three hundred pounds, with a single cylinder engine that hadn't changed much in sixty years. A large cast iron pulley mounted low on the back is where the operator would wind a rope and pull using all of his weight to start it. If the machine kicked back, the operator's hand would be drawn into the pulley causing great discomfort.

Taking parts from the pile in the shop, I'd assembled a second Gravely, painted it up real nice, and then told the guys not to use it until the timing was set back a little. It was clearly explained to them that the machine had more strength this way but may be hard to start. Within an hour the smarter of the two tried to start it and had his hand crushed by the pulley. I had my job back.

A few weeks later the shop had a new Bossman and I was back to teaching class. Time went by smoothly as I engrossed myself in the shop. Besides having a comfortable job there were a few little perks. Sometimes a Bossman would bring in a mower or a boat engine from home that needed repair. Besides letting the class see different kinds of engines, I would benefit either monetarily or with things that couldn't be obtained through the canteen. Sometimes it would be a homemade cake or a brand of coffee not sold on the compound. This new position also provided me with sole access to the tool room. The small room where the tools were stored I dubbed "my office".

Almost a year had passed, and my next parole hearing was coming up in a few months. My technique of growing up through other peoples stories seemed to be working quite well, but the relationship part of life still eluded me. The thought of substituting a chaingang Bitch for a woman seemed like a piss poor idea, but what else was there to work with. I could at least practice my rap and be a little more effective with the ladies upon my release. My last girlfriend on the street had red hair; it was only natural that the instinct to chase something similar put me on the trail of a boy in my shop that reminded me of her.

Roy was the personification of "a red-haired step child". There were no rumors about him having Bitch in him, but I felt that he was a sure thing. Opportunity came knocking one-day when he came asking for help with the book part of the course.

He didn't really care much for the small engine course, his real interest was welding. Nevertheless, they wouldn't reassign him until he had successfully completed Small engines, so I made him a deal. I'd help him study in my own way, but once he showed an obvious improvement in his grades, he would have to do a little something for me.

The training was simple. I'd have him read a chapter and then ask him questions. For every wrong answer, I'd punch him in the leg or shoulder, giving him a "frogging "as we put it. Within a few days, he stopped getting questions wrong and made a B+ on his next test. It was late in the afternoon on a Friday when I told him it was time to pay the piper. When he refused, I persisted that a deal was a deal and that he didn't have to indulge in any physical contact, just act like a woman for me. Somehow, this turned into a wrestling match that left me pinning him up against some shelves. Then the surprise came. He suddenly kissed me.

Startled, I backed away and asked, what the hell was that? With a submissive look he asked, "What's wrong, don't you want me"? Still bewildered I answered, "Yeah, Sure I want you; I just didn't expect all that"! He rubbed my crotch as he continued, "I'm not just a good kisser, I can do a lot of other things with my mouth"!

I was suddenly very horny. It had been almost four years since I'd had a woman, and my hormones were overriding my discretion. Roy looked an awful lot like a woman to me at this point, and from every indication, he planned on serving as one. I was about to serve this boy his first meal when someone knocked on the door. The shop was closing for the day and all of the tools had to be put up, including my own. He promised to take care of me Monday. It was a very long weekend.

It was late Monday morning before we had a chance to be alone in the tool room. We went through the same ritual of wrestling before he again became submissive. As he began to get on his knees, I told him that ass would be preferred. Roy said that he didn't do that. I tried being nice about it, but he still refused.

Now I was pisssed! It was bad enough that I had to ask a faggot for sex, but having to repeat myself was like begging. The thought of lowering myself to this point and then having some wanna-be bitch tell me "NO" was inexcusable. In a blind rage, I beat the shit out of him. Even after he whimpered he would do whatever I wanted, I continued beating this disrespectful Bitch. It crossed my mind at the time that this was no way to start a relationship, but the boy had to learn not to play games with a man. After lunch, he didn't return to the shop.

Late in the day, they called me up to the Voc. Coordinators office. The new Boss over all of the Voc. shops had been the Major during the canteen investigation. This is the Bossman that helped me retain my job. Today he had a funny look on his face as I entered his office, along with four Sergeants.

His first question was "What's this about you raping a boy in the shop"? "Hey, I ain't raped anybody. Who are you talking about"? One of the Sergeants added, "Roy's down in the hospital right now, and he's all banged up. He says you raped him"! "Bullshit! You can scrape every orifice on that boy; there ain't nothing from me on him anywhere. Besides, he's three years older, and weighs more than me. Don't you think I'm a little young to be running around beating up my elders?" The other Sergeant in the room asked, "If you didn't do it, how'd he get so banged up"?

I went on to explain how Roy had asked me for help in his studies, and the manner in which I'd been tutoring him, including the little punches for incorrect answers. I also added that they could check how much he'd improved in class, since they questioned the technique. Then one asked, "So how did he get so banged up"?

"I guess he just gave me all the wrong answers"!

After a short silence, they started laughing and told me I could go, as long as I promised not to tutor anyone else. This was the beginning of my reign in small engines.

At my next parole hearing, I was optimistic. They had started the new system using some kind of a scale that listed the different crimes in a column on the left of their review sheet. Across the top was the list of aggravating points such as zero in the first column, 1 in the second, 2-5 in the third and so on. The points were dictated by different factors involved in the crime committed and the age at the time of the offense. A few guys had come out of their parole hearings with immediate parole, and it only figured that I'd get a good break because of my age. It turned out that in my case the opposite applied.

The Parole Nazi

I sat across from the same parole man as the year before. He pulled out a form and began to explain it. Simple robbery carried 3-5 years if there were no aggravating points. Six to seven years, for one point, and seven to nine years, for two points. It looked as if I was no better off than the old system until he explained that my category was a completely different story. Since there was an injury during my robbery, I had fallen into the greatest most serious crime list. This one started at 7-9 years without any points. Since I was a juvenile at the time, I was automatically given two points. This made the Total time I had to serve, between 156 to 192 months. He kindly explained that since four years had already been served, then I only had to do another 8-10 years... It took a few minutes for this to sink in before I could respond.

"A year ago you told me I'd have to do between seven and nine years, closer to nine if I didn't straighten out my act. I haven't been in any trouble for over a year, and in return, you double my time. And the reason it doubled is because of my age at the time that I did it! Did it ever occur to anyone that the younger a person is when he screws up, the less responsible they are? How can you morons compare the common sense a fifteen-year-old has against that of a thirty-year-old, and then punish the younger of the two more because of his ignorance? There must be some kind of a mistake here"!

Staring at me he went on, "What ever I told you last year is superseded by these new guidelines. I didn't write them, I can only follow them to make my recommendation to Tallahassee. Maybe when I see you again in two years they'll change it and you'll get a few months knocked off. But at this moment I see no reason to recommend that they give you any kind of break." Then he smiled. His last remark royally pissed me off, and his smile was fueling the flames.

Then I realized just how much this sadistic prick was enjoying his job. My mother was right when she told me through my early years how I was the most spiteful person she'd ever known. The mere thought of this man being delighted at my personal agony made me kick into my spiteful mode. He had just fucked me, why should I let him hear me squeal like a pig. Calming down, I asked him to excuse my attitude, "You have to understand that this was a great shock to me, and I apologize for the way I just acted. I understand that you're just doing your job and that this probably upsets you as much as it does me." He went on to tell me that it could be even worse the next time he came, trying to goad me into another emotional outburst he could bask in.

I assured him that I firmly believed our next meeting would be much more productive, and hopefully a more pleasant one. I then shook his hand and I went outside where I washed my hand in the water fountain. He watched me through the window, still dumbfounded by my actions.

Time is a curse onto itself. No one really knows just how much they have. Very few notice the shift in its flow, until the very end when every second is cherished. When we are six years old, waiting a week for our birthday seems like an eternity. By our mid twenties, the bills at the beginning of the month come all too quickly, as do the holidays. When we become old and feeble we dwell on childhood memories, trying to relive the magic of moments never appreciated at the time of their occurrence. This is the true tragedy of human awareness, and my bane.

I was twenty-one years old. All of my memories of the streets had turned into the same distant memories of the elderly. The outside was just a foggy memory, a place where people came from and went back to, except for myself. My world was one of concrete, steel, and conflict. I had accepted the fact that this was now my home and that the other place called the streets was far beyond my reach.

I cursed the day that I had walked into that bank, delivering myself to the keepers of the undead. With only myself left to blame, I had relived every moment of my life over and over again. Every rotten and unpleasant act I'd ever participated in, along with every person whose feelings I'd hurt, or smile I had ruined. These were my demons, and I faced every one of them alone. There were no excuses I could think of to make them go away. The only thing to do was accept the responsibility of my actions and try to make up for them somewhere in the distant future. I hoped that someday I'd have the opportunity to make things right. But for now, I'd have to do whatever it takes to survive. As brutal or unfair as my actions may be, I will survive.

To cope with my undetermined length of incarceration, I had given up on time itself. Everyone at one time or another has watched the clock, whether in school or on the job. Watching the minutes tick by just makes the ordeal of waiting for a certain moment unbearably slow. In my case, the moment of release to the outside was my goal. So, it was necessary to remove the clock from my life. I removed any reference to dates from my locker. Month and year ceased to exist and I kept myself busy in the shop and on the compound.

My Friends

I had two friends outside of my clique that have noteworthy stories. One was my homeboy Joe. An ex-junkie, he was in for beating a fag that had approached his little brother. Joe beat the crap out of the Fag. This should have been a simple case for the courts to decide, but the Fag claimed that Joe and his friends beat him up and robbed him. This was good move on the Fag's part, since Joes little brother was only fourteen at the time. Joe got ten years while the Fag went on to chase other young boys.

A Rather ugly black Sissy named Gus had the hots for Joe. This was comical in two ways; he hated Blacks almost as much as he hated Fags. Gus was persistent and would come by at least once a day when Joe and I would sit in front of the library to make small talk. This one particular day Gus asked Joe how to get out of Disciplinary squad. Joe told him to inject lighter fluid under his kneecap. We were laughing about it as Gus left to find a needle.

We didn't see Gus almost a month after that conversation. Then one day he hobbled up to us on crutches. One of Gus's legs had been removed to prevent the blood poisoning from spreading up his leg from the knee he'd injected. Gus never had to go out on work squad again and Joe got over his dislike of Fags a little. In Joe's own words "There was just something about propping a one legged fag against the shower wall and cornholing him that gets me off".

My other friend was Mike, a rather unremarkable character from Miami. One afternoon while walking around the rec field, I was making comments about my life sentence. He just laughed it off and said I should be happy with my "Baby Life". In chaingang terms, a baby life is a basic life sentence. This means that you can spend the rest of your life in prison or that you could serve one year and then be released or paroled.

Different variations of sentences similar to mine are used, depending on the judge. For instance, 15 to life means serving 15 years before you're eligible for parole. Since you're not eligible for release for at least 15 years, the parole man doesn't come to see you for that amount of time. Mike had 25 years to life; which explained his remark about my whining.

Mike's curse was getting involved with a poor Jewish girl, or actually her family. He'd met her through her brother, whom he'd worked with. Mike moved in with her and her family. This included the mother in-law, brother-in-law and his wife's Grandpa. Grandpa was in sad shape, he was barley able to put one foot in front of the other, or control his bowels. One of Mike's designated chores was to clean up after the old man. He didn't dislike the old guy, but he hated cleaning up after him.

His mother-in-law was a greedy, vicious woman that felt cheated by life. In her mind, she should be living in a mansion with servants instead of having to rely on the earnings of her siblings. She'd moved her father in for the sole purpose of stealing his fortune. But with no insurance at the time of his heart attack, his new pacemaker had left him broke.

After stealing whatever cash he had hidden in his room, she decided to stage an accidental death to expedite her inheritance. This loving daughter read somewhere that radiation from microwave ovens could cause a pacemaker to fail. They removed the door from a microwave and rigged it to operate this way. Mikes mother-in-law distracted the old man with a conversation in the hallway while another held the microwave behind the old man simultaneously pushing the cook button. They tried this a few times, once they followed him around the house with an extension cord, but it never fazed him.

Gramps got suspicious after being pushed down some steps, and informed the family that he was leaving. Most people as evil as they may be, would just let the old guy go and wait for nature to take its course. Not this greedy Bitch, she figured he'd have his money and check book on him on his way out the door, so she hatched a new plan. She told Mike and her son to offer him a ride to the bus station. Then they would beat him in his chest until his heart stopped, take the money and dump him in an alley, making it look like a robbery. Neither of the guys wanted anything to do with this, but after hearing her lecture about the horrible beatings her father gave as a child they relented to do the job.

Gramps rode shotgun while one of the killers drove and the other sat in the rear passenger position. Traveling down the road, the driver pulled out a weighted club and whacked the old man in the chest while the other choked Gramps from behind. The old man fought like hell, got a hold of the club and swinging back at one point. One killer had a knife and began stabbing the old Dude until he stopped moving.

The car interior and everybody in inside were covered in blood, making it impossible to drop him off in public as planned. They dragged him out to a dump and threw a couch on top of him. As they walked away Mike looked back to see the victim reanimated and pushing the couch off, but they were done with the old man at that point.

Back at the house, Mom tore through her father's belongings only to find about six hundred dollars for all their trouble. She was pissed, for hours she ranted and raved until the police came knocking. They'd found the car covered in blood in the complex parking lot, and traced the registration to them. Mom hid in the back while the killers stumbled through an explanation. They were arrested and charged with first-degree murder. No one ever said a word about Mom.

Mike and his brother-in-law had the choice of pleading guilty in return for a twenty-five year to life sentence or go to trial and getting the chair. Both took the plea bargain.

A few years had passed before a lawyer found a way of getting one of them free; all they had to do was pass a lie detector test. Mike went back to Dade County Jail for this test and had someone smuggle in a couple of valiums to help regulate his reactions to the questions.

Wired to the machine, the detectives repeatedly questioned him about the murder. "Did you do it"? "NO" "Did you know anything about it?" "NO". The questions continued for the better part of an hour, as the technician analyzed the results. When they were done the lead detective said, "Well Mike it was a nice try, but you failed the test!" Mike replied, "Fuck it, I didn't think I'd get away with killing the Old Bastard anyway". That's when the Cop told him, "You passed the test with flying colors, but that remark just convicted you all over again". Mike would have to wait twenty-five years before seeing the parole man for the first time. This didn't lessen my sentence burden, but I agreed that it sucked to be him.

Construction on G-Dorm was completed and the few of us that constituted the G-Dorm counseling group moved back in. The rest of the dorm had been filled with new guys coming in from RMC. The Getto wasn't the same since the reconstruction. Instead of ten bunks to a cube, there were now thirteen. The lockers were half the size of the old ones, and the lack of personal space was quite apparent.

It didn't take long for a few of us to form a clique that would last almost the rest of my time here. There were five of us, and we found it humorous to give each other different names just to confuse anyone that may want to stick their nose in our business. My new name was Ralph, Randy was dubbed Fred, there was a George, and so on. We used our new names at all times. Some of the new cops called us by these names not knowing any better. At times, other guys would hang out with us without officially being a member of the clique. Fat Jack was one of these.

"Fat Jack" was a character onto himself. His nickname described his appearance, and to a degree, his demeanor. A rather stout baby faced guy, he'd made a very good living by working for large companies, finding a safety violation such as a shield missing from a machine, and then breaking his arm, or losing a fingertip in industrial accidents. The rewards for this ranged from seventy to two hundred grand an accident. Someone in an insurance company figured it out before he ran out of body parts. This was how he became a guest of the state, along with of us.

After a couple of years in the system, you get to know the different types of personalities that the other guys have. Hustlers, dealers, players, racists, everyone falls into some category or stereotype. But one character showed up in G-Dorm that all of us found quite unique. He was our first skinhead.

Claiming to be Aryan, he sported swastika tattoos, and a shaved head. Lean and wiry he acted crazy, or to be more accurate, we thought he was mad. No one was quite sure how to handle him, or to what extent he might go if messed with.

During a football game I noticed that the bible he always toted with him had been left open on the bench next to me. I noticed some handwritten notes covered the inside cover. It was half-time during a Tampa game and after reading some of the inscriptions, I thought the other guys might find entertainment in hearing some of the Skin Head's more private thoughts.

Standing on the front bench, I explained who the author was and went on to read "Dear God, please don't let these evil people hurt me. I'm scared and ask for your protection so that these bad men don't hurt me, and I know they all want to hurt me..." At that point the Skinhead walked in, figured out what was going on, grabbed the bible from my hands and took off screaming like a banshee. Someone in the back said, "You know that boy is crazy, I'd sleep with one eye open if I were you"!

Fat Jack mentioned that the skinhead owed him some money. Up to this point, he hadn't been sure about how to handle the collection process, but after hearing the boy's notes, he gave him until dark to pay his dues. When he didn't meet the deadline, Fat Jack decided to collect in blood.

After dinner count, everyone packed the TV room to watch the game. The Skinhead was on the bench near the front door. Fat Jack sat down with us for a moment saying that he needed an alibi, and that he had some business to take care of. Once the Bossman wandered down to the end of the dorm, Jack walked over to the water fountain on the other side of the door from where the Skinhead sat.

Pretending to walk by, Jack suddenly turned and landed a roundhouse upside the boy's shaved head. Everyone watched the kid fall to the ground on hands and knees. I expected to see this nut case lose it, come up spinning like Bruce Lee, and possibly stomp a mud hole in Fat Jack's ass. Instead, he rose up and tried to run out the open door at a speed that defied human ability. This would have made for a great escape from his attacker had he correctly calculated the position of the doorframe.

His face slammed into the wood trimmed opening with enough force to shatter his nose, split his mouth open, and knock him out. His body went rigid and tilted backwards while his nose sprayed blood at the onlookers seated on the bench he'd previously occupied. He lay sprawled out in the doorway a few moments before rising to his feet.

Grabbing his face, he ran to the infirmary emitting one continuous scream that faded into the distance. Fat Jack stood in place, stunned by what he'd just witnessed. Gathering his wits, Jack jumped onto the bench with us before the Bossman could reach the TV room to investigate the commotion. Fifteen minutes later the sergeants came for Jack. Another four hours passed before the dorm cop pointed us out to the sergeants. This ritual took place because they couldn't find a Ralph, George, or Fred listed in the Dorm roster.

We told the cops how the boy had jumped off the bench screaming and then attacked the wall with his face. "And NO, We didn't see Jack hit him"! Jack went to the box anyway, and my alias of Ralph was added to my jacket, for future reference. Neither Jack nor the skinhead were ever seen again.

In The Third Round

As the end of 1981 approached, I acquired a new enemy named Smity. He was a stout black guy that fancied himself as a boxer. While I was in B-Dorm, a friend had told me that Smity had called him out for a fight. Having known Smity for a couple of years, I refused to believe it at the time. One day he came up to me saying that he had very strong feelings for me and grabbed at my crotch. He went on to say how it would be an even thing but that he would have to play the man role in public.

Amazed by this new revelation I explained that I was honored to be trusted with his little secret, but that I only played one end of the stick. And would he please remove his hand from that stick. Realizing that he had compromised his manhood by confiding in me, I was challenged to meet him behind the rec. hall in the morning. Sure, why not? This would be interesting.

In the morning, we walked to the rear of the compound and squared off. Not believing that he was serious, I ran my mouth. Before the phrase, "You couldn't beat me with a stick" was finished, the bastard hit me. The punch wasn't really much, but the word stick tends to place the upper lip over a canine tooth. Realizing that my lip was split, I swung back only to find air where he had once stood.

The prick had hit me and then run away. Chasing him past F-Dorm, I realized just how stupid this looked. My mouth bled like hell, and he was a lot faster then I was. Trying to save some dignity, I used my shirt to soak up the blood and walked to the infirmary where an MT used fourteen stitches to reassemble my lip. Then they stuck me in the box. Two days later, they locked up my opponent. We agreed to give it six weeks before Round Two.

Six weeks to the day, we went behind the rec. hall before morning count. This time it was a more balanced fight, probably because he didn't run away. To be honest he had a slight edge on me, since we were boxing and not fighting. The fight ended when the count whistle blew. He went back to G-Dorm and I to B (where they had re-assigned me after the first fight).

This last conflict satisfied me a little, but not enough to even things for the scar on my lip. I heard from friends how Smity had been running his mouth around the compound about the second fight. Of course, his version told of a great battle, with him left the victor. As people made it a point to check on my condition, it became apparent to the general population that I showed no more damage then he did.

If anyone asked, I would respond with, "Do I look beat up to you? It was just a bullshit fight, and we came out even, no big deal." This greatly diminished the effect Smity was looking for. Instead of building his reputation by fighting a real cracker/ oldcock, he was making himself a fool and a liar in the eyes of his own peer group. The more he ranted and raved that he beat my ass the less respect the brothers gave him.

I could easily have announced his attraction to white dick, but that would appear as a cheap shot on my part. Besides a fag knows what he is, confrontation doesn't really hurt them much. Rather than expose my adversaries little secret to the general population, I elected to let him bury himself, and hurt him where it mattered most.

Smity dreamed of being a boxer. He spent every free moment he had in the gym working out. In his simple mind, an ex-con could compete professionally. A televised Boxing match from a prison had further fueled these illusions. This was his dream, his reason for getting out, the thing I would take away from him.

The more he ranted and raved about the second fight, the less people wanted to hear about it. Smity had become obsessed with his own lies. He would have to try me again, and I knew what was coming. But this time I had a plan.

We scheduled the final fight for early in the morning behind the rec. hall. The rules were no weapons or back up. I knew that he would have to bring someone with him to witness the fight this time. And true to my predictions, one of his partners was slinking around the backside of F-dorm, waiting until the fight was well under way to make an appearance.

The physical part lasted a half minute. He started slow, saving his strength for when his partner showed up. I came out with everything, knocking him down with the third punch. He looked up, surprised that I'd waste so much energy in the beginning of what was supposed to be a long boxing match. I then struck at his heart by saying, "If you think you're a boxer, you better find another dream, because I just knocked your ass down, and I ain't no boxer. Your best bet is to stick with plumbing or you'll starve on the streets"! He replied, "That wasn't shit, I tripped, the fight ain't over yet"! "Yeah, it's over, because I'm not playing the fight game any more. You can tell your friends any story you like about today, but if you ever come to me with this BULL SHIT again, I'm gonna do something to you. In your sleep or from behind you with an equalizer, I will hurt you! I'm not playing this SHIT anymore"!

Turning my back on Smity and hopping over the low wall, I noticed his friend had been listening from around the corner.

Now my revenge was complete, even Smittys' best friend would doubt him. The very person he brought with him as a witness would subconsciously underline whatever story they decided to tell about this day at a later date. To my surprise, I never heard another word about it. A month or so later, Smity moved into the other end of B-Dorm. We never spoke, or acknowledged each other's presence again. Not even during the riot.

Near the end of 1981, the compound reconstruction was complete. K-Dorm stood in the center of the camp. This new dorm had three two-story wings that housed the Juveniles, Admin.Confinement and the check-ins downstairs. One upstairs wing was reserved for the Honor Inmates. All of the cells resembled two man rooms with steel doors that could be locked electronically from the control room, the control center was located at the junction of the wings that formed a T. Along with the extra bunks K-Dorm produced, the administration focused their efforts on packing more of us together in the old dorms. Each cube had two more bunks added and rumor had it that we might go to double bunks.

In the larger dorms, this created chaos. With only a couple of hours designated at night for showers, few of us had the luxury of hot water. The chow hall, originally designed for five hundred couldn't keep up with the seven hundred plus inmates that passed through the doors for their three meals a day. Some nights the chow hall would run out of food and turn the last one or two dorms away, claiming that the shortage was caused by people from the previous dorms eating twice. Even the once impressive weekend brunch meal went to hell. They would make enough to feed two hundred guys. When something ran out the bosses would make another hundred eggs or biscuits. This would take half an hour while everyone waited. Once another fifty were served the bacon would run out, and everyone waited while the process repeated it self.

An old man that had been a bookkeeper on the streets juggled the books for the kitchen. His once very productive accounting business was now as dead as the wife he caught cheating on him. He was a clever old man that knew everything that went on in the kitchen. Very few of the guys spoke to him because of his expanded vocabulary and short temper, but being a loner with few people to relate too, he took the time one day to explain to me how the books worked.

The state allotted every compound a yearly budget based on the number of inmates it held. This yearly amount did not increase automatically. Any additional amount requested with the exception of building improvement had to be justified. This meant that the books would be audited in each department before an increased allotment per inmate could be approved.

Some of the department heads had been pocketing some rather large kickbacks by contracting through family members or friends for outside supplies. Rather than risk losing this invisible income, the department heads decided not to request additional funds for almost four years. The state awarded bonuses to these same department heads for staying within the budget, and praised DeSoto for their thriftiness.

During construction, when DeSotos population dropped below 450 the allotment for the 600 inmates caused a minor surplus. With construction complete, the population surged to over 700. Now subtract 3 percent yearly inflation, times four years and something has to give. By the old accountant's calculations, we would run out of food within the next three months.

Football season was ending. With the constant hunger that gnawed at everyone's stomach, the playoffs offered a welcome relief. This was the time that everyone could gather in the now over packed TV rooms, and for a few hours forget about our enemies sitting just a few feet away. The cops found a way to screw this up by calling extra long counts that left us sitting in our bunks, sometimes for hours.

My cynical friend Jeff insisted on a theory that they had formed a group called the "Inmate Harassment Committee." This select group of Boss men would meet once a day and come up with some way of agitating the general population. One day they would turn guys away from the chow hall for shabby haircuts, the next day it would be for missing top buttons from our shirts. The normal workday or non-football night counts were never more than fifteen minutes long. But every game night count would last from one to three hours. Jeff's theory would make sense, if there were something to be gained by packing us together, starving us, and then rattling our cage. The motivation behind the guard's actions eluded us.

B-Dorm was located closest to the chow hall alongside the fence. Whenever possible the majority of us stayed outside to play chess, learn some guitar, wrestle, or even on one occasion hold chicken fights. The superintendents house was located twenty feet away from the north end of our dorm on the other side of the fence. Sometimes we could see his wife peering out through a curtain at us, drink in hand, while her kid took shots at us with a BB gun.

The general rumor was that the Super had been banging a female sergeant while his wife turned to the bottle for company. The guards resented this woman sergeant screwing her way to the top and displayed their opinion by writing graffiti on various walls of the compound, using her first name (Linda) with the Supers' last name for president. At this point, we could care less about the freemen's little affairs but the word came down that the Super was going on a trip for two weeks and leaving this inexperienced woman in total command of the compound.

The guards grew meaner as the populations' tension swelled beyond the boiling point. This volatile combination lacked only the smallest spark to set it off. It was obvious that something had to give.

After waiting two years trouble free, the parole man paid me another visit. He informed me that because of my good behavior, he was recommending a year and a half reduction on my estimated time. Somehow, the idea of serving eleven years instead of thirteen didn't get him the joyous reaction he expected. But I was polite and performed my ritual washing of the hands afterward.

The possibility of escape had once again entered into the equation. There was no way in hell I could make it on the street after serving over a decade. My memories of the street were fading into non-existence. Once these were gone there would be only one world left for me, and it wasn't the streets. If that happened then they win and I lose. I'd rather be dead then be dependent on the state!

I had some bullets that a friend found in a cop car they were fixing over in the body shop. My shop had all of the machinery I needed to make a two-shot weapon out of a steel block I'd been saving. Common sense was losing ground in my decision making process. No one had ever successfully escaped from here. Even the two brothers that got away using the pillowcases had been captured in the Carolinas two years later. Being caught would mean an additional fifteen years added to my sentence and negate the six years I'd already served. By the same token, I couldn't let them starve me to death either. My nights became filled with visions of running through air as thick as molasses while the gun trucks surrounded me, my homemade gun malfunctioning as they opened fire. A long time ago, this same type of dream warned me about doing the robbery and I'd ignored it. Maybe this wasn't a good time to make such a desperate decision. It seemed prudent to wait a couple of weeks and then decide, after I'd cooled down a bit. Within that week, something happened that distracted me from my plans to escape.

January 10, 1982

I don't recall the teams that were playing that night but most of us had money bet on a particular game football game. Besides a long secure count, the ten o'clock count had been stretched to 11:50. As everyone piled back into the TV room to watch the end of the game we were informed that, they were still going to have a midnight count in ten minutes.

The noise grew louder in the dorm as we all complained and asked the dorm Boss to call the LT. Office to see if they could at least give us a half hour delay on midnight count to finish watching the game. The answer was NO! It wasn't just our Dorm that got loud, the whole compound yelled out with seven hundred voices emphasizing our inability to take any more of this mistreatment.

The sound from the other dorms seemed to increase in volume, as if somehow growing closer. Ten minutes later at midnight, the phones began ringing in every dorm simultaneously. Our dorm Boss put the phone to his ear then let it drop to the floor as he ran out the door. We could see him continue up the inside perimeter road towards the front gate along with the rest of the guards running in the same direction.

Then we saw hundreds of shadows coming to life, sweeping across the compound like a cloud of locust, but instead of a loud buzzing, the victorious sound of war cries filled the air, rattling the very buildings themselves. "It's a riot"! And "B-Dorm, Lets ride," could be heard amongst the roar! Funneling out the door, B-Dorm merged with the mob that had taken control of the compound.

We dragged the benches and TVs out into the yard between the dorms and finished watching the game. The canteen had been sacked and people were distributing munchies to everyone watching the game.

In the beginning it was more like a party than a riot, Guys were on the phones calling home to tell their families about what was happening, the tear-gas shot over the fence was laughingly thrown back over at the cops. We watched one guy emerge from the kitchen with a quarter of a pig thrown over his shoulder, he did two laps around the chow hall just as happy as could be until he realized that his frozen prize was uneatable. Everyone was having a good time for the first couple of hours until the first announcements began coming over the P.A. system.

Institutional policy for the control of riots dictates that the first priority is to contain the perimeter. This means to surround the compound with armed corrections and law officers to make sure that no one gets out. The next priority is to prevent damage to state property once the perimeter is secure. The Lieutenant's office all the way up to the record room was already burning when the first rioters reached that position, and no attempt was made to retrieve this ground. The front gate was too narrow for the riot squad to effectively enter in numbers, and the tear-gas was virtually ineffective in this large an open area.

The unwritten policy in a situation like this is to force the inmates into as small an area as possible. Before long, the inmates will form groups and gangs sorted by county of origin and race. Packed together in a small area and already caught up in a mob mentality, vicious fighting breaks out over territory and the opportunity for uninterrupted revenge. Once everyone wears themselves out, the guards can enter the picture and reestablish order. In this way, the guards are forgotten as the enemy and recognized as an authority figure.

The female Sergeant left in charge had no idea of how to handle this situation, nor did the Assistant Super, but the secretary of corrections who'd been visiting a nearby camp stepped in with a plan. His announcement came over the speaker system: "All inmates not participating in the riot have fifteen minutes to report to the rec. field, anyone remaining on the compound after fifteen minutes will be shot"! This message was repeated over and over again, along with the minutes remaining until the deadline.

Large groups started forming at the rear of the compound at the gate to the rec. field, now ringed with over a hundred armed Bosses, SWAT and police. Everyone went to the rec. field. The check-ins that had been hiding in K-Dorm and yelling things out the windows about our mothers had been unwillingly liberated by angry inmates, beaten unconscious, and been dragged out to the rec. field by their proud captors like trophies. Some fates are worse then death and those check-ins were about to learn this fact the hard way.

I was with a group of about forty whites from B-Dorm. We formed a circle around our property and boys with the strongest of us on the outer ring. Bob and Frank were next to me. I tended to have my doubts about their ability to fight, but I told them what was coming. Being in a race riot in high school had taught me a few things about what was coming and I informed the gang what to expect. "Pick your enemy and hit as many of them from behind as you can, because you'll never get the chance to see who hits you." This advice was questioned, but absorbed by all.

After about an hour of watching the snitches being singled out and run down like mad dogs, I went to sleep telling the guys to wake me up if anything happened. It seemed like only moments later that someone woke me and said we were moving to the Southeast corner of the Rec. Field where the Whites were forming an army.

Still in a daze, I could see large fires scattered in no particular order. Boom boxes blasted out what sounded like tribal music while the Blacks danced around the fires as if performing a ritual to some long forgotten gods. The blacks were currently forming their own army on the black top where we had made camp.

During my nap, our group had decided that we were better off joining the other groups of whites organizing at the other end of the field. We were fifty feet away from our old spot when I noticed that Frank and Bob had been overlooked, and still lay asleep not far from one of the fires. I told Jeff I was going back to wake them up and took off in a half Jog.

Putting my property and guitar down, I shook the two of them awake. Noticing a strange and sudden silence, I looking up and realized we were surrounded. Loaded with Demerol and other drugs robbed from the infirmary, some with kitchen knives, others with clubs, I stood facing a small army of about thirty Blacks. The two guys I had just awakened hadn't reached their feet yet and couldn't be counted on for much even in the best of shape.

A Zambuzi warrior grabbed my guitar as I grabbed the neck of the instrument. The guy to his left half-assed kicked me in the balls; he dropped to his knees as I returned the gesture with a vengeance. As the Zambuzi dropped the guitar to the ground I hay-makered him upside his head, dropping him like a stone. The numbers before me seemed to swell like a wave of bodies rolling up to the shore. They were pissed of that I'd reduced their army by two. I was suddenly very alone. I was already a dead man; these morons facing me just hadn't managed to stop my heart yet. But it was OK, I'd die with honor while attacking them. The state would be cheated out of their life sentence, and my soul would be free to haunt the judge and prosecutor that caused this situation. If I could only figure out which direction Ft. Lauderdale was in, it would be perfect.

Reaching into my pocket, I slid my finger into the loop of my combination lock like a set of brass knuckles and attacked the nearest one to me. As my fist closed in on his face, the lights went out. This was the real thing, not just some premonition induced by a T-shirt covering my eyes. Fighting blind, I had no idea of how the fight was going. Maybe I was dead, maybe I was winning.

There was only the vacuum of blackness. Everything seemed to have suddenly disappeared and become insignificant. The riot, the compound, even my friends had all ceased to exist. I saw no white light to head towards, and heard no sound to follow. Time held no meaning as I floated weightless in this endless expanse of night. So this is what being dead is all about, I found it rather relaxing to leave my physical form and dissolve into the void.

Wait a minute! What about the Judge and Roberts? I couldn't let them get away with what they had done! There must be a way to will myself back to Ft. Lauderdale where I could haunt them to the end of their days. Suddenly a loud buzzing seemed to surround me. Then the darkness gave way to a hundred distant pinpoints of light, like stars. They were stars. That meant that I was back. But where was Ft. Lauderdale?

A shadow flashed between the stars and myself. I'd just became aware that this was the first time in six years I'd seen stars. It seemed almost sinful not to take a few minutes from my mission to appreciate the view. Once again something flashed by me. The loud buzzing that had surrounded me seemed almost understandable; it now sounded like an army of voices shouting different things simultaneously. The shadowy figure from before began to dance back and forth before me like a curious ghost. The shadow took on the shape of a hand followed by the face of Frank. I asked Frank if he was dead too.

Frank said, "Don't be pissed man, me and Bob tried to back you up sooner but you jumped right into the middle of those guys. We thought you were dead"!

Frank explained that I wasn't dead, just hurt real bad. Some cowardly Bastard had clocked me in the head from behind with a fence post. When I kept swinging blindly a second blow to the head took me down. They told me that I laid there with my eyes open for almost five minutes while Frank and Bob stood back to back to protect what they thought was my corpse.

The B-Dorm gang had come back to rescue us, chasing the dark minions back into the anonymous night. I was paralyzed, and something was very wrong with my head, I'd been knocked senseless before but never like this. Frank and Bob took turns carrying me to the gate where the cops were now accepting casualties. Our trip to the gate seemed to take an eternity. As my two friends carried me, I could hear the sounds of fighting and the screams of the tortured. The cops came through the gate as a mob and dragged the wounded out two at a time. As the sun came up the casualties grew. Razor cuts, smashed faces, stab wounds, and one guy with a file sticking out of his back. It had slid along his ribs under the skin; he was too scared to pull it out.

Then the five worse casualties began to appear. Unrecognizable clumps of smoking flesh, you couldn't tell they were once human. Gang raped by seventy Blacks, these boys had their teeth knocked out or broken and all of their body hair burned off with butane lighters. Naked and charred their faces were beaten into such a mottled mass that you couldn't tell where their eyes, ears or mouth were if not for the blood trickling from these general areas. A mixture of semen and blood had congealed on their various orifices.

I was appalled. I'd seen rapes, dead bodies, and some mutilations, but everything together paled in comparison to these bodies that lie a few feet from me. As much as I've hated an enemy and wished the worse for someone, I could never do this kind of damage to anyone. Then someone noticed that they were still alive. I had to turn my head at that point.

The Welding Boss had recognized me and tried to put me in one of the ambulances, but I insisted that the burnt ones go first. Four of them were loaded up and taken away before the Assistant Super could stop them. He called on the gun trucks to head off the ambulance and make them return the injured. This was to keep the public from finding out how bad the situation had become. A news helicopter from channel nine was ordered to land and their film confiscated as evidence for crimes committed on the rec. field. No more ambulances were allowed in. We all clumped together with the one remaining burnt body waiting for some medical attention that never came.

Just before noon, they told us anyone needing a doctor would be escorted up to the front gate. That was where we went next, carrying some of the badly wounded with us. The sounds of fighting faded off into the distance as we walked towards the front of the compound. It was Five o'clock in the evening when an MT stuck his head in to check on us.

By now that kick to my groin had become very uncomfortable, but that barely compared to my head, which now felt like a dozen dull chisels had been driven into my brain with wooden mallets. I went down the list of wounded for the MT, trying to explain how urgently the burned guy needed attention.

The fat pudgy faced MT got in my face saying that I had no business telling him what to do, and that if we hadn't ransacked the infirmary then maybe he could do something for us. But now we'd just have to suffer and as far as he was concerned we could all do the world a favor and die! "Die like the scumbags you are"! He then went on to threaten to kick all of our asses before I told him to get out of my face. "Who do you think you are talking to me like that . . . INMATE"? With a little more aggression, I asserted, "I'm a CONVICT, if you see an inmate in this room, then you should suck his DICK! Now either do something for us or get your fat, sorry ass out of here"! The guys that were able got to their feet and agreed. Fat-Boys pig like eyes glazed over with fear as he backed out of the room. He tried to get a sergeants attention by accusing us of threatening him but he was ignored like the slug he was.

Half an hour later, a lieutenant came by to tell us that anyone requesting protective custody could stay, all others were to report to their assigned dorms. The infirmary would be open in the morning for any injuries that needed attention. Once again, I tried to explain how bad the burnt guy was, but the Lt. didn't want to hear it.

It was eight-teen hours since the riot started. The sun was going down as I stood outside of B-Dorm. Waiting for secure count, my friends filled me in on what I'd missed. The riot had started in my old home "The Getto." When G-Dorm refused to leave the TV room, a sergeant was called down to quell the rebellion.

Turning off the TV, he announced, "If anyone doesn't like it, they can take it to the Lt.'s office." Someone said maybe we'll do just that. Then the words "G-Dorm, let's ride some Crabs" rang out from the back of the TV room. This inspired the contents of G-Dorm to spill out of the TV room door and head to the Lt. Office to express their dissatisfaction with the recent count procedures. Before getting halfway to their destination, the evacuation of all corrections officers was ordered by phone.

Upon reaching the Lt. Office front door, they found the steel door barred from the inside, and the records room already on fire. Breaking down the side door to gain entrance they saw piles of books aflame and the rest of the offices deserted. It seemed that the accounting books were among those burned. The rest of the story I was familiar with except for the fighting that took place most of the following day.

My head was seriously messed up. Besides the unbearable throbbing and dizziness, both eyes felt as if they'd explode when exposed to any kind of light. Concerned friends mentioned that sleep could lead to a coma with the kind of hit I'd taken to the head. Under the circumstances, a coma couldn't be worse than this. Trying to avoid sleep, I was sitting out in front of B-Dorm with my friends when I met three new guys that I instantly took a liking to.

Most new cocks have it pretty tough, but these guys were part of a late night drop off stranded at the Lt.s Office when the riot started. All three were from Lauderdale, making them homeboys. Perry was a tall, thin, frizzy blond headed Jew. He'd basically led the other two thru the riot, then afterwards took advantage of the confusion by scribbling bunk assignments on scraps of paper to get the bunks he and the other two preferred.

289

"Waldo" (not his real name), was a blond haired, blue eyed, stocky guy, with a very quiet demeanor, that could smile while he cut your throat. The third one, Nicky was frail and weak looking, also known as the kissing bandit of Lauderdale. He liked to burglarize homes, kiss the sleeping girls before exiting, and leave a single rose as a calling card. Waldo picked G-Dorm to stay in, while Perry and Nicky liked B-Dorm.

That evening Perry kept sending Nicky to the dorm canteen for sweetie goals. I told him that was gonna cost a fortune between riot markup and interest. Perry said, "don't worry about it, the kid has money." Yeah but that's kinda taking advantage. Perry said, "If I don't take it than someone else will, might as well be a friend that will look out for him than a total stranger." I agreed, then asked if there were any granola bars.

Early next morning I found myself standing in a very long line outside the infirmary. The guy in front of me still had a file sticking out of his back. I offered to pull it out but he declined the gesture, saying that he wanted a doctor there in case something came out with it that wasn't supposed to.

They turned most of us away without treatment. As we neared the door, we had the opportunity to experience their selection process. The MT asked the file man if the steel had penetrated the ribs. When he responded, "no" he was told that they were only taking wounded with internal injuries. And that he would have to return the file since he was in the possession of contraband. He asked the MT if he could just pull it out for him". They told him that the wound just wasn't serious enough for their attention, and to stop holding up the line.

They instructed me to watch the call outs for the next few days until my name came up for x-rays. My name never appeared. When I asked what happened to my x-rays, they told me they had no record of me visiting the infirmary, besides if I lived this long it probably wasn't that serious!

For the next week, officers lined the walkways whenever we left the dorms. Similar to walking through a gauntlet, we were marched single file in a Black/White order. The local newspaper described the riot as a minor disturbance that involved a small part of the population at DeSoto. This minor rebellion was squashed within a half-hour with few casualties and minor fire damage, according to the DOC press release.

This incident would always be referred to as a "Minor Disturbance". During the riot, four of the five, burnt boys had been dragged from protective custody. The state having failed to protect them, gave them an undisclosed amount to keep their mouths shut. They were released soon after recovering.

The fifth guy had been mistaken for someone else, but since he wasn't in protective custody, they patched him up and shipped him to an easy camp. Only a few of the guys that participated in the torture were ever prosecuted. They released all but one to the streets awaiting trial. The one that was found guilty received one and a half years. The one inmate that made the statement "Lets Ride Some Crabs"' was blamed for all of the damage to property and persons and was never heard from again.

Money was pumped into DeSoto for weeks, to cover the extra expenses for personnel and reconstruction. We ate better food and more of it for almost two months. The budget was revised without an audit, since the accounting books were destroyed in the fire at the Lt.'s office.

For weeks after the "Minor Disturbance", bright light continued to give me headaches and dizzy spells. The infirmary told me that if I had a problem then I should have told them when it happened, not afterwards. No records could be found of any previous complaints I'd made and after being turned away half a dozen times, I gave up trying to get help. Along with the headaches came a short temper, which manifested itself one day in the shop with a rather slow Boy we called Elmer Fudd.

A lot of guys had been shipped out during the few weeks after the riot. Most of the new arrivals had come straight from RMC. The majority of these new cocks were to become either punks or snitches. Fudd was of the later category. After twice explaining a certain technique to the shop, Elmer Fudd stood through both explanations and asked what I was doing. "What does it look like I'm doing, Fudd"? "Looks like you're screwing something up to me"! Was his reply. I took off after his fat ass with a steel breaker bar in my hand. The boss intercepted us and read me the riot act. An argument ensued that ended with me walking out of the shop and getting an immediate job change to electronics repair, where my friends Jeff, Fred, Bob and Frank worked. Now this was a cool job.

Our main task was to fix the smashed TVs and repair the control panels that were destroyed in K-Dorm during the Minor Disturbance. Only the Boss man worked on the actual Paraguard, which was still considered top secret. Any information on how it worked was kept from us at all costs. But Jeff managed to get a hold of the Blueprints, and filled us in on how it worked.

Jeff had been trading various pieces of equipment to the Auto Body shop Bossman for computer stuff. The Personal computer hadn't yet become a reality but the first ancestor called a Timex Sinclair was starting to appear in some homes.

It consisted of a small touch pad that stored information on a cassette. Expanding the memory required a patch cord and a memory attachment. A seventy five-ohm cable fed the TV that served as our monitor. Jeff had found a way to expand the memory even more, and tied it into an electric typewriter keyboard. He immediately began to alter the few programs that were available.

One game he designed after an already existing game with different graphics, Jeff's new version was called Blac Man. There were a bunch of watermelon shaped dots in a maze with a set of lips eating them. At random points hooded looking characters would chase the lips. Boss Hog out of Auto Body Paid a pretty good price for that one. Jeff also made a space game that took three people at separate screens to play.

One boring afternoon we caught nearly a hundred tree frogs for what we referred to as G-force experiments. After clamping a piece of conduit in a vise, we'd place the "frog-o-naughts" into a capsule shaped projectile, load the capsule into the base of a conduit pipe, and launch them at a target on the far side of the shop. Using 120 psi. From our compressor, we had created a high velocity frog cannon. No one could figure out if it was G-force or Impact that caused the fatalities, so the experiment had to be retried until our source of volunteers dried up. One thing we didn't consider was the stench of a hundred frogs splattered all over the walls.

Even with these new forms of entertainment, I'd grown bored with the electronics shop. The thought of other people enjoying the shop I'd built had been gnawing at the back of my thoughts since leaving small engines. I had to take back what was mine, but it wouldn't be easy. First, an apology would have to made to my old Boss for my actions. That would be the easy part. The hard part would be dealing with Fudd, who'd been made a Voc. Aide along with Billy. Billy was actually a good mechanic, but Fudd being the snitch that he was, had turned the shop into two different groups. This had become an "Us or Them" situation with the class on one end of the shop and the aides at the other. It would take some pretty creative thinking on my part to undo the social damage that Fudd had caused.

THE SUN GOD

Small Engine shop had moved to a long metal Quonset hut at the end of the Voc. building. Large bay doors opened at each end to let the equipment in at the back, and air in through the front. In the middle was the Bosses desk and bathrooms. Workbenches separated the tool room and maintenance area from the rest of the shop leaving a narrow walkway between the two. Students were no longer allowed to get anywhere near the equipment, leaving Billy to do all of the work while Fudd checked out the tools and brown nosed with the boss.

Fudd had a lot of self-serving ideas that the Boss would implement as quickly as this leach could come up with them. This created a rather large chasm of resentment between the class and maintenance areas. Billy viewed my return as a threat to his job security and Fudd had been reinforcing this idea. Fudd had tried every trick in the book to prevent my return and the Boss made it clear that he didn't like my presence in small engines.

I was no longer allowed in my own tool room, which now had a sign hanging on the door declaring, "Fudds Room Only". They also let me know that any attempt at giving Fudd a hard time or causing him physical harm would lead to my immediate removal. The Boss was sewn up tight.

Attacking the snitch directly would not do the trick; the Boss valued Fudds' usefulness over my own. Neutralizing Fudd and making myself King of the Hill would be no small feat. This required some creative thought.

Experience dictates that any formula requires an understanding of the elements available. There was only one Bossman, as powerful as he may be, there were over a dozen other people in the shop. Without the class half of the shop we had no use for an instructor. The Boss wasn't doing his job as an instructor; he viewed his position as a glorified baby sitter. As long as Billy and myself kept the equipment running and the class passed their once a week tests he'd met his quota.

Most of the guys in the class were people I knew from the Lauderdale and Miami cliques, including Perry and Waldo. After any repairs were done, I'd hang out with them at the table towards the front of the shop. One day my classroom friends gave me the ultimatum that a choice would have to be made. I could hang with the guys in the class or the Voc. Aides, but not with both. My response was simple.

"I work back there, that's my job. My friends are up here and this is where I choose to be. Billy is a good guy that hates Fudd as much as the rest of us, but you guys forced him to be associated with Fudd. No one can force me to hang with that scumbag. I'll talk to anyone I want, and hang with anyone I want to hang with. No one tells me what to do. If you can't deal with who I hang with, then I don't need your ass around me".

I thought the whole bunch of them were going to jump me until Waldo decided to back me up saying, "My homeboy is right, no one can tell him what to do. If anyone don't like it then you'll have to fight both of us"! Within a few minutes, everyone agreed to accept my opinion. I had made myself the link between the two sides, but this was a temporary remedy at best. Something was needed that would unite both sides of the shop, something that would apply to everyone, regardless of natural avarice.

The only thing that could cover that much ground was religion. Christianity wouldn't serve my purpose, My plan required the birth of a new God, or maybe a very old one!

That weekend we watched an old Mummy movie on creature feature and the God of small engines was born! The crusades, Guyana, and Hitler all have one thing in common, the belief in an idea, and the need to be a part of something bigger than the individual. The need to belong to a group you can call your own; a group of people like yourself that can make judgments on everybody else. Once these needs have been met, everyone inside the cult becomes superior to anyone outside.

Race and language create their own barriers, drawing obvious lines between opposing groups. But in this particular case, the walls of the shop would serve as the line separating us from everyone else. Once this new border was established, the rift between the two sides of the shop would loose its significance. This would have to take place in two parts. First was to initiate interest and understanding of an icon. Next was to establish a ritual that everyone could relate to. One that would attract the attention of the whole shop. This would be the easy part.

Sitting at the table one day, I asked what anyone knew about Ra. Some smart-assed replies were made, but everyone agreed that the name sounded familiar. "You know, like in the mummy movies. Not the mummy but the God that gave the mummy life"! Someone made the remark that the whole Ra thing was some crap someone thought up for the movies. This sparked a debate over the reality of a deity versus a fictional character. I argued that Ra was worshipped before the Jews ever wrote the Bible, making Sun worship the first true religion.

Judaism was a secondary belief that had spent thousands of years trying to cover up its true origins. "Moses was trained to be the king of Egypt. This meant that he was the only one to be taught the kings magic. When he did the snake turning into a staff thing, and his snake ate the other magicians snakes, they didn't say his god was greater. They said his magic was. All of the plagues and curses were caused by the magic he'd been taught while he worshipped Ra. He just used it to help out his own people"! This proves that Egyptian Magic is more powerful than Yawehs. I'd caught their interest, the debate would continue after the guys had a chance to check out the Library.

The next day, a more informed group discussed the plausibility of there being some truth to my claims. Different guys contributed what they had learned to the group, but no one saw any real benefit in pursuing the topic much further. It looked like my plan had faltered before it got off the ground.

Later in the afternoon, Dean found a rather large bug with a long spike hanging off its mug. This proboscis dripped something we referred to as venom. Not knowing if it was poisonous, we'd been batting it around the table at each other for entertainment. Then someone said, "Let's kill it before someone gets bit". Someone else said, "Lets kill it for Ra"! It was only proper that we'd sacrifice it by fire and perform some kind of ceremony. Otherwise, we'd just be roasting a bug. Making a paper box soaked in mineral spirits, we placed the sacrifice on a dirt mound out back. Wearing a sheet from the rag box across my shoulders, I said a few words asking the Great Sun God Ra to accept our sacrifice and bestow great powers upon us, his loyal followers. We lit the holy fire and chanted Ra Ma-Ra

Ma, until the last flame went out. Returning to our class table, we then analyzed the experience.

This became a daily routine that drew the attention of some of the other shops. Within a few weeks, we had forty loyal followers. Advancing from bugs to small reptiles, the sacrifices grew in frequency and attendance. Snakes were fairly common on the compound; we had no shortage of offerings to Ra.

It was a rather messy ceremony at first with the snake jumping out of the fire a couple of times, before the idea of tying it in a knot occurred to us. Any snakes that were caught for sacrifice were deposited in a wooden box dubbed the "snake pit". Every Temple should have a snake pit. And Voc. Small Engines being the Temple of Ra had one too.

Some Christians came down to condemn our practices only to have stuff fly off the wall at them when they claimed Ra was a false God. Be it coincidence or the power of our belief it definitely strengthened our resolve. Besides the daily ritual, we found other forms of entertainment.

One kid in the shop was AJ. Sometimes referred to as GQ, he had some rich street fag that would come and throw money at him every weekend in the visiting park. I had corralled the boy in my tool room and pried out the story of how he was a poor kid that the fags had turned out. He'd met this fag gang when he was fourteen. They'd get him high and drunk, and even laid.

They advanced to blowing him or "what ever", then promising him a share of their wealth, conned him out of his ass. He didn't give blow jobs, and I never could corn hole a boy, so I settled on occasional hand jobs from him to keep his secret.

An ugly flaming sissy named Brandy had seen the boy in the gay clubs in Tampa a few years back, and was making accusations about AJ that threatened to expose him. My solution to this predicament was to stage a boxing match between these two out in my shop. Fish was a heavyset black guy and a devout worshiper of Ra that hated Brandy and genuinely like AJ. Besides giving the boy some boxing lessons, he offered to sucker punch Brandy from behind when AJ threw a punch. All the boy had to do was get Brandy positioned during the fight so that his opponents back was to Fish.

The fight was comical at best. We'd drawn a crowd of more than 50 guys and closed the bay doors to the shop. AJ threw one punch and tried to run away, but there was nowhere to run. Brandy had a good fight game going for her. She came at AJ with some serious punches. Once she pinned AJ into a corner, Fish gave the signal for our boy to throw the punch.

AJ moved his fist forward but pulled the punch back before making contact. Fish let go with a hard roundhouse that caught Brandy in the temple. Brandy dropped her hands, turned, and looked straight at Fish saying, "interfere again and you're next", then went back to pummeling AJ. A moment of silence followed this statement, "that's one tough bitch" was yelled out, followed by cheers for Brandy to kick our boys ass.

This was not going well at all. If AJ got hurt much more, he'd be removed from the shop and I'd loose my daily relief. I sent someone outside to wait a minute then return yelling "fire in the hole". Everyone piled out the back exit, and the day was saved, unlike AJ's reputation. From holding Boxing matches between Sissies to consuming purple mushrooms brought in from the cow pastures on the tractors we worked on. Every day brought some new attraction that could only be found in the Temple of Ra.

Being the high priest had its perks too. Anything that could contribute to the temple was brought to me first, for my opinion and approval. We had a couple of the sissies come down and dance for us on a few occasions. A vote was taken as to the usefulness of the sissies being made temple priestesses, but this idea was shot down since none of them were virgins.

Now I had a working shop. Billy and myself were teaching hands on repairs to the class. The guys in the shop felt that they belonged to something bigger than themselves, and since our influence had traveled beyond the walls of the temple, we felt that we had an obligation to maintain our position as the hub of our new belief. The bizarre and somewhat cruel ceremonies that we performed daily tended to keep followers from drifting away from the flock. But what about Fudd? Once the Boss saw how the shop had become more productive, he blew off his little snitch like the parasite that he was.

Some of the guys that had been released during this time had pursued successful careers in small Engine repair. When Tallahassee got wind of this, they gave the Bossman multiple special recommendations. This in turn allowed us to get Federal grant money to buy more teaching materials. I had become valuable to him while Fudd had become less of an asset. After running him out of the tool room, Fudd occupied a little chair next to the boss's desk, doing any paper work too monotonous for the Bosses attention. I had my shop back.

Dave was one of us to some degree. In his opinion, he didn't feel like he was one of us, since we were criminally inclined and he was there for vehicular homicide. According to Dave, he was playing Dukes of Hazard at two in the morning with the police, when he hit a teenaged girl on a bicycle. At over a hundred miles an hour the victim had disintegrated on impact. We'd tease him about having to pick the evidence out of his grill to cover his tracks, this upset him further fueling our harassment.

One afternoon we spent learning the finer points of tying a hangman's noose. One guy argued it required 13 loops and proceeded to tie one that way. A visiting Bossman saw this and told us it was a felony in Florida to have a noose in our possession, knocking half of the loops off, we'd secured it to the bay door as a means of pulling the door down.

On a dare, Dave had climbed up on a chair and put his head in the noose. Charley ran over and kicked the chair out from under him. We'd expected Dave's weight to pull the door down, instead the door jammed. He had the funniest look on his face while he hung there kicking, while we debated who was gonna get up off their ass and get him down. Charley put the chair back under him demanding payment for saving his life.

A few days after that Charley set Dave's shirttail on fire. I watched the flames climb above his head while he told Charley sitting behind him to put it out, since he started it. Of course, Charley refused and it turned it into a duck and roll technique as Dave tried to extinguish the blaze.

In general, we liked Dave and we were happy to hear that he might get a sentence reduction. When the newspaper came out announcing his release, the headlines read "Felon tells courtroom about prison horrors". The article went on to explain how Dave had been hung by the neck, and set on fire, barely escaping with his life. At first we were pissed, but if it got him out, than more power to him.

I frequently moved around the other shops during the day to visit my homeboys. Electronics was a common hang out with most of my friends down there, including Frank and Bob, (the two guys that stood over me in the riot). A new guy had shown up in the shop, Schooler. This kid was about 6'5 with a bad attitude and epilepsy. Epileptics can't get a license to drive unless they can prove they've gone 5 years without an attack.

He was a motor head and his parents were rich, so he drove anyway. When a cop caught him trying to get into his own car with a coat hanger after locking his keys in it, Schooler copped an attitude and hit the cop.

Only 17 years old, he thought he was bad or something. If not for his size, he'd already be someone's bitch. Jeff looked out for him in a free protection kind of way. The kid swore up and down that he didn't have seizures any more, but I'd seen him put his clothes down and duck into some bushes by the laundry. His feet shook with the ferocity of the seizure, poking out from behind the bushes. When he was done, he stood up, picked up his laundry and kept right on going.

Jeff had his boss take the kid on so he could watch him in electronics. One day he'd climbed up onto the top of the storeroom inside the electronics shop to get at a spool of wire, when he started doing the chicken. Falling head first, his head hit one table corner and bounced to another before hitting the concrete. Bob the Boy Scout jumped into action, trying to hold his head together. It had split from the middle of the forehead to top center. That's when Jeff walked up, carrying his laundry he had so neatly cleaned and folded. Bob reached for the clean white towels but Jeff ducked away and fetched some paper towels from the dispenser.

Guarding his laundry, Jeff handed Bob the paper towels and asked if his brains were exposed. Bob said he wasn't sure, then told Jeff to get some help. Instead of leaving, Jeff grabbed a couple of wires from a low power transformer and asked if they could try to make an arm or something move by applying 12 volts directly to the brain. Bob gave a dirty look and Jeff went for help.

I had walked in after seeing Schooler was carried out on a stretcher. I was just in time to hear Bob's description of the incident to the Sergeant. "I observed inmate Schooler fall from the attic after attempting to reach a spool of wire. He fell in a vertical position, passing the fuse panel at approximately 15 miles an hour; he then struck table A, then table B on the opposing corners then landed on floor C, where I began to administer First Aid. That was enough for me, I had to leave.

Schooler came back from the outside hospital looking like a cross between a clown and a monster, he wouldn't let them shave his whole head so that his blonde afro shot out from the middle of his head back. A huge Frankenstein like scar dominated the front of his head. I heard him crying to Jeff that some Zambuzi warriors were hitting him in the head trying to make him die. Thank God, he was Jeff's problem.

One day, the Ra thing got out of hand when the gang decided to sacrifice a Christian. Everyone in the shop had been enjoying the enormous good luck created by our ceremonies. It seemed like the larger the offering the better our luck. Some strange things had been happening with objects moving around on their own in front of everyone. If small animals and lizards brought this type of result, what about something bigger? The thought of human sacrifice had passed through my mind but had never been voiced. The other guys had come up with this one on their own.

We had a skinny black guy that represented the sole Christian resistance in small engines. They chased him around the building for almost an hour before I distracted them by pointing out that Ra wanted the birds in a nest that sat in the top of a frail tree just outside the rear door. By this time, everyone had worked themselves up to frenzy. Grabbing some large sharp rocks, they actually beat the tree down like stone-age men. The frenzy didn't dissipate until all of the birds lay dead in the embers still glowing on the ground at our feet. Everyone grew quiet and started staring at the ground as if too ashamed of their actions to look each other in the eye. Soon afterward, our Boss quit and the temple was dissolved. Three of us stayed in the shop to maintain the mowers. Billy and I did all of the work, while Fudd reported anything we did to the Voc. Coordinator.

This was about the time I met Norm. Norm didn't fall into any of the regular classifications, I really enjoyed his company as much as his services. This was the only fag that I ever called a friend. He could fight, he was pretty, and he could suck the chrome off a trailer hitch. Norm would come to see me in the shop a few times a week until he met Hutch. When the two of them met, they took an instant liking to each other. This chaingang affair would later turn out to be their undoing.

I'd waited a long time to get into the honor dorm. Each time an honor dorm resident left, I put in for a transfer, but never got it. One upstairs part of K-Dorm was reserved for the epileptics. After a few of them had seizures coming down the concrete steps, they were moved back to H-Dorm, by the infirmary. With ten new openings, the Voc. Coordinator managed to slip me in.

Honor and Death

K-dorm had two man concrete rooms with two steel bunks on the wall and a single commode. Each steel door had a door flap at face level, though our towels usually covered this. We had two heavy steel bookstands and a split wooden locker in the corner in each room. After living in open dormitories for years, this was real privacy. No wonder honor dorm residents stayed inside.

My first roommate was a young rich kid that was a decent guy. His older brother was also in Honor Dorm. They'd stolen cars together until the older brother was caught. This low life turned in his younger brother to get some time knocked off his sentence. They both hung out with a group of Dumb ass country boys that I never cared for much. Every day this group would meet in my room and wonder what to do for the day. Mumbling ideas for activities they'd walk in circles that grew smaller as the group formed a brain, then run off when they agreed on what to do.

Coming home from the shop one day, I found my old room mates stuff gone and some other guys stuff already moved in. Wherever he'd come from he must have been hated, because Bastard was written all over his property. Upon looking closer, I found an "o" after each bastard. Not realizing this was his name I called him Bastard with an "o" or simply room mate.

Roommate was a big dorky Mexican with a poor fitting upper plate that half slid out when he slept, adding to his already Neanderthal appearance. His idea of a good time was reading what weather was like in other countries or drawing pubic hair on the little girls in the mail order catalog. Unfortunately, he was affiliated with that dumb ass clique that liked to swarm in my room in search of a brain.

We were permitted two packages at Christmas, and two more during the year. My current package had a nice vintage guitar for band and some clothes, among them some dark blue socks. During the night after lights out, I'd washed them in the sink and set them out to dry. As I entered the dorm at lunchtime, the guards called me into the office.

"What's this we hear that you have hygiene issues?" the one guard asked. "What hygiene issues? I bathe at least once a day". "So you didn't wash your dirty socks in the sink and leave a mess in it?" he asked, between mouthfuls of state food he was chomping on from a cafeteria tray. "Well I really have no other way to wash personal laundry since I left the kitchen." Still eating he asked, "Why, what did you do in the kitchen?" "I'd put my cloths on the dish racks and run them through the dishwasher before running the plates through, while the water is still clean". The inquisitive cop looked at the tray he was eating from and started to gag. The other cop started laughing and told me not to do it again.

Running up the steps, I confronted my moron cellmate. He stuttered some stupid explanation that I was a hard person to talk to, and since he didn't want to fight he had to tell on me. I told him I wanted his snitching ass out of my cell. He refused to leave so I explained the new rules. We would not speak to each other unless absolutely necessary, he was not to touch anything of mine, or stay in the cell when my friends were over, and if I ever heard him discussing me in any way I'd do something to him while he slept. It took a few months to run him out, but in the meantime, I kept most of my business on the compound and out of the honor dorm.

I was with some friends over by H-Dorm talking about a new sissy that had come to DeSoto. During the conversation, she had come up to schedule an appointment with one of the guys sitting with us. Latin sissies are rare, and the pretty ones are even harder to come by. She had a provocative evil look in her eyes as she checked out the rest of us. After she walked away we all said "Damn, that bitch is hot, let us know what she's like tomorrow".

The next day we got our report, she was a pro, and a chaingang slut. Our friend had to wait his turn as 10 guys banged her on that first night and uncounted others received other favors of a sexual nature. He thought she might have given him something, and advised us to stay away from her until he went to the clinic to find out. Sure enough, on her first night she had spread Gonorrhea throughout the compound.

During orientation at RMC, they screen all newcomers for venereal diseases. What we didn't know was that the tests were limited to syphilis. Gonorrhea being well under control at the time in Florida and an added expense to test for, wasn't a concern to the state at the time.

Coming from Puerto Rico, this bitch had slipped though the system. This wasn't any old STD she brought with her but something a bit more sinister. After discovering a large group was infected, they rounded up everyone that had nailed her that weekend and anyone else that may have had contact with them. None of the antibiotics had any affect on the sissy and she began to get big open sores all over her.

They put her by herself in the first bottom cell in K-Dorm and burned everything that came out of that cell. We heard that the CDC was paying the institution for each case of this new virus they found. If you so much as had the flu you were locked up and given a barrage of medicines. Some kind of immune disease was all the information we could get. Whatever it was, it caused the sissies death within a few months. The compounds sexual activities slowed down a noticeable amount.

Over the next few months, my clique had acquired jobs as vocational aides and infiltrated honor dorm. Also about this time, I got into the band at the rec hall. I played rhythm guitar and sang back-up vocals well enough to play at the holiday jam for the compound with the existing band.

Bunkley played lead guitar and had a shit load of equipment and affect pedals he'd collected over the years. Tripping over the dozen or so wires and pedals he'd wrapped around himself, Bunkley struggled toward the stage they'd set up in front of the library. I'd already climbed up on the flatbed and stood in front of my mike empty handed, watching the lead guitarist hoist his accessories onto the stage.

Ten minutes into this wrestling match he walked up to his mike and asked me where my stuff was or if I planned to play at all. Into my mic, I called "Humphries". The already seated compound turned their heads to see a little sissy struggling to carry my guitar and accessories through the crowd and onto the stage. He laid the case out and placed the guitar on me, while symbolically wiping the neck of the instrument with a cloth. I looked at Bunkley and said, "Get you a roadie". The audience loved it.

Two separate bands played that day, one white and the other black. Besides that stage we also shared time in the band room for practice. We alternated the two or three week-night practices and each band had a whole weekend day. On our off days, I played an acoustic guitar that I kept in the dorm, which led to another small altercation with an old enemy.

At a team meeting, I was ordered to attend some counseling groups. These groups were mandatory before my release. The drug group was easy enough to handle. After going to three meetings the drug counselor told me, he'd pass me if I never came to group again. Human relations took a week to finish, and then there was AA.

Not only were the alcohol meetings boring, they interrupted my band nights. A Christian clique was in control of the Jaycees and the AA committees on the compound. I knew the head Christian was no saint, he'd been suspected of using the camera that was used to raise Jaycee funds for alternative purposes. My information was that he took naked pictures of the guys for their girlfriends and charged a substantial sum.

Being aware of this, I tried to find some way of blowing off my AA requirement. On various occasions, I tried to start a conversation with this guy, but basically I had nothing to offer him. The rule was one year in AA before a certificate and that was all he'd say about it.

The Local Jaycees were organizing a large function with the convict chapter. Over five hundred free people would attend this event, which included food and some kind of entertainment. The head Christian asked if I could do something mellow on acoustic with my homeboy Nick, who belonged to the inmate chapter. The other performer was our compound dentist, known as the Singing Dentist of Arcadia

Me and Nick practiced in the dorm for weeks. The day before the event, we took our guitars to the band room so we could check our volume settings on the PA equipment we'd be using for the show. Walking back into K-Dorm with our guitars we were stopped at the control room by Mr. Hays, who'd just made Lieutenant.

"What you all doing with those guitars in the dorm", he asked. "We're practicing for the Banquet they're having this week-end", I answered as I walked away from the control room towards my room. He turned up the PA "I know from the Major that no instruments are allowed in the dorm, including this one, now turn around and walk them guitars over to the rec hall where they belong".

This was the same moron that I had scammed on his first day as a CO1, and he was pissing me off. Not thinking I said, "Look, you don't run this dorm, and no one else has a problem with us keeping our instruments here, so just let it go, OK?" "But the Major..." I cut him off, The Major don't run shit either, just let it go". We put our guitars in our rooms and ran off to catch our job assignments.

We didn't get far when a voice announced our names over the PA, followed by, "report to the Majors office immediately"! We redirected our course towards the Majors office. I knew the last Major was demoted for stalking a sergeant's wife, and that the new Major hadn't been announced. I was a little curious who they picked to fill the position. Whoever it was I knew I could handle him. Opening the door, I was surprised to see "Yomans" sitting at the Majors desk.

"Now let me tell you two inmates something, I run this compound and everyone in it. That means I run you and I run you"! He shouted as he pointed at us in succession, "And as far as keeping your guitars in the dorm, you won't have to worry about that anymore because I've already reassigned you to the worse bunks on the compound! That will help you keep them guitars in the Rec Hall, where they'll be safe from the assholes you'll be bunking with. And, here's a couple of DR's for you boys to take with you.

I grabbed that moment to speak, "Yes Sir, You run me, and you run him, Hell you run the whole compound. Now I don't know what caused this misunderstanding..." He cut me off, "I'll tell you what caused it... it was your smart mouth. You ain't bullshittin your way out of this one Mr. no body, no murder. Yeah, I remember who you are! I told you there'd come a day when I'd have your ass"!

"Well Sir", I said, "it was my understanding that we had permission to practice in the dorm for the upcoming banquet we are supposed to play at. But I'll tell you what, before it causes me to lose my room in honor dorm I'd rather just send my guitar back home and forget about the whole thing. I'll go fetch my guitar right now and you can stick it in the property room. I'll give it to my folks when they come up this weekend".

God, that was about the weakest story I'd ever come up with, but he paused as a funny look came over his face. "You two are playing at the banquet this Saturday?" He asked. "Yes Sir, we were supposed to, but I don't see that happening now with my guitar going home tomorrow morning".

"You boys know that I was the one that put that together. The newspapers are gonna be there, they're expecting inmates to entertain them. I'll tell you what, you boys are going to entertain those folks Saturday, and you will keep them guitars out of the dorms. If I hear of either of you sneaking them in again, the instruments go and so do you, understand"?

The banquet went well, we gradually snuck the guitars back in, and a month later I received my AA certificate.

About this time, another red haired stepchild from Panama City had caught my interest, and Norm took this as a snubbing. Hutch had pulled some strings to get Norm into his cell across from mine in K-Dorm. It wasn't long before their intentions became obvious. I walked into the cell one day to find Norm wearing make-up and calling himself Norma. They had come up with a plan to take a truck from the Auto body shop and ram the back gate. Once on the Highway Norm would get all made up, and put on some women's clothing. This way the cops would overlook them, since the search would be for two men and not a couple. I mentioned that the truck might give them away, but they said they had that part covered.

Four times, they were set to go and I'd found some way of screwing up their plan or talking them out of it. But eventually they did it anyway. One day just before noon, the sound of a big engine could be heard racing next door, along with a bunch of guys yelling. A two-ton dump truck with Hutch at the wheel and Norm riding Shotgun came around the corner of my shop.

When they saw me, they slowed down and hollered for me to jump in the back. When I hesitated, Norm threw me his nametag as Hutch gunned the engine to gain momentum for the impact with the rear gate. Building up ramming speed, they struck the gate in the middle. The chain snapped like a piece of string as the gates flew open from the momentum of the heavy truck.

Everyone in both the maintenance and Voc. buildings ran out to yell their approval, as if we were cheering on a favorite football team. As we watched the truck with it's engine-racing turn the corner towards the highway, I could picture myself with them in the cab. God what a rush they must be having.

The truck hit State road 70 and headed East for five miles. The gun trucks couldn't pursue them with an open gate facing over two hundred riled up, close-custody inmates. This gave my friends the healthy head start they needed. Once they were fifteen miles from the camp, they pulled the truck across the highway, and flagged down the first car that came along. They told the elderly couple inside that there'd been a bad accident and they needed their car. When the owner of the car offered to give them a lift, they were promptly pulled from the car and left standing on the roadside. Escape carries up to fifteen years, but moving someone more then six feet against their will constitutes kidnapping. Kidnapping is a possible Life sentence, which they had no desire to have added to their sentence if they were caught.

Now heading West in the elderly couples' car, Norm and Hutch watched as the first group of gun trucks passed them in the opposite lane. This first group of gun trucks reached the old folks a few minutes later and radioed a vehicle description back to the second group of pursuit vehicles. Ford Courier trucks and a few state cars loaded to the hilt with guards and shotguns were just leaving the compound parking lot when they spotted the escapees vehicle passing the institution. Norm and Hutch didn't know the row of vehicles now following them were a posse.

After driving seven miles into the town of Arcadia, the two escapees sped into a grocery store parking lot to pick up another car. As they turned near the front entrance to make another pass through the parking lot, the guards opened fire in unison. The car was shot up like a pincushion while the storefront glass shattered and people ran or fell screaming. The DOC claimed that a few warning shots were fired into the air and that no one was hurt or put in danger by the state's actions. Those of us watching the news that night knew better than to believe anything we heard from them. On the TV, the shattered glass and eyewitnesses betrayed what really happened. The cops were hanging out of their vehicles shooting at the car Norm and Hutch had carjacked. After spraying the storefront, they walked up to the car and shot the hell out of it. Though neither sustained any injuries, both Norm and Hutch had a couple additional years added to their sentences and were shipped to other camps.

Some of our mutual friends were pissed at me for not having done something to stop them. They were under the opinion that I should have ratted them out or put their business on the street. That way, they would've gone to the box instead of getting more time. I felt no need to justify my actions. As a real friend, I did my best to convince them not to do it. With as small a chance there is of getting away, they had every right to make the attempt and try their luck. No one has the right to prevent anyone they care about from making a move that may not be in their best interest. If someone had prevented me from taking the same type of gamble, I would hate them the rest of my life because I would never know if I'd been robbed of the chance to be free. Somehow, no one seemed to understand my reasoning, but I'm sure Hutch and Norm did. And that's all that really mattered; it really wasn't anyone else's business.

Within a few months, everyone in my current clique was living in honor dorm. Jeff had been messing around with an electric cattle prod they'd brought in to have him fix out in electronics. He'd rigged it up with a wad of NiCad batteries and quadrupled its output, then smuggled it into the compound. Grounding all the metal in his room in honor dorm, he left one hot wire attached to the radio antenna. (We commonly attached wire to the antennas to get better reception).

As each of us entered the room, he would try to get us to grab the wire, but we were a little brighter than that. Then along came a Goober named Dave. Dave was a skinny tall kid with a severe under bite. Always trying to be cool, he figured that we were the guys to know. His visits amused us, and we taunted him by saying his name in the beginning and end of every sentence directed to him. Jeff started it, "Dave, we need you to peel some insulation off of that wire on the antenna, Dave".

"OK what do I use to strip it?" "Dave, use your teeth, Dave." He put the wire in his mouth and sparks flew off his teeth as the whole locker containing the mechanism and batteries rattled and hummed like a transformer. The power from this gizmo knocked his slow ass out for almost two minutes. After regaining consciousness, he'd lost his memory of what had happened. We reassured him that he was ok now, but he seemed to have had some kind of seizure just outside our door. To calm him we gave him some coffee, and then asked him to fix our reception.

This time his teeth locked down on the wire end for almost half a minute. After pulling the deadly wire out of the kids mouth, Jeff held the wire to different parts of his head trying to map out his motor control or something to that effect. All the time the metal locker in the corner rattled and hummed until the batteries began to die and our visitor stopped moving altogether.

After a half hour Dave still wasn't moving and we were getting concerned. If we pushed his body out in the hallway he'd be right by our door, if we dragged him any distance someone would see us. We were starting to argue about it when he moaned. We gave him some coffee and asked how long he'd been having these seizures and that we were concerned they may be getting worse. He muttered something about us not being his friends. So we kicked his ass and sent him on his way. What audacity!

The parole man paid me another visit and knocked off another year and a half, bringing my parole date to within two years. I'd been down for over eight years before earning medium custody. This meant that now I could go outside the fence with unarmed supervision. It was nice to know that I was getting close to getting out, but before going to work release, I'd have to prove myself by working a job assignment outside the fence. That meant the end of small engines.

Boss Hog

My Boy at this time was the same red haired one Norm had been jealous of. He was a good bitch, keeping our cell in Honor dorm clean and fetching the groceries from the canteen. Being very desirable, it was tough to get possession of him in the beginning. Only one other Man had ever owned him and that was Sparky. I'd made a deal with the boy to teach him how to play guitar in return for whatever I wanted.

It was like being married. He'd bitch about me being a slob and not caring about his feelings. And he didn't think he should "put out" on command like some kind of a sex slave. You just about had to get the boy drunk before he'd act right. In spite of this, I still looked out for him.

His guitar had a bad bridge, so one of the cops brought me a replacement part in return for fixing a boat motor. The Auto Body Boss next door to Small Eng. had a hair up his ass that day, and told me to stay out of his shop. Ignoring his request, I went back over to give my boy the part. "Boss Hog" as he was called, dragged me into his office and started writing me up.

"Why are you doing this to me", I asked.

"Because I can, I told you to stay out of my shop and you came back over anyway"!

"Look man, I'm real close to getting minimum custody and this would jamb me up. How about we just forget about this and you'll never see me over here again"?

318

"That's too bad about your custody problem. When I'm done with this DR you can kiss your release goodbye, they'll never let you out", he said this while handing me a pencil. Flicking the pencil in his face I yelled," Look here Ass Hole, I ain't signing shit, are you forgetting all the favors I did for you"? "Now you can add assaulting a corrections officer to your charges", he growled while reaching for the phone.

This instructor weighed about three hundred pounds and carried a six-foot hickory stick with him everywhere he went, hence the nickname Boss Hog. The stick had been sitting across his desk during our exchange of words. I grabbed it and reared back to make a lethal blow. Yelling, "I haven't gone through all of this just to have some fat punk fuck it all up! If my life is over then so is yours"! He covered his face and started sobbing, "Please don't hit me, PLEASE, Don't!

I was already fucked. Assault with a pencil was enough reason to lose my custody status, but grabbing the stick meant assault with a deadly weapon. Glancing through the plate glass window above his desk, I could see the whole class watching me. With twenty witnesses my fate was sealed, the mistake had already been made. I might as well get the satisfaction of painting the walls with his brains. My bat like weapon was coming down on Hog's head when a thought came to me. "There might still be a way out". I lowered the stick and gave it a shot.

"Hey, you're the one that traded some computers to a friend of mine for the stereo from the Library. And those binoculars that are missing from the warehouse aren't they in your closet at home? Correct me if I'm wrong, but aren't those binoculars part of a federal grant? The Fed.'s are still investigating their disappearance. Go ahead and call the troops in. They might just forgive me when I tell them what you've got at your house"!

He sniveled, "I can have them out of there before they get to my house"! I thought you told everyone your wife worked fifty miles from your home; she won't get there in time. In fact, since she's an accessory, your kids might just end up in a foster home with people like me for a few years"!

"NO ONE will listen to you, you're just a convict".

I continued, "Remember the Vocational coordinator, the one that used to be the major? Isn't he the one catching the heat for your little theft? He'll listen. Fat boy you might as well pack your shit, cause your going to the box"!

Handing him his stick I included, "tell your whole family to pack too. You fucked with my life and now I'm gonna fuck yours and your families"!

I hoped my bluff would delay his phone call long enough to get to the coordinators office. Reaching the office proved to be a little anti-climatic. The coordinator was out at the officers' quarters partying. I told his aid to get word to him that it was an emergency, as I turned to watch the back gate. Any time now the goon squad would come running through it, to take me away. Then someone tapped me on the shoulder from behind.

Turning around I saw one of Hogs little Henchmen standing there all big-eyed.

"Boss Hog wants to see you", he stammered.

"Well I don't want to see him, tell him his ass is mine"! A few minutes later, he returned and told me that if I came back and apologized, then everything would be cool. Not sure if this some kind of a trap, I pretended to think about it before deciding to take my chances. After all, what did I have to lose?

I sat in silence inside Hogs office for almost fifteen minutes before he asked, "well".

"Well what? I'm here ain't I"?

"I don't hear an apology".

"That's because I'm not sorry. The only reason we're both here at this moment is because we can both fuck each other. I do regret lowering myself to your level, but you left me no other choice".

"That's not an apology".

"That's as close as it gets".

"You know this will never work again, don't think you can hold this over my head! Those items you mentioned will be gone tonight"!

"What Items"? I said over my shoulder, as I left his office.

My custody rating was dropped from close to medium. Whenever some one is reclassified to Medium custody, they have to exercise it. This means that at least once a week they'd gather up a few of us to do certain outside jobs. For a few weeks, they took some of us out to clear the tree line around the municipal Golf Course. Sometimes I'd be dropped off at people's houses to fix a tractor or boat engine while the other guys were put to work. This continued until they decided I could be placed on minimum custody.

At least three days a week was still spent out in small engine shop with Billy and Fudd. Without a Bossman, we could pretty much do what we wanted. Different guys from ground crew would come out to pick up or drop off the small push mowers used on the compound. One of these characters was Hiller.

Hiller was a wanna-be Aryan weight lifter, not being very bright, he knew that his only chance of making it on the compound was to get big. Now that he'd gained some size, the boy walked around and presented himself as some kind of a badass. One of his main goals in life was to impress me that he was someone to be respected and reckoned with. Not being very bright, this left him open to a few of my better practical jokes.

The Temple of Ra had been inactive accept for an occasional sacrifice. I still kept a few snakes in the pit, and sometimes disciples would come by with strange bugs or reptiles they found. One time someone dropped off a banana spider. Never having seen one before we were amazed at it's' size. This spider was bright orange with black hair on its' joints and body. Laid out flat on the table, the tips of the spiders' legs covered a ten inch area. The guy that brought us this marvel of nature had jammed it into a large coffee cup to get it past the gate, breaking most of its legs. Instead of sacrificing it, we decided that Ra would rather have "Boris the Spider" as a pet, so we splinted its legs with toothpicks and string, trying to nurse it back to health.

On our new pets second day, Hiller stopped in and asked what the orange thing with sticks tied to it was. This was too easy!

"That's a Florida Orange Spider". "What's a Florida Orange Spider"? Hiller asked. "They're native to Florida. Because of natural coloration, they can hide in orange trees waiting for their prey to walk under them. Then they pounce on your head and bite you in the back of the neck so the poison can get to the brain faster." "That thing isn't even real, you're full of shit"!

At that remark Fudd prodded the spider, which began to scurry around the table on its splinted legs. Hiller's eyes got big, then he ran off to tell everybody about Florida Orange Spiders.

After drawing a crowd, Hiller came back to prove to everybody that Florida Orange Spiders do exist. A couple of the group knew it was a banana Spider and told Hiller he was an idiot. They also explained to him that they don't hide in orange trees jumping on people's heads. When they asked where he got these ideas. Hiller pointed at me. I responded that all I did was show him a Banana spider and he ran off screaming.

Knowing how stupid he looked Hiller grabbed a shovel off the wall and threatened to smash Boris saying, "It doesn't matter what it is, if it's dead." We wrestled the shovel away from Hiller and sent him on his way. Boris died sometime during the night from his original injuries. We buried our pet with a full ceremony, as I pondered my next form of entertainment.

A few days later one of the guys from masonry showed up at the shop carrying another beast under his arm. He had a six-foot rat snake jammed into a cardboard container slightly larger than a shoebox. The box was wrapped in twine after splitting at the seams from the snake's frantic attempts to escape. The Mason wanted to store this monster in our snake pit until after work. He needed the snake kept alive until he could skin it for belt material in hobby craft. The snake pit wasn't set up for anything that big. We had maybe a half dozen water bandits in the pit, all less than two feet in length. He promised to replace any bandits that were killed or eaten. Then he paid five bucks for four hours of snake storage.

Our new snake had a head the size of a large dog, with a full set of teeth that could snap the head off a rat with one strike. Rat snakes are notorious for snapping off fingers from the unwary, or people stupid enough to tease them. Normally not very aggressive, this one had gone quite mad during his internment in the box.

The pit was only eighteen inches square, with two hinged half doors on top. Getting the snake into the pit was a real wrestling match, but keeping him in was just as bad. Old Yeller was strong enough to push the lid open with his head, and menacing enough to hold us back. When Fudd tried pushing its head down with a broomstick, the snake grabbed it from him and spit it out. Billy knocked it in the head with a shovel and shut the lid saying, "We didn't get enough money for this"! Just to be safe we placed a cinder block on the lid and watched as the snake shook and rattled the box.

We drew a crowd over from the other shops for a repeat show of Billy's' Snake charming act but after a few more whacks in the head, Old Yeller had become completely unmanageable. Then along came Hiller.

"Hey guys, what's in the box"?

"You won't believe me, but it's a rare type of snake".

"I want to see it", Hiller said, as he started to remove the cinder block. Everyone yelled "NO" at the same time causing Hiller to hesitate.

"What's so special about this snake"?

"It's a Florida Orange Cobra"! I yelled.

"Don't even try that on me, there's no such thing as a Florida Orange Cobra. Ain't no such thing"!

"Haven't you read in the paper about those parrots, monkeys, and snakes that got away from the zoo down in Miami"?

"Yea, I heard something about that; they're living in the everglades or something".

"Well, some of them did some breeding and because of the natural coloration thing" . . . .

"Don't even try that one on me! Let me guess, they turned orange so they could hide in orange trees, Right"?

"I don't know if Cobras can even climb trees, but they turned the same color as that high grass so they can hide in it". This one hasn't turned color all the way yet, he's still kinda yellow. But it is a real Cobra, and if you open that lid you're a dead man".

"Bull Shit, no snake would bang around inside a box like that, it's probably a possum or something. I'd bet on it"!

"Put your money where your mouth is. I'll bet five bucks that box has the meanest snake you ever saw in it"! Everyone in the shop offered the same bet. I'm not about to bet on it, but I still want to see this cobra", Hiller said as he removed the cinder block.

One-half of the lid lifted an inch and then closed again as if on its' own. Hiller paused to stare at this strange phenomenon, when the lid was flung open. The boy froze with his eyes fixed and mouth open, as a large yellow head slowly rose up out of the pit to eye level. Letting out a loud raspy rush of air, Old Yeller had become the personification of every child's nightmare and a few adults.

Hillers' arms waved backwards in a pinwheel motion as he leaned back to get away. Falling backwards, he crab-walked on his feet and elbows, never taking his eyes off of the snake, until reaching the far wall of the shop.

"Oh Shit; you do have a Florida Orange Cobra"!

Billy slapped the great yellow head a few times with his shovel, before the snake retreated into the Pit, saying, "It's a rat snake you dumb ass. Boy you are the stupidest white boy I ever met".

After the cobra incident, Hiller stopped coming around to see us.

All good things must come to an end, as did my tenure in the small engine shop. Before making work release, I had to prove I could be trusted on minimum custody.

With the new classification came my job out in the motor pool. The motor pool boss said that it was time I learned how to drive, as he handed me the keys to a two-ton dump truck and sent me out to practice in the dump. My first driving lesson had come at the age of twenty-four.

This was a great job. Along with driving privileges, most of the Motor Pool guys attended the rodeos. We'd cook the burgers and tend the concession stands while the bosses collected the money. This was done for local charities. The second day of my first rodeo a couple of large busses pulled up and starting unloading an army of special children. The kids ranged in age from six years old, to early teens. They all had trisomy twenty-one, sometimes referred to as "mongolism".

I'd never seen this many kids with the same affliction together in a group. Looking through the faces you could tell where some of them were hardly affected by their condition and were just like any other kid. Others were severely retarded with muscle control problems. The worst of them were wheelchair ridden.

They all had big smiles. They were thrilled to get out and see something as different as a rodeo with real cowboys and a variety of animals. As the kids were organized into lines in front of our stand, we saw how the other people treated them. Parents began pulling their kids away from this new group saying things like, "Don't get near them, you might catch something", "They don't belong here with real people", and "Don't worry, we won't have to sit near "THEM"!

Instead of just walking away, these good town folks milled around bitching about these kids. Within minutes, they started taunting them. A few of the kids that were less afflicted were beginning to sense that something was wrong. Group hysteria was building.

Convicts as a whole happen to like kids. They also identify with the underdogs or in this situation the outcasts. All of us working the concession had been an outcast at one time or another and we took these vicious comments personally. These kids were harmless, having been dumped in an institution by parents that were unable or unwilling to care for their sick kids. We were enraged by the public's behavior to the point of madness.

It started simply enough, we asked the people to move away from the stand if they weren't buying anything. Then we told them to go somewhere else if they didn't like the view. It grew more personal as we defended the special kids with threats of violence. The Bosses formed a wall in between the crowd and us, and ordered us back to work. They told the locals that our concession was closed until we were done serving the kids off the bus.

We gave each one of them the special attention they deserved, much to the resentment of some passerbyes. It's a sad day when a gang of murderers, robbers and thieves has to take a stand against law-abiding citizens in defense of the sick and the weak. And they call us the scum of the earth! A week after the rodeo incident the state sent me to work release.

Work Release

Located across the highway from Tampa stadium, the work release complex was once a nurses training camp. Two male units, one female unit, and a mental rehabilitation building filled these grounds along with an HRS building. I was placed as a permanent, meaning that I worked in the kitchen until my sentence was short enough to qualify for the regular work release. After a week in the dish-room, they made me sandwich man.

It was my job to make the bag lunches for the hundred plus guys that went to work every morning. Some of the guys wanted to pay me to put a little something extra on their sandwiches. I was supposed to limit the sandwiches contents to meat, cheese and condiments, along with an apple or other fruit. For a weekly fee, I would throw in lettuce, tomato, onions etc. As word spread that five bucks a week would give them what they wanted, my income grew tremendously. The permanents were taken to Department store once a week for street clothes or what ever else might be needed. I found it hard to keep the spending down with my new surplus of pocket money.

Twice a week in the afternoon I'd donate my time to a voluntary program that visited problem kids in the local schools and juvenile institutions. There were three of us that went on these trips. The other two guys were a couple of flakes. I would watch the kid's roll their eyes in disbelief as these two morons made up killer stories trying to impress teens that knew better.

When my turn came, I'd tell them the truth about not having women and being hungry. Sometimes I'd have to catch their attention by telling how we smuggled the drugs in. But included the fact that your best friend would steal them from you if given the chance. Being their age when busted helped me relate to them. I had the chance to say all of the things to them that I wish someone had said to me before walking into that bank over nine years before. And they all listened.

I realized I could never undo the things from my past, but if I kept one kid from making the same mistakes I'd made, then my time in here hadn't been wasted. In my mind, every kid I kept out of the states hands was my way of cheating the state out of the money they'd collect to keep that kid locked up. Regardless of my intentions, the results were still positive enough to be recognized. The Sheriffs office sent me a commendation for how effective I had been in the prevention of teen-age crime. Besides my GED, this was the first piece of paper I was really proud of. The school trips ended when I made regular work release.

The idea behind work release was to let a convict get into the routine of working on the streets. You work an eight-hour job, and stay at the center for nights and weekends. For some reason they sent me to Tampa work release. I didn't know anything about Tampa or anyone in it. This left me in a predicament as far as work went. I had to rely on the in-house counselor in charge of job assignments.

The job counselor told me that he had a job opening as a laborer for a masonry company he dealt with on a regular basis. After explaining that I was a DOT certified mechanic, he laughed and said that those state certificates meant nothing. If I didn't take the job he assigned me, then I'd be sent back to my institution. He explained that as a hiring incentive the government gave a large tax credit to any employer that hired a convict. It was mandatory that I obtain one of these tax forms before applying for a job.

Everyone in the center had to go to the state employment office and register for the tax incentive, then report to the job site to confirm employment. After returning the form to him, He would give the final OK. Against his advice, I declined his masonry job offer, I searched for my own job as a mechanic.

This was no small task in an unfamiliar city. To make matters worse I had to confirm a job over the phone before going to an interview. Before getting permission to go to a personal interview, the job counselor would make a call to tell my perspective employer what kind of crime I'd committed, poisoning the well, so to speak.

After a few weeks of job hunting over the phone, I thought I had a small engine job. Since we weren't allowed to go out on an interview, I told the Job Counselor that I was going to the employment office to get his form filled out. Bus maps in hand I mapped out a route that would take me by the shop I had called, and then back by the employment office.

Walking the last half mile and then into the shop I asked for the owner. A rather large man with a limp walked out and asked about my experience. I told him what I knew and what I was capable of. He was very impressed until I told him where I was living. A look of hatred suddenly emanated from his face as he told me that the job had already been taken.

"Excuse me, but you just said that I was the kind of man you were looking for. Is it something I said"?
He replied, "You better leave now or I'm calling the police"! I was Free, White, and Twenty-one, but this guy hated me because of something I'd done almost a decade before. I was experiencing my first exposure to prejudice, and I didn't like it. This guy needed his

ass kicked and I felt qualified to fill my new job description. Then a little voice in my head told me to walk out and let it go. "Don't throw away everything you've worked so hard for because of one ass-hole"!

"I'm sorry I wasted your time, Have a really nice day", I told him as I left. I'd never been treated like this in my life. Now I had some idea of how it must feel to be black, and I wondered how Blacks could have a good attitude after being treated this way most of their lives. This thought stayed with me all the way to the employment agency. The next morning my new job as a mason tender started.

Being scared of heights was not to my advantage on the new job. They tried everything to get me out on the scaffolds, but to no avail. Even having me tend to twelve masons by myself didn't work. They figured that I'd get tired of being overworked and conquer my fear of heights, but I took it in stride. This was better than weight lifting for building strength. If only my feet could handle the running around with the additional weight.

Every night would find me back in the room soaking my tired dogs in a mop bucket full of hot water and Epsom Salts. This continued until the building was almost finished. Word had come down that the next site wouldn't be large enough to keep all of the employees. After securing an interview with a go-cart track in the north end of Tampa, I decided to ask the boss if he could lay me off. He told me that he planned to keep me for the next job since I was such a hard worker. When I explained the deal to him he relented, while telling me that I could always come back to work for him if the mechanic job didn't pan out.

The Job Coordinator was pissed off when I told him I'd been laid off. He told me to stop wasting his time with interviews and to get another card filled out at the employment office. Bus routes in hand I took another unauthorized trip risking an escape charge.

The ad read: Mechanic/ Foreman with small engine experience needed, and then the address.

This job was in very north end of Tampa, I had to walk a mile beyond where the buses stopped. After a brief interview, they told me I had the job but they wanted to see my work before considering me for the foreman position. They agreed to tell the center that they had hired me over the phone and that they understood I was an ex-con.

When I got back to the center, the Job Coordinator was furious. He'd never heard of anyone getting themselves hired over the phone without an interview. He then called my new employers in front of me and gave them full details of my crime, along with some of the reasons I'd been in the box. But they still wanted me. Perplexed he told me I could work there, but I needed to have a new card filled out before I started. A week later, they made me Shop Foreman with salary and full benefits.

I was called to the coordinators office one night, only to find five guys in suites waiting for me. They asked how I liked my job. After telling them about some of my responsibilities, they congratulated the Coordinator for doing such a wonderful job in placing me in my present situation. After they left, he asked me how many more guys they needed where I worked. I told him he'd have to talk to my boss about that. While I worked there, they never hired anyone else from the work release center.

Being salary meant that I had no specific hours. Monday through Friday, I was required to be there, but I told the center I worked Saturdays too. After catching up on my paper work, I'd play the video games out in the game room or piddle around in the shop.

For promotional reasons, a few of us from the track would go out to the sunshine speedway at night to show off our larger go-cart dubbed the Mirage. Built like a Formula One racer these things had a rotary engine that could push it to over seventy miles an hour. Of course, our track had very tight turns that kept the top speed well below that. Besides handing out free lap tickets, we got to see all of the races at the speedway free, sometimes not getting home until two or three in the morning. It was on my return from one of these trips that they informed me I was being released.

The state needed to release a large number of prisoners because of overcrowding and somehow my name had come up on their list. The parole papers were waiting for me to sign in the office. Once I signed them, I would have twenty-four hours to report to my parole officer in Ft Lauderdale. As a condition of my parole, I had to have a job waiting for me. The company I worked for had another track in Broward County, where the mechanic had agreed to swap places with me in a few months. On this short notice, the job might not be there.

The state had decided to limit the length of parole to two years for anyone released after 1984 with a few exceptions. Because of my special circumstances, my contract demanded six. I could either sign the papers now or be sent back. Of course, I signed them.

I called my folks to tell them I was coming home, and was met with silence. After nine and a half years, they believed it less than I did. At six the next morning I was pushed out the door into the pouring rain with two guitars, three large cardboard boxes, a check for the money I'd earned working, and no ID. I called the sales manager at work and explained my circumstances. He co-signed the check for me and reserved a ticket for the flight back.

We had a steak dinner with beer at his house. Both he and his family looked at me strangely when I asked how their TV came in so clearly. I'd never seen cable TV or a VCR before. This was quite an improvement over the broadcast television I was used to. Just after dark, my host gave me a ride to the airport and I was on my way home on a small turbo prop heading for Ft. Lauderdale.

So many things were running through my head on my flight home. Part of me couldn't believe that the whole thing was over. Reviewing everything I'd experienced during the last ten years, I was rather pleased with the way things had panned out. I had persevered well beyond my own expectations. The system had failed to break me; instead, it made me stronger. Strong enough to still be me after all of their attempts to erase who I was.

Trying to imagine what I would be like now if none of this had happened was beyond my abilities. There was no high school graduation or prom that I could recall, nor any kind of normal relationship to remember. All of my growing up had been done in the chaingang. The need to bury my emotions and survive using my wits, no longer existed. But the person I was before didn't exist either. I had no idea of who I was outside of the barbed wire. The fact that I was institutionalized, hit me like a truck. I had no idea what it was like not to be a convict!

Looking at the other people on the plane, I confirmed that my panic was properly concealed. Good, they couldn't tell. Maybe things just had to be put in the proper perspective. For starters, this parole thing would have to be handled the same way a transfer to another camp would be handled. Figure out where I stand and make a place for myself. It was like being a newcock all over again. Just keep your mouth shut and act like everybody else until you get the routine down.

As the lights of Ft. Lauderdale grew closer, I had to laugh; maybe they had won after all. . . . .

After Note

Growing up in prison had definitely left its marks. Adapting to the streets after my release was a slow and tedious process. Crime was never an option compared to gainful employment and I've managed to avoid returning to prison. Only one time in the late 90's did I have a brush with the law.

I live in Palm Beach and have worked as a mechanic at local dealerships for the past few years. My daughter is a pre-med student in a Florida college. Times are hard for me just as they are for everyone else, but I find comfort knowing that every day I wake up on this side of the fence!